"THE EUROPEAN REVOLUTION"
&
CORRESPONDENCE WITH GOBINEAU

ALEXIS DE TOCQUEVILLE was born of a noble family in Paris in 1805. He became an assistant magistrate in the French government, and in 1831 he received permission to go to America to study the penal system, together with a fellow magistrate and friend, Gustave de Beaumont. He traveled in America for nine months. He then wrote *Democracy in America,* the first volume of which was published in 1835 and was immediately recognized as a masterpiece. He was active in French politics, serving briefly as Minister of Foreign Affairs in the Republican government established after the Revolution of 1848. He described this period in his *Recollections.* As a result of the *coup d'état* of Louis Napoleon, he retired from public life. He died in Cannes in 1859.

Tocqueville spent the last years of his life working on a major study of the French Revolution and its consequences. He completed only the first volume of this study before his death. This volume was published under the title *L'ancien Régime et la Révolution* in 1865, and was translated into English the same year. *The Old Regime and the French Revolution* appears in English translation by Stuart Gilbert in the Anchor series.

The editor of this volume, John Lukacs, a historian and essayist, is the author of a large diplomatic history and many studies and reviews of Tocqueville. He is now working on a volume on historiography.

Alexis de Tocqueville

"THE EUROPEAN
REVOLUTION"

&

CORRESPONDENCE
WITH GOBINEAU

*Introduced, edited and
translated by John Lukacs*

DOUBLEDAY ANCHOR BOOKS
DOUBLEDAY & COMPANY, INC.
GARDEN CITY, NEW YORK
1959

COVER BY LEONARD BASKIN
TYPOGRAPHY BY EDWARD GOREY

Library of Congress Catalog Card Number 59–6275
Copyright © 1959 by John Lukacs
All Rights Reserved
Printed in the United States of America

CONTENTS

[vii]

CORRESPONDENCE WITH GOBINEAU

CONTENTS

CONTENTS

"THE EUROPEAN REVOLUTION"
&
CORRESPONDENCE WITH GOBINEAU

Introduction

1

Nearly a century after his death the reputation of Alexis de Tocqueville is in rapid, if in somewhat confused, growth. This is heartening even to those who feel that Tocqueville's fine, noble voice is breaking through the ideological din, alas, too late, since intellectual reputation is one thing but actual influence another. Still, the revival of Tocqueville's reputation is a lesson to the despairing and to the cynical. It suggests that even in the most confusing of times, amidst the clatter and loud babel of the twentieth century, pretension and shoddiness ultimately fade while, in contrast, true wisdom gains permanence and even some influence through an invisible evolution which goes on through generations. It is an evolution with which our impatient human selves are unable to keep track but which is, nonetheless, ascertainable.

Everywhere the hierarchy of the past century is undergoing a rapid and radical revision: the present appreciation of Tocqueville is part and parcel of that revision.

A few hitherto obscured, thin, and vague figures are emerging from the Victorian murk now substantial and vivid while many others who have been filling the foreground now appear as somewhat less than great. We experience a re-vision, in the literal sense of that word. With it Marx and Spencer and Bentham and Tolstoi and Darwin and Garibaldi and Ranke and Bancroft pale; Tocqueville and Metternich and Burckhardt and Henry Adams grow.

Yet such rapid revisions have their own dangers. There is that nervous superficiality so often a consequence of the procedures of modern "communications." Right now the reputations of these great men run the risk of being buried under tons of paper, accompanied by academic singsong. Tocqueville's reputation may have already reached that peculiarly modern state of intellectual eminence where he is frequently quoted but seldom really read. Yet Tocqueville's literary heritage is singularly ill adapted to a safe resting place at a respected referential plateau: for Tocqueville's voice is at times poetic, frequently religious, and almost always exhortatory. The contents of this book will, I hope, illustrate this often overlooked quality of his genius.

2

The main dates of Tocqueville's life may be given as follows:

29 July 1805	Born in Paris of an ancient noble family of Normandy; his father a legitimist of acute intelligence; his mother Malesherbes's granddaughter; his uncle, Chateaubriand.
1812–23	Domestic tutoring by an extraordinary priest, the Abbé Lesueur; formal schooling at Metz. First important friendships.
1823–27	Reads in law; first journeys to Italy and Sicily.
1827–30	*Juge auditeur* at Versailles.
1830–31	The July Revolution. With his friend Beaumont, Tocqueville successfully elicits an official assignment to study the American penitentiary system.
1831–32	American journey. Resigns from his judicial post.

1833, 1835 Journeys in England and Ireland.

1835 First volume of *Democracy in America*.

1836 Marries Marie Mottley, a middle-class Englishwoman.

1837 Fails to be elected to the Chamber.

1839 Elected as Member for Valognes.

1840 The second volume of *Democracy* is published.

1840–48 Honorable career in the Chamber.

1841 Elected to the *Académie*. Travel in Algeria.

1848 February and June revolutions. His political prestige rises.

1848–49 Member of the Constitutional Committee.

1849 For five months Tocqueville is Foreign Minister of France.

1850–51 Illness; journey to Sorrento.

1851 Arrested briefly during Louis Napoleon's *coup d'état*.

1853 Retires to the country. During a winter sojourn near Tours he begins *The Old Regime and the Revolution*.

1854 German journey.

1856 Publication of *The Old Regime*.

1857 Journey and extraordinary reception in England.

1858 A grave hemorrhage. He moves to Cannes.

16 April 1859 Dies at Cannes.

No mere chronology will reflect Tocqueville's tremendous literary dedication. The overwhelming part of his writings was unpublished until after his death. A very large part remains unpublished today. It is only now that a committee headed by J. P. Mayer, the foremost Tocqueville scholar of our days, is producing his first complete Collected Works.

Unpublished until 1893 were his private Recollections of 1848–49, the famous *Souvenirs,* which rank, with Saint-Simon and Saint-Évremond, among the greatest of memoirs. Tocqueville left a more than half-finished second volume of his *Old Regime and the Revolution,* besides astonishingly rich dossiers full of travel notes, state papers, drafts of essays, maxims, and sketches. His friend Beaumont said about him that "for one volume he published he wrote ten; and the notes he cast aside as intended only for himself would have served many writers as text for the printer." Perhaps above all stands his impressive correspondence, of which, we are assured by Mr. Mayer, perhaps three fourths has not yet been published. Tocqueville letters are still being discovered in French family archives and in the stocks of book and manuscript dealers. In the Collected Works they may cover as many as eight volumes. They are, in many ways, the most important, the most original sources of Tocqueville's thought.

The most important letters were written to his French friends, to Kergorlay, the Stoffelses, the Circourts, Mme. Swetchine, Corcelle, Freslon, Molé, Rivet, Rémusat, Lanjuinais, De Broglie, Ampère; to his British friends, Mill, Reeve, Senior, Hatherton, Brougham, the Grotes, the Lewises. Among the most complete and, for our purposes, the most interesting, are his letters to Arthur de Gobineau. Among the most complete of his posthumous book-length manuscripts are the finished chapters and outstanding fragments of the second volume of *The Old Regime and the Revolution.* Hitherto untranslated into English, this forms the first and the Gobineau letters the second part of this book.

The main purpose of this Introduction is to justify this dual selection, grouped together under the title *"The European Revolution."*

3

Everything Tocqueville wrote he wrote with some moral purpose in mind. It is, therefore, important to group and sum up his writings with their corresponding moral concerns. These are clearly traceable from his many letters; moreover, he often suggests his moral purpose in the forewords and, frequently, in the very pages of his published books. It may be said that these are built around three great principles which preoccupied him during his entire life: their following order is not, therefore, one of topical or chronological precedence.

First, Tocqueville believed that a new age of social democracy was about inevitable; that the principle of social equality had triumphed over the traditional aristocratic order of Europe; that this democratic future was full of hitherto unseen dangers but that, on the other hand, through the proper exercise of self-government, liberty and an orderly social democracy were not irreconcilable. To a broad illustration, and to an exposition of these principles, he devoted *Democracy in America*. Here his purpose was less a book about America than a book about democracy, written for the sake of France.[1]

Second, Tocqueville came to conclude that the origins of the great European revolution which broke out in 1789 ought to be traced less to aristocratic misrule than to an ideological revolution. This was a revolution which, paradoxically, the European aristocracy itself had embraced and furthered; its overwhelming political condition had been the thoughtless and continued extension of the central powers of the State, which process, in France, had pre-

---

[1] *"Democracy in America,"* wrote the Stalinist historian Alpatov in an article entitled "Tocqueville: Historian of the Nobility" (1949), "was a book directed against the American people. But it was primarily directed against the French people."

ceded the Revolution by at least a hundred and fifty years and which was still going on. To these propositions he devoted the two volumes of *The Old Regime and the Revolution*. Here his purpose was less a book about France than a book about the great Revolution, written for the sake of Europe.

Third, Tocqueville was convinced that the nineteenth century was wrong in believing that liberty and Christianity were irreconcilable. He saw that the new forces of social democracy, unlike the transitory bourgeois forces, might not be opposed to religion at all. His prophetic conclusions about the potential harmony between democracy and religion (and especially the Roman Catholic religion) appeared in *Democracy in America;* his judicious criticism of the false eighteenth-century optimism about human nature appears in *The Old Regime* and also in his *Souvenirs,* which latter he wrote for himself alone; even more, these concerns appear in his letters, in his American correspondence, and in the letters written during his last decade of life, especially to Corcelle, Mme. Swetchine, De Broglie, and Freslon. But above all these is his monumental defense of Catholic Christianity and of liberty in his debate with Gobineau—written, I shall add, for the sake of Western Christendom.

It is the second and the third of these grand concerns which the contents of this book should illuminate. Yet, confronted as we are with the extraordinarily coherent and consistent nature of Tocqueville's philosophy, it is evident that these great concerns cannot be academically separated. He considered the French Revolution of 1789 but part and parcel of a greater, European Revolution which, sixty years after the storming of the Bastille, may have been still in its first phase. The European Revolution, in turn, was but a manifestation of a great global movement toward social democracy, at the core of which remained the fundamental problem of liberty and Christianity; and the problem of their compatibility was, to Tocqueville, inseparable from the prospects of what we now call "Western civilization."

I believe that some of the finest examples of Tocqueville's thoughts along these lines may be found in the uncompleted parts of *The Old Regime and the Revolution*, which have hitherto not been published in English. While, except for a few notes, the first volume (published as an Anchor book under the title *The Old Regime and the French Revolution*) illuminates the scene of France, in the second volume his illustrations begin to spread out from France, first of all to Germany; their ultimate concern is civilized Europe. I know that the most inspiring expressions of his philosophic propositions about the prospects of that Europe may be found in his correspondence with Gobineau. This complementary connection should, I think, justify the combination of these two separate parts of the Tocquevillean heritage in this volume.

For this volume I have, therefore, chosen the somewhat flat-sounding title of *The European Revolution*. I believe that this at least corresponds with the main concern in Tocqueville's mind and that it is properly applicable to the parts of his work on the French Revolution that I have translated for this volume, as well as to the letters exchanged with Gobineau, beginning on page 188. It has been disagreeable to apply a self-made title to a volume which comprises the writings of such a clear and precise author. Yet I believe it to be preferable to such indistinct, if more exact, titles as *From the Unpublished Writings* or *Fragments from the Writings of Alexis de Tocqueville*. A further justification is suggested by Tocqueville's letter to Ampère, dated 1 February 1856, from which it appears that even at that late date Tocqueville wished to call his book *The Revolution*. Another justification is provided by his letter to the Comte de Circourt on 14 June 1852, where, in parentheses, Tocqueville says about the French Revolution: "We may now venture to call it the European Revolution."[2]

4

In the winter of 1850–51, ill and weighted down with the gloomiest thoughts about the future of France, Tocqueville retired to Sorrento. There the idea of a book about Napoleon first arose in his restless mind. His first jottings on Napoleon, Chapter I of Book IV (pages 143–46), were written there. Not until December 1852 did Tocqueville turn from a book about the Consulate and the Empire to the larger plan of a book describing the main features of the Revolution. Retiring to a country house near Tours in 1853, he found a treasure of valuable and electrifying sources in the provincial archives by accident. He was providentially assisted by the famous archivist, Charles de Grandmaison, in residence there. His ideas for *The Old Regime and the French Revolution* then crystallized. The first volume appeared in June 1856 while he went ahead with the second. Both stemmed from the same dedication; both were to sustain the same kind of exposition and argument. He had practically finished the first book of this second volume in early 1858. He then planned to put the second into final

[2] This whole passage deserves to be quoted here. It concerns a book by the Abbé Baruel, *Mémoires sur le Jacobinisme*. "His first proposition," wrote Tocqueville, "is that the French Revolution (we may now venture to call it the European Revolution) was the result of a conspiracy. It seems to me that nothing can be more untrue. I do not say that during the course of the eighteenth century there were no secret societies and underground machinations undermining the old social system. Beneath all great movements you will find underhand conspiracies: they form the subsoil of revolutions. But I feel certain that those secret societies were the symptoms of the disease, and not the disease itself—the effects, and not the causes. The change of opinions which produced the change in events was effected in broad daylight by the combined efforts of all classes; writers, nobles, princes, all deserting the old system without knowing what other to adopt."

shape, but soon thereafter a blood vessel burst in his lungs; the chance to finish the work was not given to him.

This is not the place to trace minutely the evolution of this volume. We must, nevertheless, clarify the status of the materials therein. Parts of its first and of its third book had been included in the incomplete *Oeuvres Complètes* published by his friend Beaumont within a decade of Tocqueville's death, and two brief fragments were added in the form of appendices to two English editions of *The Old Regime* or, as the 1873 Reeve edition was entitled, *France before the Revolution.* But it was only for the present *Oeuvres Complètes,* directed by Peter Mayer, that all of the relevant materials were carefully collected and published by a masterful editor, M. André Jardin. They are as follows:

Original outline by Tocqueville, dated 1856.

Book I. Seven chapters up to the meeting of the Estates-General; several notes.

Book II. From Tocqueville's notes on the history of the Revolution. Four chapters, comprising various notes.

Book III. Two chapters about the end of the Directorate and the coming of Napoleon.

Book IV. From Tocqueville's notes on the Consulate and the Empire. Three chapters.

Book V. General notes and reflections about the Revolution. Three chapters.

Appendix. Various notes.

Books I and III had been nearly completed when their author died. Save for certain notes, they are translated here in their entirety. The half-finished chapters of Books II, IV, and V are translated here in part. Unlike the more formal practice, it is here, within the body of this Introduction, that I register my indebtedness for the generosity of Peter Mayer and of MM. Gallimard, who helped to make this Doubleday Anchor edition possible.

Thus it is evident that, though original in English, this

book is not a full reproduction of the exhaustive and excellent documentary collection in the *Oeuvres Complètes* of which it is to be hoped that a complete English edition will someday be forthcoming. In the fragmentary chapters of Book II and on a few occasions in Chapters III and IV of Book I, I condensed one or two passages and incorporated some of Tocqueville's notes. On pages 173-76, therefore, a Comparative Table indicates, for scholarly purposes, the correspondences with the *Oeuvres Complètes* volume. It was my intention to make this great summation of a book as readable as possible. This is also why this is a "free" rather than a "literal" translation, a discriminating rather than definitive text: I have aimed less at the exact textual definition of Tocqueville's words than at a conscientious and truthful rendition, in modern English, of his sentences —and *sententiae* they are, too, in the classic meaning of the word.

5

This unique interpretation of the French Revolution is, of course, a history; and its writer a historian. He has been so recognized by some of the greatest historical thinkers of the generations following him, among whom Burckhardt, Droysen, Dilthey, Gooch, Huizinga, Dawson stand out. To the singular quality of Tocqueville as a historian his otherwise ungenerous critic, Émile Faguet, paid unwitting tribute when he wrote that the task which Tocqueville "set for himself was to penetrate beneath accidental history to solid history, or beneath history to the physiology of peoples." From this correct analysis Faguet had, however, already deduced the wrong conclusion: that Tocqueville was, really, a cautious sociologist rather than a bold historian.

[3] The notes marked with a (т) are those of Tocqueville; the others are those which I considered unavoidable for elementary purposes of reference.

Yet the whole key to Tocqueville's singular historical talents lies here. When Faguet wrote sixty years ago, the texture of history had not yet changed. At that time it seemed still reasonable to keep concentrating on "surface" history, on the history of the politically conscious classes; as Seeley and Freeman, Victorian contemporaries, had put it, history was past politics and politics present history. Since then, however, it has become more and more obvious that, with the social and democratic character of our age, the requirements of historiography have changed, that it is no longer possible to concentrate exclusively on the actions of leading protagonists of the politically active classes, that it is less and less possible to separate what Faguet called "surface" history from what lies "beneath" it. And this Tocqueville already knew. The importance of *The Revolution*, therefore, is not only that it is an extraordinarily instructive interpretation of the French Revolution; it is, also, an extraordinarily instructive *new type* of history.

Within it Tocqueville implicitly and, at times, explicitly refutes many of the propositions of modern "professional" historiography. He is among the earliest observers who note that political history is no longer enough. He sees that the politically active classes may frequently become powerless and that their abdication of leadership is a development often more decisive than are the alleged "demands and decisions" of the people. Revolutions are seldom made by the conscious "dynamism" of the people, yet Tocqueville rejects the fatalistic notion that accidents govern history and also the deterministic notion that people are moved by predetermined economic motives.

History is made by men, to whom God has given free will. Tocqueville refutes the notion that history is a methodological "science." He conceives his historian's duties as primarily moral ones; but, then, he is also an artist at the same time. It will be seen from his Notes in this book how often he speaks of "what I am going to paint," "what I am trying to portray." He wished to be a true painter and not a methodical chronicler; he sought to find the great latent tendencies of the human heart rather than to be an academic accountant of the obvious. His literary and historical purposes were not narration, entertainment, information but description, proposition, comprehension. This novel conception of historiography with its nobly instructive purpose was immeasurably furthered by the lucidity and the almost Cartesian symmetry of his style: unlike Descartes, however, he was not willing to substitute clarity for charity.

Tocqueville was neither an academic sociologist nor a professional chronicler but a modern historian. And yet, because of the deplorable habit of this modern age to think in terms of intellectual categories, it is seldom that he is so recognized. It is not only that he was not a "professional" historian, but he and his principles hardly fit into any of those modern preconceived categories. An interesting list could be compiled with the names of those who have asserted that Tocqueville was a conservative, a liberal, a historian, a sociologist, an aristocrat, a bourgeois, a Christian, an agnostic, for in quite a number of instances the commentators contradict themselves, and at times Tocqueville is assigned to contradictory categories in the same book, essay, or review.

From this book it should appear, for instance, that, while Tocqueville did not believe that the voice of the people is the voice of God, neither did he believe that it was that of the devil. He was not one of those who believed that a nation has the right to go beyond her natural interests to propagate ideas and to arrogate to herself the singular role of impressing them on the world, yet he did not believe in narrow concepts of national interests either. He was not a French nationalist or a European imperialist, yet he did not believe that the achievements and the ideals of every nation and of every civilization are of the same worth. And he condemned the old regime as well as the Revolution.

Yet it is not possible to try to find a solution along liberal lines, as so many have done: to say that Tocqueville was the classic moderate, that his greatness consists of his having trodden a cautious narrow path between opposite categories. For Tocqueville was not between them. He was *above* them. He transcends these categories. No man with such absolute principles as that of Tocqueville would be a consummate compromiser, a trimmer, a mere moderate. He did not believe that the voice of the people was divine, yet he believed that it *could* echo the divine. He did not wish to steer a middle way between ideological and strategic concepts of national destiny, nor was he a moderate cosmopolitan, midway between being an internationalist or a nationalist: instead of cocking his liberal ear to ideological platitudes about one classless world or to sentimental invocations of nation or race, he fixed his patriotic eye on the providential limits of human and national ambitions. And if he condemned both old regime and Revolution for their vices, he also found virtues of lasting inspiration in both.

The Revolution, therefore, is exhortatory history. As in his letters to Gobineau, not only the occasional tone but the essential purpose is exhortatory. I have already said that it is hardly possible to comprehend the writings of Tocqueville without considering the moral purpose of their author. In turn, it is only with these moral purposes in mind that we will be able to correct some of the mistaken conceptions about him. If the main concern of *Democracy in America* was the future of democracy, that book also reveals that Tocqueville was more than a "conservative" democrat or a "liberal" aristocrat. If the main concern of *The Revolution* was the future of France and of Europe, it also reveals that Tocqueville was more than a late-comer to the historical academy or an early forerunner of sociology. And his main concern was with the future of Western Christendom; reflected in his correspondence with Gobineau, this reveals that Tocqueville was neither a "progressive" Catholic nor an aristocratic agnostic, but that he was a great Christian thinker with a noble heart.

6

Until now relatively little interest has been devoted to this correspondence. This is somewhat surprising since a dialogue between archetypes is frequently an incentive to curiosity, and at first sight these two correspondents represent nineteenth-century archetypes of thought. The categories are these: Tocqueville, a nineteenth-century liberal, a moderate critic of democracy; Gobineau, a nineteenth-century reactionary, a forerunner of Hitlerism. In a brief Note on Gobineau (pages 179–87) I shall suggest that he ought not to be assigned to these archetypal categories; I have already suggested that such categories will prove obstacles to our understanding of Tocqueville. I think that this correspondence will show that he was a conservative in the highest sense of that word; and, above all, that he was a Christian. And it is because of his conservative and principled defense of liberty and his liberal and generous defense of Christianity that this correspondence may be of high interest today.

The first letters between Tocqueville and Gobineau date back to 1843. There is no direct evidence that they met before. It is likely that Gobineau was introduced to Tocqueville through their mutual royalist friends, Kergorlay and Rémusat (with the former Gobineau was to launch a short-lived review devoted to the cause of provincial liberties and to governmental decentralization). Still, it is probable that Gobineau had met Tocqueville already in 1836 in Switzerland, and an article by Gobineau in 1841 about Greece interested Tocqueville very much. At any rate, their correspondence rather faithfully mirrors three different periods of their relationships.

In 1843 and 1844, Tocqueville considered enlisting the

collaboration of the young Gobineau in a work which he tentatively undertook for the *Académie des sciences morales et politiques*. It was to be a study of the new moral concepts and social habits developing in Europe during the dissolution of the old aristocratic order and with the new growth of democracy. At that time Gobineau was still very young, somewhat cynical, a radical; he was an agnostic, close to being an atheist ideologue. Despite their mutual affection, important divergences between their basic principles therefore existed. For this, but also for other reasons, Tocqueville decided to lay this work aside. Yet their friendship persisted. In June 1849, Tocqueville chose Gobineau for his principal secretary, *chef de cabinet*, in the Foreign Ministry. Five months later Tocqueville requested that the career of his young friend be unaffected by his own resignation. Gobineau remained in the diplomatic service, writing lengthy letters to his mentor from Switzerland during this second period of their relationship. By that time Gobineau had become quite a conservative—or, rather, an anti-democrat.

But their most important discussions about race, religion, and the future of Europe begin in April 1852 and continue until Tocqueville's death. By this time Gobineau had become a new kind of radical—a radical of the "Right."

All the published letters of the first and third periods are reproduced in this book. From them the disagreements of Tocqueville and Gobineau will of course appear. Yet something should be said about their personal relationship. Tocqueville, who remained childless, was exceptionally affectionate and generous to his young relatives and talented young friends. Despite his distaste for Gobineau's ideas and even despite his concern with some of Gobineau's personal traits, there is a tone of noble mentorship in these letters which never gives expression to personal rancor or irritation, however tempting. Tocqueville was never insincere. "We belong to diametrically opposed spheres," he wrote to Gobineau. Yet "in the realm of fine and high sentiments we shall always belong to the same camp." That Gobineau knew this to be more than a genteel phrase appears not only from his frequent expressions of gratitude in his letters to Tocqueville, but also from private letters written earlier. "It is impossible to even imagine a more profoundly good and affectionate man," he wrote to his family about Tocqueville; "I am, thus, completely dedicated to him."

Even when Tocqueville rejected the racial doctrines of his young friend so openly and directly, he could write about him thus to Beaumont:

> * * * has just sent me a thick book, full of research and talent, in which he endeavors to prove that everything that takes place in the world may be explained by differences of race. I do not believe a word of it, and yet I think that there is in every nation, whether in consequence of race or of an education which has lasted for centuries, some peculiarity, tenacious if not permanent, which combines with all the events that befall it, and is seen both in good and in bad fortune, in every period of its history . . .

Here, then, is a correspondence which ranks in importance with the great dialogues of modern history, with the dialogues between Machiavelli and Guicciardini, between Proudhon and Marx, between Burckhardt and Nietzsche. It is a co-respondence in the literal sense of that word. What does it represent?

7

It represents not only the aristocratic and the conservative and the sensitively pessimistic but the much less known Christian and democratic and contemplatively optimistic side of Tocqueville. His letters express the truth that the gloomy and Germanic twentieth-century notion of the "decline of the West" has been, in reality, a sentimental and bourgeois notion. Despite his frequent personal pessimism, Tocqueville manfully rejects the argument suggested by Gobineau (and later proclaimed by so many others) about the inevitability of the decline of Europe. Which is, perhaps, the highest and most exhilarating point reached in this correspondence.

Now it is not only that Tocqueville's predictions have proved almost always right and Gobineau's almost always wrong, that Gobineau (as did almost every nineteenth-century prophet) failed to recognize what may well be the two most astonishing developments of the twentieth century: the rise of American power and the reascendance of Catholicism all over the world. More than any other great dialogue of the nineteenth century, the Tocqueville-Gobineau correspondence is a crystalline, microcosmic representation of the great divisions of the twentieth.

It is evident that, by now, a general reaction has set in everywhere in the West against the basic assumptions of the French Revolution, against the enlightened illusions of the eighteenth century about perfectible human nature, against the inorganic optimism about the potential creation of an efficient Garden of Eden in this world, against utilitarianism, against individualism. There were many who foresaw that a reaction against these so often insubstantial and godless illusions had to come. Yet few foresaw the violent forms this reaction would take, for instance, in the form of a Hitler. That what Tocqueville had to say is very relevant to the twentieth century is obvious to the point of a platitude. But what is not so obvious is that Tocqueville, who was so justly critical of the illusions of the eighteenth century, had already begun to worry about the potential spiritual disasters of this reaction against them. He, who so often extolled the virtues of Faith and the follies of Reason when pushed to extremes, already foresaw the dangers of that new sort of political fideism which characterizes the mass movements of the twentieth century. And today when the Communist appeal in the West has shrunk to a minority of warped minions, we should recall that Tocqueville predicted that shrinking a century ago.

We should recognize that the main struggle may no longer develop between the two seemingly so logical antipoles of "Left" and "Right" (which, in themselves, are already outdated nineteenth-century designations) but between two divergent forces of the so-called "Right." We should liberate ourselves from accustomed ideological categories as we observe Europe in the last hundred years. The most outstanding figures have been men of the "Right": a Bismarck, a Churchill, a Mussolini, a Hitler, perhaps an Adenauer, a De Gaulle; so were most of the outstanding thinkers, from Nietzsche to Ortega; artists, poets, writers, historians, from Wagner to Yeats, from Ibsen to Orwell, the great anxious talents moved steadily "rightward" during their lifetime; and for the first time since the Counter Reformation conversions have been flowing almost unilaterally toward Catholicism. Of course it is true that meanwhile the European aristocracies, and with them all class differences, have gradually disappeared, that the practices of popular sovereignty, of universal suffrage, of universal education have become accepted everywhere as part and parcel of the modern welfare state: that, therefore, the structure of European society has become more and more social and democratic. But this structural development is not specifically European but global. What is specifically European within it is a spiritual movement to the "Right," a movement which is, at its best, instinctively conservative and which, at its worst, has been shot through with disgust against the tiring regimen of Reason. It is within these divergences that the meaning of the European Revolution appears.

In 1789 the issue could still be understood as "Right" versus "Left." But these designations no longer make sense when we try to apply them to such crucial episodes of recent European history as the rising of a few German patricians (but not of the millions of former German Marxist voters) against the totalitarian Hitler in July 1944. Nor are they applicable to the Polish or Hungarian revolutions of 1956, where despite twelve years of absolute Communist indoctrination the bankruptcy of the Communist appeal has been so evident; where it was obvious how much stronger and how more enduring are the political emotions of nationalism than the exhortations of international communism; where it could be said (and this is true of many more nations than meet the eye at first sight) that the main inherent divisions are between different concepts of anti-communism and between different concepts of *national* socialism. Consider the confusion of commentators who alternately speak of the "right-wing" or the "left-wing" rebels of the Communist parties in Poland and Hungary. But the essential difference is no longer between "Right" and "Left."

The essence of the division has been already manifest, here and there. It appears, for instance, between the totalitarian doctrines of Hitler and the authoritarian thought of a Salazar; in the divergence of the career of a Churchill from, say, that of a Mosley; in the difference between the actions of a De Gaulle and that of a Doriot; between the reactions to the twentieth century of Eliot on one hand and Knut Hamsun on the other; between the patriotism of a Péguy and the ideology of a Brasillach. Closer to the sources are the contrasts between the doctrines of Mosca and Gentile, between the principles of Burckhardt and of Nietzsche. The Tocqueville-Gobineau contrast is the first of these. This is why it is so important, prophetic, illuminative. From this earliest chrysalis of a correspondence one may glimpse the essential difference between those who, like Tocqueville, love liberty more than they dislike democracy and those who, like Gobineau, dislike democracy more than they love liberty.

Tocqueville foresaw that in the Western world the greatest dangers to the free human spirit may no longer come from the entrenched rule of aristocratic minorities but from the emancipated majorities themselves. To him it was always evident that such democratic institutions as universal suffrage, popular education, and the advancement of social equality were not automatic guarantees of freedom. So far there is little disagreement between Gobineau and Tocqueville or between Tocqueville and the great nineteenth-century conservative or even liberal thinkers. The quality of Tocqueville's aristocratic heart and mind,[4] however, was such that it made him rise above despair, self-pity, or sentimental rationalization: he refused to despair of democracy or to reject it. Again, this is not the position of a "moderate"; it is the attitude of a generous man. Nor is it expressible within the nineteenth-century parliamentary categories of "Right" and "Left."

It may be that in our days things are getting simpler: as the old categories of liberal politics dissolve, there might remain but two camps, conservatives and radicals. Tocqueville belonged to the first; Gobineau to the second. It is true that, in many ways, they did not represent human or even intellectual antipoles; at first sight it seems that just as the difference between Girondists and Jacobins, "Trots-

---

[4] There exists a Tocqueville notation on a fragment discovered posthumously by M. Redier, which is of fundamental importance to the understanding of Tocqueville. Dated November 1841, and entitled *Mon Instinct, Mes Opinions,* it says, among other things: "My mind favors democratic institutions, but my heart is aristocratic: I despise and fear mobs . . . I belong neither to the radical nor to the conservative party. Yet, after all, I incline rather to the second than to the first. For I differ with the conservatives rather in their means than in their end, while I differ with the radicals both in their means and in their end."

kyites" and "Stalinists," the difference between all kinds of "conservatives" or "Rightists" is, simply, a difference of shades. But it was Tocqueville himself who coined a maxim, the profound meaning of which transcends the geometrical conception of opposites. *"Ces sont les nuances qui querrellent,"* he said, *"pas les couleurs."* Two shades of color, though close in their articulate appearance, clash; but, of course, since they are different in purpose. Their purpose is different not in kind but in essence. Tocqueville knew that complex mystery of the human soul and will which makes it impossible to capture the difference of human beings and of their desires within fixed methodological categories or to illustrate them on mathematical scales. Mathematical logic, for instance, would compel us to say that every anti-anti-Communist is, by necessity, a pro-Communist. But this is nonsense.

This, too, Tocqueville knew. He despised communism or, indeed, all "Leftist" radicalism; but he would not overestimate their prospects. He saw that with the rise of social democracy the radical proletarian elements would gradually become property owners and adopt petty bourgeois ideals of spiritual and material security, but that during this pursuit of security they might thoughtlessly surrender whatever slight appetite for personal liberty they might originally have had. "I do not think that there is in France a man less revolutionary than I," wrote Tocqueville to Stoffels in 1836, "nor one who has a more profound hatred for what is called the revolutionary spirit." "Which spirit," he added, "by the way, combines very well with the love of an absolute government"—a prediction not only of Lenin but also of Hitler, and of course of Napoleon III. The plebiscitary success of the latter in 1848, largely due to a broad national movement which could with some justice be called today a sort of ideological anti-communism, not only confirmed Tocqueville's worst fears, it not only showed the world how the causes of liberty and of democracy might diverge; it also suggested to Tocqueville the forms which the European Revolution could take.

From some of his letters we can glimpse an astonishing insight into Russia. He considered Russia, notwithstanding all of her European veneer, essentially outside of and inimical to Western civilization. He would not have been surprised to see Russia turn Communist one day. But he saw the dangers of European civilization coming not from without but from within. And our now so natural concern with the deadly power of Bolshevik Russia should not obscure this truth. We should always remember that it was from Western Europe that Marxism traveled to Russia; that there the Bolshevik Revolution succeeded only because of the awful European War of 1914–18, when the European nations tore each other apart; that Lenin was sent back to Russia by nationalist Germany; that the rulers of the same Germany helped the Communist Russia regime survive; that it was Hitler, the revolutionary leader of the "New Europe," who twenty years later invited Stalin to advance into Poland; that nationalist revolutionary Germany and not Communist Russia was primarily responsible for the Second World War, from which the latter so naturally profited; that, unlike other and more spontaneous totalitarian movements ever since then, no Bolshevik regime has ever succeeded in Europe without the assistance of external, Russian, arms.

In this sense I do not hesitate to say that Tocqueville was an anti-anti-Communist. "The insane fear of socialism," he wrote in 1852, "throws the bourgeois headlong into the arms of despotism. As in Prussia, Hungary, Austria, Italy, in France the democrats have served the cause of the absolutists. But now that the weakness of the Red party has been proved, people will regret the price at which their enemy has been put down." By that time new kinds of radicals had arisen: Proudhon, Veuillot, Gobineau, different from each other but no longer "Leftist." The Leftist monopoly on radicalism was coming to an end; and it is practically finished now, a century later.

Most of these new radicals had accepted the Caesarean dictatorship of Napoleon III, which Tocqueville resisted from the beginning. Shortly thereafter he was proved to have been right. Yet this fame faded soon after his death, especially in France. By the end of the century he was regarded as something of an archaic liberal, bypassed by the new radicals of the "Right." It is a paradox, and a very meaningful one, that some of these early new "radicals of the Right," including even professed Catholics, regarded the racial Darwinism of Gobineau as "inspiring" and "traditional," while they neglected Tocqueville, whom one of them, Léon de Montesquiou, declared to have been *too* democratic, "a criminal." And the pregnant nature of this paradox persists in our generation when among the few who expressed their partial doubts about Tocqueville we find not only Harold Laski and a Soviet hack, Alpatov, but, perhaps symptomatically, Wyndham Lewis and Ezra Pound.

The European Revolution, beginning to unfold fully after 1848, has been a unique movement.[5] Tocqueville knew that it is anti-aristocratic; but he also knew that it is anti-Communist. Its origins came from intellectual pretension; it was furthered by intellectual confusion; yet in its late, popular phase it has been a revolution against Reason. It had, ever since its very first manifestation in seventeenth-century England, a Germanic character; it even

---

[5] When did it begin? From *The Old Regime* it clearly appears that Tocqueville is among those who believe that it began well before the French Revolution. I wish to suggest here that continental Europeans have, unfortunately, not devoted enough interest to the English Civil War of the seventeenth century, though, as the twentieth century progresses, the radical importance of that Anglo-Saxon revolution stands out more and more while the enduring importance of the French Revolution seems to pale. This is a pity, since today some of the effects of that

had condensed and angry manifestations outside Europe, in the Russian Slavophiles and in the American Populists; and though its hitherto most disastrous wave, with Hitler riding its crest, has now subsided, it is by no means certain that it has run its course, that other waves are not going to form. Yet these need not prove necessarily disastrous. Tocqueville, who knew that history is unpredictable, had a very deep trust in that unique quality of resilience which characterizes European civilization. He refused to share the savage pessimism of Gobineau.

Their dialogue is, of course, conducted on an aristocratic level. Yet it has something in common with the dialogue between Proudhon and Marx, a dialogue on the radical level; and it has much in common with another great contemporary dialogue, the one between Burckhardt and Nietzsche, in fragments on a higher level. For Europe, against the hard logical categories of Marx, Proudhon's warnings about popular instinct, "which grasps more easily the simple notion of Power than the complex notion of Social Contract," stand out. Instead of her complacency with constitutions, contracts, and colonial alliances, Europe should have heeded them before 1914. Against the exaltation of emotions, Burckhardt's warnings against "the terrible simplifiers" stand out. Instead of her complacency with the "organic and social" architects of anti-Communist states, Europe should have heeded them before 1939. But the warnings of Tocqueville are, perhaps, timeliest now.

For, by now, social democracy has triumphed almost all

---

ideological and nationalist, anti-aristocratic and anti-Communist, social and democratic seventeenth-century revolution are returning to the continent of Europe through a roundabout way: from America. Here it should be added that, despite his instinctive comprehension of the history and society of the English-speaking peoples, Tocqueville did not seem to have fully understood the meaning of 1641. From his few scattered notations on the subject it appears as if it were about the *only* instance where his judgment may have been consistently wrong.

over the world. That this is no time for nostalgic evocations of the order of the past, Tocqueville knew more than a hundred years ago. While so many pre-eminent minds were still struggling against democracy, Tocqueville concluded that democracy was here to stay and that the question was this: What kind of democracy? He foresaw that neither bourgeois society nor the bourgeois mode of thought, nor bourgeois liberalism, nor a neo-medieval romanticism would by itself prevent the devolution of democracies into national, and later continental, socialist tyrannies. But Christianity could. His chief dream remained to reconcile modern democracy with the Church. He believed "that the faults of the clergy are far less dangerous to liberty than their subjection to the State." And he said—and here he remained, until now, frequently misunderstood—that to hate democracy is, therefore, not merely impractical: it is also immoral. But he was not only ahead of Marx in a moral sense; he was ahead of him by a hundred years.

8

In the end his letters to Gobineau represent the Catholic Christian Tocqueville. If *The Revolution* gives evidence of the genius of Tocqueville the historian, his letters to Gobineau especially after 1852 indicate that he was then a believing Christian. This is important, since he has seldom been so classified by his commentators. Again, the accustomed categories have proved an obstacle in understanding Tocqueville; some of his commentators have been misled by the circumstance that during the last decade of his life many of his closest friends and correspondents were so-called "liberal" Catholics. Many of his commentators are, for instance, baffled by the circumstance that after 1852, when French Catholic opinion was divided in two camps, Tocqueville sided neither with the "rigorists" nor with the "liberals," neither with Veuillot, nor with his friend Montalembert, and that he was privately often critical of both. The agnostic Sainte-Beuve implied that Tocqueville could hardly have been a Catholic. The Marxist Laski, on the other hand, said that Tocqueville "believed almost despite himself." Curiously enough, one of the earliest unequivocal assertions of Tocqueville's Catholicism came not from a liberal Catholic but from the pen of the Abbé Baunard, from an ultramontane rigorist who wisely chose to include Tocqueville among the outstanding nineteenth-century defenders of the Faith.

Now it is not given to us human beings to affirm the extent of faith in others. We should not, and cannot, attribute various degrees of faith to our fellow men, dead or living. Nor are we allowed to assert the sincerity of their faith or the lack of it from our own attribution of their unexpressed motives. All we, men, are allowed to do is to record their expressions or denials of faith in their words and deeds. I believe that Tocqueville's expressions in these letters are a very important part of that record.

But beyond the argument about Tocqueville's personal Christianity stands his remarkably novel and rational affirmation of the Faith. For there is nothing nostalgic or sentimental in his rational conclusions. Contrast the generosity of the conservative Tocqueville in these letters, his belief that everywhere human nature was the same, with the dour conservatism and the muscular Christianity of his contemporary, Sir James Stephen, who claimed that Teutonic blood was the basis of liberty. All the great converts and religious thinkers of the past hundred years deplored the weakening of religion in Europe, as did Tocqueville; yet Tocqueville sensed early that the great dangers in the new age of social democracy would come less from faithlessness than from lovelessness. Gobineau, in his *Les Pléiades*, speaks of the "folly of the Western concept of Love." To Tocqueville, instead, it is the Christian message of love, Saint Paul's eternal exhortation that without charity faith is nothing, which is the greatest and the truly unique treasure in the heritage of Western Christendom.

Not that one should dismiss the Catholicism of Gobineau. It is true that his Catholicism had a curious tinge (it was perhaps a Hispanic tinge, like that of Maurras, perhaps a Bavarian one, like that of Döllinger). His anticlerical biographer, Schemann, in trying to explain Gobineau's Catholicism away, claimed that Gobineau was an *Ur-Katholik*, an Old Catholic, that he strove to bring about a harmony between Catholicism and Germandom, that he wished to eliminate the Jewish element from the Old Testament. There is something to this. There were also certain German Catholic churchmen, a prelate of Mainz, the Bishop of Rothenburg, the famous F. X. Kraus,[6] who were enthusiastic early members of the racialist *Gobineau-Vereinigung*. They were soon proved wrong. But so was Romain Rolland when he wrote (in 1923) that Tocqueville and Gobineau belonged to successive generations. Though he rightly sensed that the new Gobineauists (he pointed out Montherlant) represented a dangerous tendency, as indeed their performance in 1940 was to show, his tired suggestion that Tocqueville was but a fine figure of the past proved mistaken, after all. The impact of Tocqueville survived that of Gobineau.

It is an impact which is by no means merely intellectual. "Do what you will," wrote the young Tocqueville to his friend Kergorlay, "you can't change the fact that men have bodies as well as souls—that the angel is enclosed in the beast . . . Any philosophy, any religion which tries to leave entirely out of account one of these two things may produce a few extraordinary examples, but it will never influence humanity as a whole. This is what I believe, and it troubles

---

[6] In 1899 this very influential German nationalist prelate wrote in his recently published (1957) Diaries: "For long I haven't agreed with Tocqueville; he seems to have made his peace with Democracy too cheaply and too soon."

me, for you know that, no more detached from the beast
than anyone else, I adore the angel and want at all costs
to see him predominate . . ." The world is indebted to the
Abbé Baunard and to M. Antoine Redier for a truly pains-
taking description of Tocqueville's Catholic Christian death.
He was buried on the feast day of Saint Anselm, another
solitary writer in Normandy, who became Archbishop of
Canterbury, another believer in the noble alliance of Saint
George and Saint Denis. Early in the cold, unsure Christian
dawn of the eleventh-century Anselm, like Abelard, fought
"in season and out of season" for political and for intellectual liberty, against the ambitious tyranny of William II
Rufus. He was neither a political nor a Gnostic mystic; he
embodied the best in the Western and French, in the European Christian tradition. "Christ loves nothing so much in
this world," he said (and so did Alexis de Tocqueville),
"as the liberty of his Church." "I do not try to understand
in order to believe," Saint Anselm wrote, "I believe in order
to understand."

"I cannot believe," wrote Tocqueville, "that God has for
several centuries been pushing two or three hundred million men toward equality just to make them wind up under
a Tiberian or Claudian despotism. Verily, that wouldn't be
worth the trouble. Why He is drawing us toward democracy, I do not know; but embarked on a vessel that I did
not build, I am at least trying to use it to gain the nearest
port."

THE REVOLUTION

The projected second volume of
The Old Regime and the Revolution

[From Tocqueville's posthumous notes]

Original concept; general approach to the subject

> Should be reread at times, to keep me on the
> main course of my thoughts (1856).

My aim is:

1. The true portrait of a man, extraordinary rather than great, who as yet has not, I believe, been drawn with adequate fidelity or depth. Novel side of my aim.

Whatever reflects him, in his thoughts, in his passions, in his true *self*, must attract my particular attention.

2. How he was aided by existing conditions and by the opinions prevalent during his times.

3. The means he employed.

But for him and because of him, I want to paint, above all, the great Revolution, in which he played such an important part. To judge and describe it with a freer spirit than has been employed hitherto; to profit from contemporary sources which shed light on important features. This task could be great and original if it were only well done.

Further, I want to paint the peculiar physiognomy of France in the midst of this revolution: what it was that this revolution added to our national character; how our national character contributed to it. A new view, if I succeed in treating it with the detached freedom of which I may be capable especially now when I am no longer interested in politics, when I have none of those passions which would urge me to embellish or distort features, when I have no other desire than to discover what is true and describe it.[1]

[1] (T) A marginal addition to the two last paragraphs: "We are still too close to these events to know many details (this seems curious, but it is true); details often appear only in posthumous revelations and are frequently ignored by contemporaries. But what these writers know better than does posterity are the movements of opinion, the popular inclinations of their times, the vibrations of which they can still sense in their minds and hearts. The true traits of the principal persons and of their relationships, of the movements of the masses are often better described by witnesses than recorded by posterity. These are the necessary details. Those close to them are better placed to trace the general history, the general causes, the grand movements of events, the spiritual currents which men who are further removed may no longer find since these things cannot be perceived from the memoirs."

BOOK ONE

[Before the Revolution]

CHAPTER I

Of the Violent and Uncertain Agitation of Minds before the Revolution[1]

In the ten or fifteen years before the French Revolution throughout Europe the human mind was affected by strange, incoherent, irregular impulses, in a mood not seen for centuries. These were symptoms of a new and extraordinary disease which would have singularly alarmed the world if only the world had understood it.

The general idea of the greatness of man, of the omnipotence of his reason, of the limitless powers of his intelligence had penetrated and pervaded the spirit of the

---

[1] (T) In Tocqueville's files there is a notation which very clearly expresses the intention of this chapter. "This chapter, at first sight, seems to depict both France and the rest of Europe. Yet it does not really deal with France. It should not, either, since I had written my first volume to sketch the origins of the Revolution in France. I must therefore sketch the intellectual developments outside France, also to avoid an impression of repetition. Thus in the beginning I should say something like this: 'Many things that I had previously said about France should be understood as having involved all of Europe . . .'"

century; yet this lofty conception of mankind in general was coupled with a particular contempt for the contemporary age and for contemporary society. The pride of humanity was madly inflated; the esteem of one's own times and one's own country was singularly low. All over the Continent that instinctive attachment and involuntary respect which men of all ages and nations are wont to feel for their own institutions, for their traditional customs, and for the wisdom or the virtues of their forefathers had almost ceased to exist among the educated classes.

These talked unceasingly about the decrepitude, the senselessness, and the ridiculous nature of existing institutions, about the vices and the corruption of existing society.

Traces of this state of mind may be discovered throughout the literature of Germany. Philosophy, history, even the novels are full of it. *Waldemar,* that insipid philosophical novel written by Jacobi in 1779 which, no matter how ridiculous, made a great contemporary impression, is full of diatribes against the times and full of predictions of a coming catastrophe. "The actual state of society," wrote Jacobi, "is to me nothing but the aspect of a dead and stagnant sea: that is why I would desire a flood of barbarians, if need be, to sweep away these reeking marshes, to uncover a virgin soil."

Hornich (a man of common sense who later in the novel is discarded by the author) is quite alarmed when he hears this. He has reason to be. I think that the author would have been even more alarmed over that barbarian flood had he really believed it.

He says, furthermore: "We are living amidst the debris of institutions and forms—a monstrous chaos, reflecting decay and death everywhere."

These things were written in pretty country houses by wealthy people, surrounded by literary society in their drawing rooms, passing their time in endless philosophical discussions which affected, excited, and inflamed them until they shed torrents of imaginary tears most of the time.

That book shows very well how far these oddities of an idle, excitable, intellectual society spread across Europe. Its ponderous exaggerations merely illustrate in a German setting all the faults of French thinking at the time.

It was not the princes, not the ministers, not the rulers, not those, in short, who in different positions were directing human affairs who perceived that some great change was at hand. The idea that government could become different, that what had lasted so long might be destroyed and superseded by what as yet existed only in the brains of a few writers, the thought that the existing state of things might be overthrown for the sake of establishing a new order in the midst of disorder and ruin, would have appeared to them as an absurd dream. The most that these governing people could envisage was some sort of gradual reform.

It is curious to see in the official correspondence of that era able and clear-sighted administrators laying their plans, framing their measures, and making scientific reform projects for a time when the government they served, when the laws they applied, when their own society and they themselves would be no more.

It is a common fault of otherwise intelligent and practical men that they judge by certain measures people whose purpose is to change or to destroy those very measures. Yet when passion begins to rule, the opinions of men of experience are often less important than are schemes in the minds of dreamers.

Do not suppose that this disgust with one's own times and with one's own country, which had so strangely afflicted almost all the peoples of Europe, was a superficial or a transient sentiment. Ten years later the French Revolution had inflicted on Germany violent upheavals, death, and destruction. Even then one of those Germans in whom enthusiasm for France had turned to bitter hatred exclaims, mindful of the past, in a confidential outburst: "What was is no more. What new building will be raised on the ruins? I don't know. But what I do know is that it would be horrid if out of this terrible era would come again the apathy and the worn-out forms of the past. . . . One cannot stage a play by repeating the first act. Let us progress!" "Yes," replies the nobleman to whom these words were addressed, "the old society must perish."

The ten or fifteen years which preceded the French Revolution were, all over Europe, years of great prosperity. Useful enterprises developed everywhere; the taste for material enjoyment spread; industry and commerce, supplying these wants, flourished and grew. It would appear that when there is much bustle and pleasure the human mind would not indulge in abstract considerations of society but would think more about personal affairs. This impression is false. For the contrary took place. All over Europe, almost as much as in France, the educated classes reveled in philosophical discussions. Where one would expect this the least, people were philosophizing passionately. In the great commercial cities of Germany, in Hamburg, Lübeck, and Danzig, the merchants, traders, and manufacturers would meet after the labors of the day to debate great questions about the existence, the condition, the happiness of man. Even the women, amidst their petty household cares, were sometimes transported by these grandiose problems. It seemed as if everyone wished to escape whenever he could from his private affairs to devote himself to the greater concerns of humanity.

In France literary affairs filled a large space even in the busiest lives. The publication of a new book was an event in the villages as well as in the large cities. Everything was a subject of inquiry; everything was a source of emotion. It seemed that arsenals of passion were accumulating in every breast, seeking but an occasion to break out.

Thus a traveler who had been round the globe was an object of universal attention. When Forster, one of Captain

Cook's companions, went to Germany in 1774 he was received with tremendous enthusiasm. The smallest villages feted him; crowds pressed about him to hear his adventures from his own lips, but still more to hear him describe the unknown countries he had visited and the strange customs of the men among whom he had been living. People kept asking themselves: Is not their savage simplicity worth more than all our riches and our arts? Are not their instincts better than our virtues?

A certain unfrocked Lutheran priest, one Basedow, ignorant, quarrelsome, a drunkard, a caricature of Luther, claimed to have invented a new system of schools which, he said, would change the ideas and habits of his countrymen. He presented his scheme in vulgar but enthusiastic language. He took care to announce that his aim was the regeneration not merely of Germany but of the entire human race. For this purpose it would be sufficient to follow his simple method, with the help of which all men would become enlightened and virtuous. Soon all Germany is in movement. Princes, nobles, merchants, magistrates, free cities abet the great innovator. Lords and ladies of high estate write to Basedow for advice. Hordes of mothers place his books in the hands of their children. Everywhere the old German schools founded by Melanchthon are forsaken. A college designed to educate these reformers of mankind is founded under the name of "Philanthropinon," flourishes for a short while, then disappears. The enthusiasm evaporates, leaving behind confused and disturbed minds. That such a man could produce such effects would be inconceivable were it not that the power of innovators in revolutionary times comes much less from themselves than from what they encounter in the spirit of the mass.

We know how, on the eve of the French Revolution, Europe teemed with strange fraternities and secret societies, either newly formed or resurrected under long-forgotten titles. Such were the Swedenborgians, the Martinists, the

Freemasons, the Illuminati, the Rosicrucians, the Disciples of Strict Abstinence, the Mesmerists, and many other varieties of these.

Many of these sects originally had been formed with limited concerns in mind. Yet all of them were now busy with the destiny of mankind. Most of them had originally been philosophical or religious societies: all of them were now fascinated by politics. Their means differed but they, all, proposed the same objective: a regeneration of society and the reform of government. Physicians say that during great plagues all kinds of maladies end up by producing some symptoms of the dominant epidemic. This is what happened in the intellectual world.

Another thing should be noted. This was a time when the sciences, as they became more positive and more certain, had discredited miracles—when the inexplicable was usually regarded as false, when in every sphere reason claimed to supersede authority, reality imagination and free inquiry faith. Yet every one of the sects I have just mentioned had some sort of mystique of its own. Some of them were imbued with mystical conceptions: others fancied they had found the way to change some of the laws of nature. All sorts of enthusiastic fads passed for science, philosophic cranks found all kinds of listeners, impostors could rouse crowds of believers. Nothing shows better the perplexed and agitated condition of minds grasping for this and for that, like a traveler in the woods who fears that he lost his main path and who, instead of going ahead, desperately tries to hack out new paths in all kinds of directions.

Today it is impoverished workers, obscure artisans, ignorant peasants who join secret societies. At the time I am speaking of they consisted entirely of princes, great nobles, financiers, merchants, and men of letters. When in 1786 the secret papers of the Illuminati were seized from their leader, Weishaupt, some typically anarchist documents were found among them: personal property was described as the source of all evil and absolute equality was exalted. In the same sectarian archives there was a list of members: it consisted of the most distinguished names of Germany.

Many contemporary writers, unable to discern the general causes which had produced these strange developments, attributed them to a conspiracy of secret societies. As if any particular conspiracy could ever explain the sudden destruction of all the existing institutions! The secret societies were certainly not the cause of the Revolution. They must be regarded, instead, as one of the most conspicuous signs of its coming.

They were not the only signs.

It would be a mistake to suppose that the American Revolution was hailed with ardent sympathy in France alone. Its echo reverberated to the very ends of Europe: everywhere it was regarded as a beacon. Professor Steffens, who thirty years later took so active a part in the German rising against France, relates in his *Memoirs* how in early childhood the first thing that excited him was the cause of American independence.

"I still remember vividly," says he, "what happened at Elsinore and in the harbor on the day when the peace was signed that secured the triumph of freedom. The day was fine; the harbor was full of ships of every nation. We were up, expecting the sunrise with eager impatience. All the ships flew their colors—the masts ornamented with pennants, everything covered with flags; the weather was calm, with just enough wind to cause the gay bunting to flutter in the breeze; the cannon booming, the cheers of the crews made a festival of the day. My father (who was a doctor) had invited some friends to his table; they drank to the victory of the Americans and to the triumph of popular liberty, though there was some obscure concern with what would result from this triumph. This was like the bright and pleasing dawn of a later so bloody day. My father sought to imbue us with the love of political liberty. Contrary to our domestic habit, he had us brought to the table; there he impressed us with the importance of the event we were witnessing and bade us drink with him and his guests to the welfare of the new republic."

Of the men who, in every corner of old Europe, felt themselves thus moved by the deeds of a small people in the New World, not one thoroughly understood the deep and secret sources of his own emotion, yet everyone heard a signal in that distant sound. What it announced was still unknown. It was like the voice of John crying in the wilderness that new times were at hand.

Do not assign specific causes to these events: they were but different symptoms of the same social disease. Everywhere the old institutions and the old powers no longer accurately fitted the new conditions and the novel desires of men.

Hence that strange unrest which led even the great and the successful to consider their own state of life intolerable. Hence that universal desire for change, flooding every mind, though no one knew as yet how that change could be brought about. An internal and spontaneous impulse seemed to shake at once the whole structure of society; it shook to their foundations the customary ideas and habits of every man. One felt that it could not be halted. Yet no one knew which way things would fall, and the whole of Europe trembled like a huge mass before toppling over.

CHAPTER II

How This Vague Agitation of Human Minds
in France Suddenly Became a Positive Passion,
and What Form This Passion First Assumed

In the year 1787 this vague agitation of minds which I have
just described, and which for some time had perturbed the
whole of Europe without any definite direction, suddenly
became in France an active passion toward a specific goal.

But, strangely enough, this goal was not the one which
the French Revolution was to attain, and those who were
first and most affected by this new passion were the very
men whom the Revolution was to devour.

At first they were looking not so much for equality as
for political liberty. And the Frenchmen who were first impassioned and who set society in motion belonged not to
the lower but to the upper classes. Before filtering down to
the people, this new fury against absolute power took hold
of the nobles, the clergy, the magistracy, the wealthiest of
the bourgeois, who, being closest to the master of the State,
had more means than had others of resisting him as well as
more hopes of sharing his power.

I shall not relate how, by 1787, Louis XVI was led by
financial considerations to invite the members of the nobility, the clergy, and the upper rank of the bourgeois, and
to submit to this Assembly of Notables the state of affairs.
I am discussing, not recounting, history. . . .

Henri IV had once used the same means to adjourn the
Estates-General and to obtain, in their absence, a sort of

public sanction to his measures; but now times were different. In 1596, France emerged from a long civil war; she was worn down by her efforts and distrustful of her own powers; she sought only rest and asked of her rulers no more than a semblance of legality. Then her notables helped France to forget the Estates-General; but in 1787 they suddenly revived that image in her memory.

At the time of Henri IV the princes, nobles, bishops, and rich bourgeois whom the King summoned for advice were still the masters of society. They could therefore control the movement they had helped to bring about; they were able to support as well as resist royalty. Under Louis XVI these same classes retained merely the externals of power. Its substance had slipped from them forever. They were, so to speak, hollow bodies, still resonant but easy to crush. They were still capable of exciting the people; they were incapable of directing it.

Since this great change had come about imperceptibly, it was not yet recognized by anyone. The notables failed to see it; their opponents were uncertain. The whole nation had been for so long separated from the government of her own affairs that she had but a confused view of her own condition.

No sooner were the notables assembled than, forgetting that they were the nominees of the sovereign, chosen by him to give counsels and not injunctions, they began to act as if they were the representatives of the nation. They demanded the public accounts; they censured the acts of the government; they attacked most of the measures, though they had been requested merely to facilitate their execution. They had been asked for their assistance; instead, they proclaimed their opposition.

Public opinion instantly rose in their favor; it threw its whole weight on their side. One could now witness the singular spectacle of a government which, trying to become popular, was proposing measures favorable to the popular interest without, however, ceasing to be unpopular; and of an assembly resisting these measures with the support of public favor.

Thus the government proposed to reform the salt tax [*la gabelle*], which weighed so heavily and often so cruelly on the people. It would have abolished forced labor [*la corvée*], reformed the *taille*, and suppressed the half tithes, from which the upper classes had earlier succeeded in exempting themselves. In the place of these taxes to be abolished or reformed, a real estate tax was proposed on the same basis of our real estate tax of today. The internal customs houses, which had restricted trade and industry, were to be removed. Finally, beside the royal Intendants, who administered each province, an elective body was to be placed with the power of not only watching but also, in most cases, directing the conduct of public affairs.

All of these measures were either resisted or postponed by the notables. But it was the government which remained unpopular, and it was the notables who received the public acclaim.

Fearing that he had not been understood, the Finance Minister, Calonne, explained in a public document that the new laws would relieve the poor from a part of their taxes and would shift that portion onto the rich. That was true, but the Minister remained unpopular. "The clergy," he said elsewhere, "are, before everything else, citizens and subjects. They should pay taxes like everyone else. If they have debts they should sell some of their properties to discharge them." That again was aimed at one of the most sensitive points of public opinion. The public was unmoved.

The notables opposed the reform of the *taille* on the ground that it would impose an excessive burden on other taxpayers, especially on the nobility and clergy (whose taxation had already been reduced to nearly nothing). The abolition of internal customs houses they peremptorily opposed on behalf of certain provinces allegedly deserving special consideration. If they loudly approved in principle the creation of Provincial Assemblies, they also desired that instead of the three estates sitting together these small local bodies should be kept separate, always under the presidency of a nobleman or a prelate. "For," said some of the committees of notables, "unless guided by the superior minds of the upper estates, these assemblies would tend to democracy."

Meanwhile the popularity of the notables remained unshaken to the end. As a matter of fact, it constantly increased. They were applauded, incited, encouraged. When they resisted the government, they were loudly cheered on to combat. And the King, when he dismissed them, felt obliged to offer them his thanks.

Many of them were said to have been amazed at this sudden increase in power and public favor. They would have been more amazed if they could have foreseen what was about to follow. For the very proposals which they had fought with so much popular applause came from the very principles which were to triumph in the Revolution; and those traditional institutions with which they opposed the reforms proposed by the royal government were the very institutions which the Revolution was to destroy.

These notables were popular not because of the content but because of the very existence of their opposition. They criticized the abuses of the royal power; they censured its extravagance; they demanded an account of its expenditures; they spoke of the constitutional laws of the country, of the fundamental principles limiting the unlimited powers of the Crown and, without exactly calling for national participation in the government through the Estates-General, they continually kept suggesting that idea.

This was enough.

For some time already the government had been suffering from a malady which is the natural and incurable disease of powers that undertake to regulate, to foresee, to do everything. It had become responsible for everything. However men might differ about the grounds of their complaints, they were united in blaming the common source, but what up to now had been no more than a general inclination suddenly became a universal and impetuous emotion. All the secret sores caused by the constant contact with dilapidated institutions, chafing habit as well as ideas in a thousand places; all the subdued hatreds kept in existence by divided classes, by questionable conditions, by absurd or oppressive distinctions, now broke out against the supreme power. For a long time their passions had sought to come out into the open. Now a path seemed open; they rushed forward blindly. It was not their natural path, but it was the first they found. At this moment the hatred of arbitrary power seemed to have become the sole passion of Frenchmen, and the government their common enemy.

CHAPTER III

How the Parliaments, Aided by Precedent,
Overthrew the Monarchy[1]

The feudal government, whose ruined structure still sheltered the people, had been a government in which arbitrary power, violence, and great freedom all existed. Under its

[1] The word "parliament" should not confuse the reader. The parliaments of 1787 were still closer to being medieval courts than to political bodies: their function was judicial rather than legislative.

laws freedom of action had often been restricted, but speech was almost always free, independent, and bold.

The legislative power was always exercised by the King, but never without checks. When the great old political assemblies of France had ceased to exist, the parliaments took their place; and before they were to codify a new law officially decreed by the King, they stated their objections and expressed their opinions.

Many investigations have been made into the origins of this partial usurping of legislative functions by the judicial power. They are to be found only in the general habits of those times which could not suffer or even conceive of a human power so absolute and secret that it could not even permit a discussion on the terms of obedience. So the function of the parliaments grew naturally from contemporary ideas and from the habits of subjects and kings.

An edict, before being enforced, was sent down to the parliament. The agents of the Crown explained its principles and advantages; the magistrates discussed it; all this was done in public, in open debate, with that virility characteristic of the institutions of the Middle Ages. It frequently happened that the parliament sent deputies to the King several times in succession, asking him to modify or withdraw an edict. If sometimes the King came down in person he allowed his own law to be debated vigorously, at times even violently, in his very presence. But when he finally made his will known, there was silence and obedience; for the magistrates recognized that they were but the chief officers and representatives of the sovereign, that their duty was to advise but not to coerce him.

What happened in 1787 was that these ancient precedents were suddenly put into action again. The old governmental machine was again set in motion; yet it soon became apparent that the machine was propelled by some new and unknown power which, instead of making it run well, was going to destroy it.

Thus the King, following custom, had the new edicts brought down to parliament; and the parliament, equally according to custom, remonstrated.[2]

The King replied; the parliament insisted. For centuries things had gone on in this way, and the nation could hear from time to time this sort of political dialogue carried on above its head between the sovereign and his magistrates. The practice had only been interrupted during the reign of Louis XIV, and for a short time; but what was new now was the subject of the debate and the nature of the arguments.

This time the parliament, proceeding to codify the edicts, called for all the accounts of the finances, what we would now call the state budget; and since the King naturally declined to deliver the entire government to a body which was neither elected nor officially responsible and so to share the legislative power with a tribunal, the parliament then declared that the nation alone had the right to raise taxes, and thereupon demanded a national assembly.

The parliament thus captured the very heart of the people, but certainly not for very long.

The arguments put forward by the magistrates to support their demands were not less new than the demands themselves. The King, they said, was merely the administrator and not the possessor of public wealth; the representative and principal officer of the nation, but not its master; sovereignty resided only in the nation itself; the nation alone could decide great questions; its rights were not dependent on the will of the sovereign; their source was

---

[2] (T) The Edicts of 17 June 1787 were:
1. For the free trade of grain.
2. To establish provincial assemblies.
3. For the commutation of forced labor.
4. A land subsidy.
5. A Stamp Act.
The parliament accepted the first three and resisted the last two.

the nature of man; they were as indestructible as human nature itself.

When the King exiled the parliament from Paris, that body protested that liberty of speech and action was the inalienable right of men and could not be wrested from them except through tyranny or through lawful judicial procedure.

It should not be supposed that the parliaments presented these principles as if they were something new. These were, on the contrary, very industriously traced back to the vaguest origins of the monarchy. The judgments or decrees of the parliament of Paris were crammed with historical quotations, frequently reproduced from the Middle Ages, in barbarous Latin. They were full of capitulations, old royal ordinances, rules, and dusty precedents dragged out from the attic of the past.

It was a curious spectacle to see these "newborn" ideas, enclosed and swathed in these swaddles of antiquity, brought forth again.

It was the old tradition of monarchy that parliament should be allowed to remonstrate in a frank and almost rude fashion. The parliament, moreover, was used to making a great deal of noise for small results. What it said usually went beyond what it meant; it was allowed a sort of oratorical exaggeration. The most absolute sovereigns had tolerated this license because of the impotence of those speaking. Since the kings were assured of obedience, the indulgence of free speech could be permitted. Within this established society, a sort of dramatic comedy was played before the nation. But now the play and the audience were different.

Now the parliament carried this old freedom to a degree of license never heard before, for a newborn fire was burning in their hearts, unconsciously inflaming their language. I dare to say that despite the military and police forces at the disposal of many of our modern governments not one of them could afford to have its ministers and its measures continually attacked in such terms.

Especially on the subject of taxation and against the collectors of the revenue the parliaments had always argued violently. Their language would, at first, seem inconceivable were it not that the speeches only repeated with more violence what had been said so many times before on the same subject. Since under the old monarchy most of the taxes were levied on private landowners, people had been accustomed to look upon taxation as a levy on the profits of certain men and not as the common burden of the nation. Taxes were commonly denounced as "odious exactions"; their vices and burdens were exaggerated; their collectors were called thieves of the public, enriching themselves out of the poverty of all.[3] The government which had granted the tax farmers their very rights scarcely said anything different. It acted as if this business were not its own, as if it wished to ignore the clamor which pursued its own agents.

When, therefore, the parliament of Paris spoke in this manner about taxes, it merely followed an old practice, repeating what had already been said a hundred times. The play was the same, but the audience was different and larger. And the clamor, instead of dying away as it usually did within the classes who, because of their privileges, were hardly affected by taxation at all, was now so loud and so repetitious that it finally filtered down to the classes which

[3] (T) From an additional note by Tocqueville: "The inflated sentimentalism, the exaggerated expressions, the incoherence, and the ungainly images, those constant citations from antiquity which were to be characteristic of the language of the Revolution were already habitual at this time. Tranquillity or moderation was completely absent. The overwhelming inclinations of all minds were to commonplaces; nor was it permissible to express anything simply; it was necessary that the expression should overflow beyond the original idea or sentiment. . . ."

bore the heaviest burden; and it began to fill them with fury.

Parliament and King were hardly in accord except on one point. They agreed on the edict creating new local powers under the name of Provincial Assemblies. How astonishing this agreement is in retrospect! That the King should propose and parliament accept such a radically destructive law shows better than anything else how in these times when everyone, including women, were busying themselves with political discussions common sense about human nature was absent from society and from government alike.

(Here, in a rapid sketch, show how the edict concerning the Provincial Assemblies was to destroy the entire political system of old Europe by suddenly substituting democracy for aristocracy, republic for monarchy.) I am not speaking of the value of this reform; I am saying only that it was such an immediate and radical change of old institutions that the mutual agreement of parliament and King to go ahead with it suggests that neither of them knew where they were going; they walked hand in hand in the dark. . . .

If the parliament employed new arguments in trying to establish its old rights, the government did not hesitate to employ new means in defending its ancient prerogatives. (Here bring in whatever I can find in the speeches of the King, ministers, writings of their official friends that tend to incite the rich against the poor, the unprivileged against the privileged, the bourgeois against the noblemen . . . From a pamphlet attributed to the Court for example: "The parliament want to retain their exemption from taxation; this is nothing but a continuation of that formidable alliance between the nobility of sword and gown under the pretext of liberty to humble and enslave the commons, whom the King alone defends and intends to elevate.")

It seems that both parliament and King wished to instruct the people in the quickest and easiest way possible.

The first wanted to teach them about the vices of royalty, the second about the crimes of aristocracy. The first attacked a power which it did not really wish to destroy, the second affirmed new and pernicious powers which it did not really wish to employ.

While these discussions about the very essence of government were going on, the daily work of the administration threatened to stop; money was lacking. The parliament had rejected measures relating to taxation. It refused to sanction a loan. In this perplexity the King, since he saw that he could not win over the Assembly, tried to coerce it. He went down to them and, before commanding their submission, less eager as he was to exercise than to reaffirm his rights, he caused the edicts to be debated once more in his presence. Yet, after having thus permitted this well-established and so customary privilege to be contested before him, the King chose to resume the exercise of his most disputed and least popular ones. His own act had opened the mouths of the speakers; now he sought to punish them for having spoken. Then occurred a most typical scene which shows how the most easygoing government may unwittingly assume the traits of tyranny.

Two men especially stood out by the boldness of their speeches and by their rebellious attitude: they were M. Goislard and M. d'Eprémesnil. It was decided to arrest them. Informed of this decision, they fled their homes and took refuge in parliament itself, where, in the full dress of their order, they were merged in the crowd of magistrates. The *Palais de Justice* was surrounded by soldiers. The Vicomte d'Agoult, commanding these, appeared alone in the great chamber. The entire parliament was assembled, sitting in all its solemnity. The number of the magistrates, the venerable tradition of this court, the dignity of their dress, the simplicity of their demeanor, the extent of their power, the majesty of the very hall filled with so many historic memories all contributed to make the parliament at that moment the greatest and most respected body after the Throne.

In the presence of such an assembly the royal officer stood, at first silent. He was asked who had sent him there. He answered in a rude but unsure tone: he had come to arrest two members. They should be pointed out to him. The parliament sat motionless and silent. The officer withdrew, re-entered, then withdrew again; parliament, still motionless and silent, neither resisted nor yielded.

Night had fallen. The soldiers lit fires around the approaches to the palace as if it were a fort besieged. Crowds began to assemble at some distance. The populace was perplexed but not yet excited, thus standing aloof to contemplate by the light of those campfires a scene so new and strange under the monarchy. The oldest government in Europe thus showed the people how to challenge the majesty of the oldest institutions and how to violate in their very sanctuary the most venerable of ancient privileges.

This lasted until midnight, when D'Eprémesnil finally rose. He thanked the parliament for the effort it had made to save him; he did not wish to impose on it any longer. He commended the public cause and his children to their care and, descending the steps of the court, surrendered himself to the officer. It seemed as if he were leaving this assembly to mount the scaffold. A scaffold, indeed, he was one day to mount, but in quite different circumstances!

The only living witness of this strange scene told me that at these words of D'Eprémesnil the whole Assembly burst into tears. It was as if a new Regulus were marching out of Rome to return to the horrid death awaiting him in Carthage. The Marshal de Noailles sobbed aloud; yet many tears were to be soon shed at the occasion of greater tragedies.

These parliamentary tears were exaggerated, though they were not false ones. For at the beginning of a revolution the vividness of emotions always supersedes the importance of events, while at its close the opposite is sadly true.

France was at that time divided into thirteen judicial provinces, each of which had a parliament. All of these parliaments were absolutely independent of one another; all of them had equal prerogatives; all of them possessed the same right of discussing the mandates of the legislator before submitting to them. This will seem natural if we consider the time when most of these courts of justice were founded. The parts of France were then so dissimilar in their interests, dispositions, customs, and habits that the same legislation could not be simultaneously applied to all of them. Since distinct laws were usually enacted for the particular provinces, it was natural that in each province there should be a parliament to test and apply them. Later, France having become more homogeneous, one law sufficed for all; but the rights of discussing and applying the laws remained different.

Thus a royal edict, accepted in one part of France, might still be modified or contested in twelve others. That was the right, though it was not the custom. A kind of tacit agreement prevailed, for men are usually wiser than the laws they make. For a long period of time the particular parliaments did not debate the general laws of the kingdom unless the interests of their own province seemed to be affected by some particular provision. But now each province chose to distinguish itself by its own acts of resistance. An edict accepted by the parliament of Paris was rejected by the provinces; another accepted by the provinces was fought by Paris. Assailed by many adversaries wielding many different weapons at once, the government searched in vain for means by which it could disable the entire opposition with one stroke.

But more remarkable than its diversity was the uniformity of the resistance. Each of the thirteen courts took a somewhat different route, but the goal which attracted them was the same. The remonstrances published by them at that time would fill many volumes; yet open the book where you will, you seem to be reading the same page. Everywhere I found the same ideas expressed almost literally in the very same words. [All of them demanded the Estates-General in the name of the inalienable rights of the nation; all of them approved the conduct of the parliament of Paris, protested against the acts of violence directed against it, encouraged it to resist, and imitated, as well as they could, not only its acts, but its philosophical language.]

Listen to the tumult of these magistrates all over France; it sounds like the confused noise of a mob. Listen attentively to what they are saying; it is as the voice of one man. This uniformity of the parliaments was not merely the medium of the Revolution, it was its symptom. It suggested that beneath the still existing diversity of a multitude of institutions the nation was already homogeneous: a nation obeying the same impulses, following the same ideas.

This action of the parliaments, at once multiple and uniform, surging forward crowd-like, but pressing toward a single goal—this judicial revolt was more dangerous to the government than any other insurrection, including military revolt. For it turned against the government those regular civil and moral powers which are the habitual instruments of authority. The strength of an army may prove coercive for a day, but it is through the everyday practice of the courts that the established order prevails.

Another consequence of this resistance of the parliaments, aside from the mischief they themselves committed, was what they allowed others to commit. They established, for instance, the worst form of freedom of the press; that freedom, namely, which springs not from a right, but from weakness in the execution of existing laws, from the paralyzed will of authority to halt excesses. And they let the rights of assembly prevail so that the different members of each estate and the estates themselves could at once remove the barriers which divided them and unite in a common course of action.

.   .   .   .

Then came the six edicts of 8 May 1788 [they included the adjournment of the parliaments].

To analyze them in a few words, to show that they were not so bad by themselves. Indeed, they realized some of the most important and propitious reforms (separation of powers, equality of taxation)[4] which the Revolution was to carry through.

Those times had not yet come when despotism, appealing to democracy, is supported by the people as long as it maintains equality and security.[5] In an instant the spirit of the nation rose . . .

The nobility were the first and boldest champions in the common struggle against the absolute powers of the King.

Absolute royal government had established itself by replacing the rule of the nobles. The latter were the first who were being humiliated and annoyed by obscure government officials who, under the title of Intendant, continually interfered and intruded into the smallest local affairs behind their backs. Yet, apart from their own grievances, the nobles were carried away by the common passion which had become universal. What is important is the nature of their attack. Their complaint was not that their peculiar privileges had been violated but that common law had been trampled under, the freedom of the press curbed, personal liberty menaced, the Provincial Estates abolished, the Estates-General suspended, that the nation had been treated like a minor and deprived of the management of its own affairs.

During this first period of the Revolution, when hostili-

---

[4] Tocqueville was in error here (pointed out in the Jardin edition).

[5] Tocqueville's courageous reference to the dictatorship of Napoleon III.

ties had not yet been declared between the classes, the language of the aristocracy was exactly the same as that of the other classes, indeed, perhaps even more extreme at times. Their opposition had something republican about it. Thus did the prevailing ideas and the common sentiments influence these proud men accustomed to greatness.

A man who had until then been a violent enemy of the nobility was present at one of the meetings where the nobles had sacrificed their rights amidst the applause of the commons. Relating this scene, he exclaims with enthusiasm, "Our nobility (how truly a nobility!) has come down to point out our rights, to defend them together with us: I have heard it with my own ears; free elections, equality of numbers, equality of taxation—every heart was touched by their disinterestedness and kindled by their patriotism."

[When public rejoicings took place at Grenoble upon the news of the dismissal of the Archbishop of Sens, 29 August 1788, the city was instantly illuminated and covered with transparencies, on one of which stood the lines:

> *Nobles, vous méritez le sort qui vous décore,*
> *De l'État chancellant vous êtes les soutiens;*
> *La nation, par vous, va briser ses liens*
> *Déjà du plus beau jour on voit briller l'aurore.*[6]

[In Brittany the nobles were ready to arm the peasants in order to resist the royal authorities. When the first riot broke out in Paris (24 August 1788), feebly and indecisively repressed by the army, several of the officers who belonged to the nobility resigned their commissions rather than shed the blood of the people. The parliament complimented them on their conduct and called them "those

---

[6] Nobles, you deserve your now brilliant fate,
  You are the main support of the trembling State.
  To break the Nation's chains you show the way;
  Your dawn announces a most glorious day.

noble and generous soldiers whom the purity and delicacy of their sentiments had compelled to resign their commissions."]

The opposition of the clergy was not less determined, though more discreet. It naturally assumed the forms appropriate to the clerical estate.

[Wherever the three estates combined in opposition, the clergy made their appearance. Usually the bishop spoke little, but he took the chair which was offered him. The famous meeting at Romans, the one which protested with the greatest violence against the edicts of May, was also presided over by the Archbishop of Vienne.]

At the outset of the struggle the middle classes had shown themselves timid and undecided. Yet it was especially upon them that the government had relied for assistance. The propositions of the government had been framed with particular regard to the interests and the passions of the middle classes. Long accustomed to obedience, these did not easily embark on a course of resistance. Their opposition was cautious. They still flattered the power to which they were now opposed and acknowledged its rights while they contested their employment. They seemed partly tempted by its favors and ready to yield to the royal power, provided some share of government were bestowed on themselves.

Even when they appeared to be in front, the middle classes never ventured to march alone; they carefully advanced with the upper classes. Impelled by fervor which they did not care to show, they sought to hide behind the passions of the upper classes and to turn these to their own advantage.

Yet later, as the struggle was prolonged and the class question appeared, the middle class became more excited and bolder, until it outstripped the other classes, assuming the leading part and keeping it until the people rose onto the stage.

During this period not a trace of class warfare is to be seen. This concord may have been sincere. One sole passion paramount to other passions pervaded all classes: a spirit of resistance to the government as to the common enemy, a spirit of opposition throughout, in small as well as in great affairs, assuming all kinds of shapes, including those which disfigured it.

Some, to resist the government, laid stress on what remained of old local privileges. Here a man stood up for some old privilege of his class, there another for some special right of his profession. In his ardor everyone grasped the weapon of argument nearest at hand, even when it was the least suited to him. It almost seemed as if the object of the impending revolution was not to destroy but to restore the old regime. For it is difficult for individuals carried along by great movements to see amongst the causes the real motive by which they themselves are moved. Who would have imagined that the passion which caused the assertion of all these traditional rights was the very one which irresistibly led to their complete abolition?

Let us now close our ears for a moment to these tumultuous sounds of the middle and upper classes of the nation. Let us listen to the first sounds of the tempest rising within the people.

No sign that I can discover from this distance of time would show that the rural population was at all agitated. The peasant silently plodded onward in his wonted tract. This vast majority of the nation was quiet and unseen. Even in the towns the people remained aloof from the excitement of the upper classes and indifferent to the noise going on above their heads. They listen; they watch, somewhat surprised, curious rather than angry. But no sooner does the agitation make itself felt among them than it assumes a new and unknown character.

I have said elsewhere in this book that riots were frequent under the old regime; that the government was so well entrenched that it easily allowed these transient outbursts. Yet now came a time when old habits assumed new features. [Corn riots had always occurred in France; still they were staged by mobs without leadership and without definite aims. But now there broke out an insurrection such as we have witnessed so often since, with the tocsin, with the nocturnal cries, the inflammatory posters; a fierce and cruel apparition: a mob infuriated, yet organized and directed to some end, pouring into civil war and shattering everything in its way.

[Upon the news that the parliament had prevailed and that the Archbishop of Sens had retired from the Ministry, the populace of Paris broke out in disorderly manifestations, burned the Minister in effigy and insulted the watch. These disturbances were, as usual, put down by force; but the mob took arms, burnt the guardhouses, disarmed the troops, attempted to set fire to the Hôtel Lamoignon, and was driven back only by the King's household troops. The Reign of Terror was already visible in disguise. Paris, which in our own times a hundred thousand soldiers can hardly keep subdued, was then protected by an indifferent sort of police called the watch. The household troops and the Swiss Guards were quartered outside the city. This time the watch was powerless.]

In the face of this new kind of popular opposition, the government at first showed signs of surprise and of annoyance rather than of defeat. It employed all its old weapons, proclamations, *lettres de cachet*, exile, but it employed them in vain. Its show of force was enough to irritate but not enough to instill fear. Moreover, a whole people cannot thus be frightened.

The government attempted to excite the passions of the multitude against the rich, the citizens against the aristocracy, the lower magistrates against the courts of justice. It was the old game, but now it was played in vain. It offered favors and money, but the instincts of political passion prevailed over those of venality. New judges were appointed, but most of the new magistrates refused to sit. Efforts were made to divert the public attention, but it remained concentrated. Unable to stop or even to check the liberty of the press, the government sought to use it for its own purposes; at no small cost it had a great number of pamphlets published for its side. Nobody read these, but the myriad pamphlets that attacked it were devoured.

Finally an incident occurred which precipitated the crisis.

The parliament of Dauphiné had resisted like all the other parliaments and had been smitten likewise. But nowhere did the cause which it defended find more unanimous support or more passionate champions.

[Class grievances were there perhaps more intense than in any other place, but the prevailing excitement lulled all private passions. In most of the other provinces each class conducted its own warfare against the government separately; in the Dauphiné they formed a political body and prepared for resistance. For long centuries the Dauphiné had the privilege of its own estates, suspended since 1628, but not abolished. Certain nobles, certain priests, and certain citizens of their own accord had dared to call upon the nobility, the clergy, and the commons to meet as Provincial Estates in a country house near Grenoble named Vizille. There three estates immediately declared themselves constituted; thus the cloak of legality was thrown over their illegal proceedings. Forty-nine members of the clergy were present, two hundred and thirty-three members of the nobility, three hundred and ninety-one of the commons. The assembly then proceeded to deliberate and protested in a body against the edicts of May and the suppression of the parliament. It demanded the restoration of the old Provincial Estates which had been arbitrarily and illegally suspended; it demanded that in these estates a double number of representatives should be given to the commons; it called for the prompt convocation of the Estates-General and decided on the spot that a letter should be addressed to the King stating the grievances and demands of Dauphiné. This letter, couched in immoderate language and in a tone of civil strife, was immediately signed by all the members. Similar protests had already been made, similar demands had been expressed with equal violence; but nowhere as yet had there been so signal an example of the union of all classes. "The members of the nobility and the clergy," say the minutes, "were complimented by a member of the third estate on the loyalty with which, laying aside former pretensions, they had hastened to do justice to the commons, and on their zeal to support the union of the three estates." The President replied that the peers would always be ready to act together with their fellow citizens for the salvation of the country.]

The Assembly of Vizille produced a great effect throughout France. It was the last time that an event outside Paris has had a decisive influence on the destinies of the nation.

The government feared that what the Dauphiné had dared to do might be imitated everywhere. At last it gave up trying to conquer the resistance of the opposition; it declared itself defeated. Louis XVI dismissed his ministers, abolished or suspended his edicts, and recalled the parliament.

It must be emphasized that this was not a concession of particulars. It was a renunciation of absolute power. It was an admission of divided powers, of which the consequent decision to convoke the Estates-General was to be a guarantee given the nation. One may say that from this very moment the Revolution had triumphed, although it had not yet shown its true colors.

In reading the writings of authors before the end of 1788, one is astonished to find them speaking of a great revolution already accomplished before 1789. Yet if one considers the history of 1788 one sees that the changes which occurred during that year were greater than those of previous centuries. This was truly a very great revolution but one destined to be obscured by history, lost as it was in the immensity of the revolution about to follow.

Numerous and prodigious indeed were the faults that had been up to this point committed by the government of Louis XVI. But that government, having allowed itself to be driven so far, cannot be condemned for giving way. If it resigned its absolute powers, it did so because it had no way to defend them. It could not employ the law since its own tribunals were in opposition, it could not prevail by mere force since the chief officers of the army lent only a reluctant support to its policy. Moreover, under the old regime, the absolute power of the Crown had never assumed the aspect of military tyranny; it had not been born on the battlefield, and it had not rested on support of the military; it was essentially a civil despotism, governing artfully rather than violently.

The unchecked power of the King had prevailed only by dividing the classes, by hedging them round with the prejudices, the jealousies, the hatreds of each so as never to have to do with more than one class at a time, and to bring the weight of all the others to bear against it.

It was enough that these different classes should lower, if only for a moment, the barriers by which they had been divided; that they should be in accord but for a single day. The absolute power of the government was defeated on the day they thus met.

The Assembly of Vizille was the outward and visible sign of this new union and of what it portended, and although it took place deep in a province in a far corner of the Alps this particular incident became the principal event for all France. It exposed to every eye what had before been visible but to few; everyone could see the true disposition of the nation. At that moment the outcome was already decided.

CHAPTER IV

*How, Just When They Thought Themselves
Masters of the Nation, the Parliaments Sud-
denly Discovered that They Amounted to
Nothing*

When the royal authority had been defeated, the parliaments at first imagined that the triumph was their own.
They returned to their benches as conquerors and thought
that all they had to do was to enjoy the sweet fruits of
victory.

The King, having withdrawn his edicts establishing new
judges, ordered that at least the judgments and decrees
which they had already rendered should be respected. But
the parliaments declared that whatever had been adjudged
without them was not lawfully adjudged at all; they summoned before them those recalcitrant appointees who had
dared to aspire to their seats and, borrowing an old expression of medieval law, they "noted them worthy of infamy."
All France could see that the King's partisans were punished for their fidelity to the Crown, and people did not
forget that henceforth obedience to authority was no
longer a guarantee of personal security.

The intoxication of the parliaments is easy to understand.
Louis XIV in all his glory had never been the object of more
universal adulation, if that word can be applied at all to
immoderate praise produced by truly altruistic passions.

When the parliament of Paris was exiled to Troyes
(August–September 1787) it was received there by the

public corporations, which treated it as if it were the unique sovereign, and pronounced the most extravagant compliments: "August senators!" "Generous citizens!" "Virtuous and charitable magistrates!"

The treasury officials of Troyes: "Our descendants will know that this temple (the *Palais de Justice*) was the sanctuary of your pronouncements; they will know that their ancestors witnessed your patriotic resolutions. Your noble example evokes in every French heart the desire to die for the nation if must. . . . You are the consolation of the nation's ills." The Church also came to compliment them. The Chapter of the Cathedral of Troyes: "As painfully as the other estates we have witnessed this national occasion of mourning, you suspended from your functions, torn from the breasts of your families . . . shameful scenes these were to us! As long as these august walls retain the echoes of public dolor, we in our sacred temple contribute our own expressions of grief . . . We follow you and cover you with our benedictions; our duties of hospitality shall not obscure the extent of our admiration and love. Nation and Church solicit a durable monument for what you have done."

Even the University came forth, in gowns and mortarboards, to drawl its homage in bad and nasal Latin: "*Illustrissimi Senatus princeps, praesedes insulati, Senatores integerrimi!* We share the general emotion! We are here to express our lively admiration of your patriotic heroism. Hitherto the highest courage was that military valor which calls legions of heroes from their homes; we now see the heroes of peace standing in the sanctuary of justice; like those generous citizens who were the pride of Rome in their day of triumph, you have earned a triumph which secures your immortal fame."

Inevitably the parliament became intoxicated with these new and sudden delights of political popularity. The first President replied to these addresses with august haughtiness and royally assured the speakers of the good will of his court.

In several provinces the arrest or the exile of the magistrates led to riots. Everywhere their return provoked almost insane explosions of popular rejoicing. For in France passions always lead to popular exaggeration, and the greatest public cause loses some dignity amidst such spectacles.

[At Grenoble, when the courier arrived with the news of the restoration of the parliaments, he was triumphantly carried through the town; he was overpowered with caresses and acclamations; women, unable to reach him, kissed his horse. In the evening the whole town was spontaneously illuminated. All the public bodies and guilds paraded before the parliament, proclaiming bombastic compliments.

[At Bordeaux on the same day there was a similar ovation. The people unhitched the horses from the carriage of the first President and carried him to his chambers. Those judges who had obeyed the King's orders were booed. The first President reprimanded them in public. In the midst of this scene the oldest member of the parliament (La Colonie) exclaimed, "My children, tell your descendants about this day, the memory of which will keep alive the fire of patriotism." This was a man, ninety years old, whose youth had been spent under the reign of Louis XIV. What new ideas and new phrases are born within the life span of one man! They ended by burning a cardinal in effigy on the market place; this, however, did not prevent the clergy from singing a *Te Deum*.]

Suddenly the acclamations ceased. The enthusiasm disappeared; silence and solitude gathered about the parliaments. Not only were they now objects of indifference but all sorts of charges were brought against them, including the very ones which the government had so vainly attempted to propose earlier. [France was inundated with pamphlets in which not only is praise lacking but in which the very liberalism of the parliaments is viciously attacked.

In some of these the revolutionaries sound almost as if they are royalists: "These judges know nothing of politics; in reality they aim only at power. They are at one with the nobles and the priests; they are as hostile as these to the commons, which means to the entire nation. They fancied that their attack on despotism would cause all this to be forgotten. Indeed, the demands they made of the King were in some respects excessive. They are an aristocracy of lawyers who want to be masters of the King himself."]

For the parliament of Paris the fall was especially sudden and terrible. [Within a few days all the enthusiasm ceased. Consider its solitude, the deathlike silence which encompassed that parliament, its sense of impotence and despair and the scornful vengeance of the Crown when, in reply to renewed remonstrances, Louis XVI said: "I have no answer to make to my parliament or to its supplications. With the assembled nation I shall discuss measures in order to permanently consolidate public order and the prosperity of the Kingdom."

[The same measure which recalled the parliament restored D'Eprémesnil to liberty. The reader will remember the dramatic scene of his arrest, his address in the style of Regulus, the emotion of the audience, the immense popularity of the martyr. He was confined on the Isle Sainte-Marguerite, off Cannes: the warrant for his discharge arrives, and he is off. On the road he is at first treated as a great man, but as he proceeds the radiance that surrounded him fades away; once he is in Paris, nobody cares about him. Later his name becomes a joke: a pamphlet attributes some of his earlier deeds to an escaped madman by the same name.

[The parliament, wretched at the discovery of its unpopularity, tried to regain the sympathy of the public. The same language which had so often served to excite the people in its favor was again employed. The cry for the responsibility of ministers, for personal freedom, for the liberty of the press, all was in vain. The amazement of the magistrates was extreme; they could not comprehend what was happening before their eyes. They kept talking about constitutional privileges, yet they failed to see that this was a popular term only so long as it suggested opposition to royal power. But "privileges" also suggests opposition to democratic equality—consequently it was now a hateful word.] The magistrates did not see that the same wave which had swept them so high now washed them under as it roared away . . .

Originally the parliament had consisted of jurists and lawyers who were chosen by the King from the ablest of these professions. A path to high honors by merit was thus opened even to men born in the humblest conditions. Like the Church, the parliament was then one of those powerful democratic institutions which were born and had implanted themselves in the aristocratic soil of the Middle Ages, establishing deep roots of human equality.

Later the Kings, to make money, put up to sale the right of administering justice. The parliament was then filled by a certain number of wealthy families who considered this national judiciary a sanctuary of their own. They guarded it from the intrusion of others with increasing jealousy. In this way they obeyed that strange impulse which seemed to impel many political bodies to dwindle more and more into a tight little aristocracy while the ideas and the habits of the nation were moving more and more towards democracy; regulations which would have been unimaginable in feudal times reserved membership in the high courts for noblemen. Certainly nothing could be more in contrast to the ideas of the time than a judicial caste which had purchased its very rights. No practice had been more often and more bitterly censured than the sale of these offices.

Yet, vicious as this principle was, it had a practical merit which the better constituted tribunals of our own time do not always possess. The judges were independent. They obeyed no passions but their own.

When all the intermediate powers which could balance or mitigate the unlimited power of the King had been destroyed, the parliament alone remained.

It could still speak when all the rest were silent; it could stand erect at a time when all the rest had long been forced to bow. Thus it had become popular just when the government lost its popularity. And when the hatred of despotism had become the fervent passion and the common sentiment of every Frenchman, the parliaments appeared to be the sole remaining bulwarks of liberty. All of their faults suddenly seemed political guarantees. Their vices, their love of power, their presumptions, and their prejudices were the means which the nation wished to employ.

But when absolute power had been definitely defeated and the nation felt assured that she could defend her rights alone, the parliaments at once became again what they were before: a decrepit, deformed, and discredited institution, a legacy of the Middle Ages, again exposed to the full tide of public aversion. To destroy it all the King had to do was to let it triumph for a day.

CHAPTER V

How, Once Absolute Power Was Defeated, the Real Spirit of the Revolution Became Immediately Manifest

The bond of a common passion had linked all the classes together for a moment. No sooner was that bond relaxed than they fell apart and the true spirit of the Revolution, hitherto disguised, suddenly revealed itself.

After having triumphed against the King, the next thing was to ascertain who should gain the fruits of victory; now that the Estates-General was conceded, who should dominate that assembly?

The King could no longer refuse to convoke it, but he still had the power to determine the form it was to assume. No one contested this right of his. Necessity allowed him to do so. One hundred and seventy-five years had elapsed since the last convocation. It had become a vague tradition. No one knew precisely what should be the number of the deputies, the relationships of the three estates, the procedure of their election, the habits of deliberation. The King alone could have settled these questions. He did not settle them.

The Cardinal de Brienne, his prime minister, had strange ideas on this subject and caused his master to adopt a resolution unparalleled in history.

He regarded the problems, whether the voting was to be universal or limited, whether the assembly was to be numerous or restricted, whether the estates were to be separated or united, whether their rights would be identical or different, as if these were mere matters of erudition. Consequently an order in council charged all public bodies to make researches on the structure of the old Estates-General and on the forms used by them in the past. He added: "His Majesty invites all the learned persons of the kingdom, and particularly those who belong to the Academy of Belles-lettres and Antiquities, to send to the Keeper of the Seals papers and information on this subject."

Thus was the constitution of the nation treated like an academic problem, to be solved by an essay competition.

The call was heard. Immediately everyone had something to say; and as this was the most literary country in Europe at a time when contemporary passions were clothed by heavy cloaks of erudition, a deluge of publications was the result. Every provincial group deliberated on the answer to be given to the King; every corporate body put in its claims; all the classes tried to dig up from the ruins of the old Estates-General the forms which seemed best adapted to guarantee their own peculiar interests.

The conflict of classes was inevitable; but this conflict, which properly belonged within the Estates-General, where it might have been kept within bounds and limited to certain issues, now found no limits before it. Fed by vague and general ideas, it quickly became very violent. This was understandable if we consider the excitement underneath, but no visible symptom had as yet prepared men for this conflict of classes.

Between the time of the royal renunciation of absolute authority and the elections about five months elapsed. In this interval few things changed outwardly, but the movement which drove sentiments and ideas toward a full revolution of society developed with increasing speed.

At first all that men talked about was the constitution of the Estates-General; pretentious and hastily written books, forced attempts to reconcile the Middle Ages with the demands of the present appeared. Then the whole question of the old Estates-General was dropped; this moldy heap of precedents was thrown aside, and people began to examine abstract philosophical principles in order to establish what the legislative power ought to be. With each of these steps the horizon expanded; beyond the constitution of the legislature the question of the whole framework of government arose; beyond the frame of government the whole of society was to be rebuilt from its very foundations. At first people discussed a better balance of powers, a better adjustment of the rights of classes; but soon they advanced, they hurried, they rushed toward unlimited democracy. At first Montesquieu was most frequently quoted; in the end no one was cited but Rousseau. He became and was to remain the singular authority in this first period of the Revolution.

The notion of government had become simple: everything was subordinated to numbers. Politics were reduced to arithmetic propositions. Thus was the seed of the coming events implanted in every mind. The germ of every opinion later prevailing during different phases of the Revolution could already be found.

["In all things the majority of numbers is to give the law." This was the keynote of the whole controversy. "What could be more absurd," a contemporary writer, one of the more moderate ones, exclaims, "than that a body of twenty million heads should be represented in the same manner as one of one hundred thousand." Establishing that there were in France eighty thousand ecclesiastics and about one hundred and twenty thousand nobles, Sieyès merely adds: "Compare the number of these two hundred thousand privileged persons to that of twenty-six million souls and judge the question on its merits." Everything was statistical, though everybody framed his own statistics. "The relation of privileged persons to those not privileged," said Lafon-Ladebat, "is as one to twenty-two." According to the city of Bourg, the commons formed nineteen twentieths of the population; according to the city of Nîmes, twenty-nine thirtieths. It was obviously a mere question of figures. From this political arithmetic Volney deduced universal suffrage; Roederer, universal eligibility; Péthion, the unicameral nature of the assembly. Their calculations frequently led them beyond their hopes and even beyond their wishes.]

The government itself had brought in this discussion; it could no longer set its limits.

At first the third estate only expressed its occasional jealousy of certain privileges; it never spoke against persons. But by degrees the tone became bitter and jealousy turned into furious hatred. A thousand conflicting desires coalesced to form the mighty weapon which a thousand arms were

suddenly to lift and hurl at the aristocracy. At first the nobility were reproached for having carried their rights too
far; in the end the very existence of such rights was denied.
At first it was proposed to share power with them; soon
they were refused all power. Not only must the nobles remain masters no longer; they were hardly allowed to call
themselves citizens. They became foreigners who had imposed themselves on the nation and whom the nation now,
at last, rejected . . . In his famous speech on the third
estate Sieyès said: "Why aren't all these families, with their
foolish pretensions of claiming descent from the original
conquerors, sent back to the forests of Franconia? Then a
purified nation may console herself by feeling that she is,
at last, composed of the true descendants of the Gauls and
the Romans."

Perhaps for the first time in history one saw the upper
classes isolated and separated from the others to such a
degree that they seemed a mere handful of sheep cast out
from a flock. For the first time perhaps the middle classes
were bent on *not* mixing with the upper ones; on the
contrary, they kept jealously away from all contact. These
two symptoms, had they been understood, would have revealed the immensity of the revolution which was coming
—or, rather, which was already here.

The privileged ranks were attacked in countless publications. They were defended in so few that it is somewhat
difficult to find what was said in their favor. It may seem
surprising that these assailed classes who held most of the
great offices and owned a large portion of the land should
have found so few defenders within or without their ranks,
especially when one considers how many eloquent voices
were to plead their cause after they had been conquered,
decimated, and ruined. But this is explained by the extreme confusion into which the aristocracy was thrown
when, after having marched for a short time together with
the rest of the nation, the latter suddenly turned in fury

against the former. The nobles were surprised to find that they were attacked with arguments which had been their own; what had been the amusements of aristocratic leisure became terrible weapons directed at aristocratic society.

Like their adversaries, these nobles were ready enough to believe that the most perfect form of society would be the one based on the natural equality of men, in which merit alone, and not birth or fortune, should determine rank, in which government would represent the general will and numerical majority would determine the law. Their interests may have been different, but their opinions were the same; they knew nothing of politics except what they had read in books, and always in the same books. Had they been born plebeians, these same noblemen would have made the Revolution.

Thus, when they suddenly found themselves attacked, they were singularly embarrassed in their defense. Not one of them had ever considered by what means an aristocracy may justify its privileges in the eyes of the people. They did not know what to say in order to show that only an aristocracy can preserve the people from the oppression of royal tyranny and from the miseries of revolution; that the privileges which seem established in the sole interest of those who possess them do also form the best guarantee for the tranquillity and prosperity even of those who do not have them—of all this they were ignorant. All these arguments, so familiar to those with long experience of public affairs and with an understanding of government, were new and unknown to the nobles of France. They spoke, instead, about the services which their ancestors had rendered six hundred years before. They evoked the antiquated titles of a now detested past. They pretended that they alone knew how to uphold the honor of arms and the traditions of military valor. Their language was often arrogant since they were used to being leaders, but it was also irresolute since they were not sure about their rights themselves.

The spirit of jealousy and contention now rose among those who were thus isolated themselves—the nobles against the priests (the first voice raised to demand the confiscation of the property of the clergy was that of a noble), the priests against the nobles, the lesser nobility against the great lords, the parish priests against the bishops.

The discussion evoked by the King's edicts, after going round the whole circle of human institutions, always ended in these two problems, the essential core of the whole struggle:

Was the third estate to have more representatives than each of the two other estates so that the total number of its deputies would be equal to those of the nobility and clergy combined?

Were the three estates thus constituted to deliberate together or separately?

This duplication of the third and the fusion of the three estates in one assembly appeared at that time less important than they really were. Minor circumstances had concealed their novelty and their magnitude.

For centuries the Provincial Estates of Languedoc had been assembling in this manner, with no other result than that of giving to the bourgeoisie a larger share of public affairs and of creating a sense of common interests and easier contacts between them and the two higher estates. Instead of dividing the classes, they were thus drawn together.

The King himself appeared to have spoken in favor of this method, for he had just applied it to those provinces previously without estates of their own. It was not yet clearly seen that a modification of the traditional constitution of the nation in a single province was different; that it might bring about a total and violent overthrow of the constitution when it was applied to the whole state.

It was evident that a third estate, if equal in number to the two other estates in a general national assembly, would at once prove preponderant there. It would not only participate but become the absolute master. For the third estate would stand and move united between two bodies divided against each other, and even against themselves: the third with identical interests, aims, passions; the two other orders with different interests, various aims, and frequently contrary passions. The third had the current of public opinion in its favor; the others had this current working against them. This pressure from without was to keep the third estate together while it pulled away from the nobility and the clergy those persons who were seeking popularity or new power. In the parliament of Languedoc every bourgeois carried within himself a sort of counterweight, for the aristocratic influence still prevailed in his habits and opinions. But here the reverse was true, and the third estate was bound to be the dominant estate even without an absolute majority in numbers.

The action of such a party in the Assembly was bound to be not only dominant but also violent, since this was a place full of potential hatreds. To live together with contrary opinions is no easy task to begin with. But to enclose in the same political arena bodies already formed, each with its specific origin, its own history, its peculiar customs, its particular spirit, to place them constantly face to face, to try making them check each other and thus to compel them to carry on an incessant debate with no intermediaries in-between will not lead to discussion but to war.

So this majority, inflamed by its own passions as well as by those of its adversaries, was all-powerful. Nothing could arrest or even retard its movements, for nothing remained to contain it outside the royal power, which, however, was already disarmed and destined to yield before a single assembly concentrated against it.

This was not to bring about a gradual change in the balance of power but to upset it at once. It was not giving the third estate a share in the exorbitant powers of the aristocracy; it was a sudden transfer of total power to new hands. It meant the surrender of the direction of affairs to a single passion, to a single interest, to a single idea. This led not to Reform but to Revolution.[1]

Mounier, who alone among contemporary reformers seemed to know what it was he wanted to do, who had a correct idea of the conditions of an orderly and free government—even Mounier, who had divided the three estates in his plan of government, favored their joint session. He candidly gave his reasons: above all, he said, an assembly was needed to destroy the remains of the old constitution, all of the particular rights and all of the local privileges, which could never be done with an upper house composed of the nobles and of the clergy.

At any rate, it would seem that the doubling of the votes of the third and the fusion of the three estates in one body must have been two questions inseparable from each other. For why should the number of representatives of an estate be increased if they were to sit and vote apart from the other two?

The government imagined it could separate them.

At that time M. Necker so advised the King; he was, momentarily, the idol of the nation. His traits are effaced by distance now. Still, he was one of those men who never really know where they are going, for they do not follow their own inclinations but the ideas which they think are influencing the others.

There is no doubt that he desired both the doubling of the third and that the three estates should vote together. It is probable that the King inclined in the same direction. He had just been conquered by the aristocracy. It was the

[1] This may refer to the words (made since famous by Taine) uttered by the Duke of Larochefoucauld-Liancourt on the night of 14–15 July 1789 when he woke the King with the news of the Bastille. "So it is a revolt," said the King. "Sire," said the Duke, "it is a revolution."

aristocracy which pressed him hardest, which had roused the other classes against the royal authority and had led them to victory. These blows had been felt, and the King did not have a clear enough vision to see that his adversaries would soon be the ones compelled to defend him. Therefore, like his minister, Louis XVI was inclined to constitute the Estates-General in accord with the wishes of the third estate.

But they did not dare to go that far. They stopped halfway, though not from any clear perception of the dangers but confused by the inarticulate clamor around them. Still, when was there ever a man or a class who had the resolution and who clearly saw the moment when to descend from a pinnacle in order to avoid being hurled down from it soon?

It was decided that the third should return twice as many members as each of the other estates, but the question of the common session was left unsettled. Of all possible courses this was certainly the most dangerous one.

Nothing serves despotism better than the mutual hatreds and jealousies of classes. Absolute power thrives on them: on condition, however, that these sentiments are bitter but suppressed, sufficient to prevent men from concerting their action but insufficient to make them take up arms. Yet governments will succumb when it comes to a violent collision of classes, once they make war on each other.

Surely it was very late to resort to the old constitution of the Estates-General, even if it were reformed. Yet with this resolution, however rash, the government had tradition in its favor, and it still had its hand upon the instrument of the law.

If the doubling of the third and the joint voting of the three estates had been conceded together, no doubt a revolution would have been made, but it would have been made by the Crown, which, by leading the demolition of old institutions, might have avoided a catastrophic ruin. The upper classes would have submitted to an inevitable necessity. Feeling the pressure of royal power as well as that of the third estate, they would have understood their powerlessness at once. Instead of foolishly struggling to retain everything, they would have been fighting to save something.

Would it not have been possible to do throughout France what was actually done by the three estates in the Dauphiné? There the Provincial Estates had chosen, by a general vote, the representatives of the three orders to the Estates-General. Each estate had been elected separately and stood for itself alone; but all of them combined to name the deputies to the Estates-General, so that every noble had commoners among his constituents and every commoner nobles. The three delegations, though remaining distinct, thus acquired a certain homogeneity. If the estates had been constituted in this manner, might they not have coexisted in the same assembly, without coming to a disastrous collision?

Still, too much importance should not be given to these legislative expedients. Not mechanical legal structures but the ideas and the passions of men are the motive forces of human affairs. It is always in men's souls that one may find the symptoms of forthcoming events.

No matter what measures would, at that time, have been taken to form and regulate the assemblies of the nation, possibly the war between the classes would still have broken out in all its violence. Their animosities were perhaps already too fierce and the power of the King already too weak to make them agree. Yet it should be said that what was done could not have been better calculated to make the conflict inevitable.

Consider how improvidence and incapacity led to results which could not have been achieved by the most skillful revolutionary planning! The third estate was given the chance to prepare for the encounter and to pull itself together. The ardor of its members increased; it doubled their power. They were encouraged in the beginning and threatened in the end. They had been lured by the prospects of victory which, then, was withheld from them. Thus were they invited to seize it.

For five months the government left the two classes to reinvigorate their old hatreds and to recapitulate the long stories of their grievances, until they burned against each other with fury; then they were brought face to face, and the first subject they were to debate was, of course, the over-all one.

I am less struck by the genius of those who made the Revolution because they desired it than by the singular imbecility of those who made it without desiring it. When I consider the French Revolution I am amazed at the prodigious magnitude of the event, at the glare it cast to the extremities of the earth, at its power, which more or less stirred every nation.

When I, then, turn to that court which had so great a share in the Revolution, I see there some of the most trivial scenes in history: harebrained or narrow-minded ministers, dissolute priests, futile women, rash or mercenary courtiers, a King with peculiarly useless virtues. Yet I see these paltry personages moving, pushing, precipitating immense events. They themselves have little share in them. More than mere accidents, they might almost pass for primary causes; and I marvel at the almighty power of God, who, with instruments as weak as these, can set the whole mass of human society in motion.

CHAPTER VI

*How the Instructions to the Estates-General
Impressed the Idea of a Radical Revolution
Deep on the Minds of the People*

The most impressive features of the otherwise imperfect institutions of the Middle Ages were their diversity and their sincerity. They always gave all the liberties they seemed to promise. They were not very artful, but neither were they cunning.

At the same time when the third estate was invited to participate in the assembly of the nation, it was accorded an unlimited facility to express its complaints and declare its requests.

In the cities which were to send deputies to the Estates-General, the entire population was called upon to give its advice about the abuses to be corrected and the demands to be made. Anyone might express his grievance in his own way. The means were as simple as the political procedure was bold. Down to the Estates-General of 1614, in every town, and even in Paris, a large box was placed in the market place to receive the complaints and opinions of anyone, which a committee sitting at the Hôtel de Ville was to sift and examine. Out of all these diverse remonstrances a document was drawn up which, under the humble title of "Grievances," expressed with the greatest liberty and frequently with singularly bitter language the complaints of all and of each.

The physical and social institutions of those times rested

on such deep and solid foundations that this sort of public inquest could occur without much risk. There was no question of changing the principle of the laws but simply of straightening them out here and there; no question of breaking the powers of the King and of the nobility but simply of redressing their occasional abuses. What was called the third estate at that time consisted of no commons, not even of the rural class (the latter were represented by their lords), but of the bourgeois of certain towns. They were allowed complete liberty to express their grievances, since they were unable to enforce redress: they exercised such a broad democratic freedom because in all other respects the aristocracy reigned supreme. The communities of the Middle Ages were, in reality, aristocratic bodies which contained (and, in part, it is here that their greatness lay) small fragments of democracy.

In 1789 the third estate to be represented in the Estates-General no longer consisted, as in 1614, of the urban bourgeoisie alone but of twenty million peasants scattered over the whole kingdom. Until then these had never taken any interest in public affairs; for them politics was not even the accidental memory of another age: it was, in every respect, a novelty. Thus ancient liberties were being extended to new people with their ancient effects in mind, and the results turned out to be the exact opposite of those of three hundred years ago.

Meanwhile, on a certain day, the church bells of every rural parish of France called the people to the market place. There, for the first time in the history of the monarchy, they were called upon to compose what was still called in the medieval fashion the *cahier* of grievances of the third estate.

In those countries where political assemblies are elected by universal suffrage, every general election must deeply involve the people unless their freedom of voting is a lie. But here not only a universal vote but a universal deliberation and inquest were to be taken. Every citizen of one of the greatest nations in the world was asked not what he thought of this or that particular problem but what he had to say against every law and every social and political institution of his country. I think that no such spectacle had ever been seen before.

All the peasants of France thus set themselves to recapitulate all their sufferings and their just complaints. The spirit of the Revolution, having excited the citizens of the towns, rushed now through a thousand rills, penetrating the rural population to its very depths. But there the form it assumed was different; it became peculiarly appropriate to those just affected by it. All of those general and abstract theories which filled the minds of the middle classes here took concrete and definite forms. In the cities the cry was for rights to be acquired; in the country it rose for wants to be satisfied.

When the peasants came to ask each other what their complaints should be about they cared not for the balance of powers, for the guarantees of political liberty, for the abstract rights of man or of the citizen. They dwelt at once on objects close to themselves, on burdens which each of them had had to endure. One thought of the feudal dues which had taken half of his last year's crops; another of the days he had been compelled to work for his landowner without pay. One spoke of the lord's pigeons, which had picked his seed from the ground before it sprouted; another of the rabbits which had nibbled his green corn. As their excitement rose with the common recitation of their miseries, to them all these evils seemed to proceed not so much from institutions as from a particular single person who still called them his subjects, though he had long ceased to govern them—who had privileges without obligations and who retained none of his political rights save that of living at their expense. And to see in him the common enemy was the passionate agreement that grew.

Providence, which seems to have resolved that the spectacle of our passions and of our misfortunes should be a lesson for the world, allowed the commencement of the Revolution to coincide with a great drought and an extraordinary winter. The harvest of 1788 was bad, and the first months of the winter of 1789 were marked by a cold of unparalleled severity—a frost, like that of the northern extremities of Europe, hardened the earth to a great depth. For two months the whole of France lay hidden under a thick fall of snow, like the steppes of Siberia. The air was icy, the sky lonely, dull, and sad. This accident of nature helped give a gloomy and sharp tone to human dispositions. All the grievances against the institutions and the rulers of the country were felt more bitterly amidst the frozen misery that prevailed.

And when the peasant went out from his darkening hut with its chilly fireplace, from his famished and cold family to meet some of his fellows and discuss their common condition, it seemed easy for him to do so: he fancied that he could easily, if he dared, put his finger on the source of all his wrongs.

CHAPTER VII

How, on the Eve of the National Assembly, All Hearts and All Spirits Rose Together

Two questions had thus far divided the classes—the doubling of the third and the joint voting of the estates. The first was decided, the second postponed. That great Assembly, which everyone had regarded as the fulfillment of his own hopes and which all had demanded with equal fervor, was about to meet. The event had long been anticipated; yet to the very end it remained doubtful. Now it came. Everyone felt that things were passing from words to action, from anticipation to reality.

At that solemn moment men paused to consider the greatness of the endeavor which was already near enough for them to discern the vast portents of what was to be done and to comprehend the vast effort which was to be required.

Nobles, clergy, bourgeois alike now clearly saw that the object was not to modify this or that law but to remodel them all, to breathe a new spirit into them, to change and to rejuvenate every institution: as they used to say, to re-generate France. No one knew as yet exactly what would be destroyed or what would be created, but everyone felt that immense demolitions would take place and immense structures would rise.

Nor did their thoughts halt there. None doubted that the destiny of all mankind was engaged in these coming en-deavors.

Nowadays when the perils of revolutions have made us so humble that we scarcely believe ourselves worthy of the freedom enjoyed by other nations,[1] it is difficult to conceive the degree of pride in these forefathers of ours. When one reads the literature of the time, one is amazed at the tre-mendous opinion which Frenchmen of all ranks had at that time of their country and of their race, at their superb self-confidence. Hardly any of the projects of reform brought to light examples from abroad. Nothing was to be learned from mankind; the French were the teachers. (The very tendency of contemporary political thought to uniformity unconsciously led to this sort of thinking.)[2] Every French-

---

[1] Another courageous allusion to the dictatorship of Napoleon III.

[2] (T) Marginal notation: "Badly expressed but the idea is true—it belongs here."

man was convinced that not only was the government of France to be reformed but that new principles of government were to be introduced into the world, applicable to all the nations of the earth and destined to remodel the entirety of human affairs; that in his hands lay not only the destiny of his own country but the fate of mankind.

These sentiments were extravagant but they were, perhaps, not altogether mistaken. For a great enterprise was really opening. Its magnitude, its beauty, its risks were now visible. This great sight gripped and enraptured the imagination of the whole French people. In the presence of this immense design there was a moment when thousands of individuals completely forgot their particular interests to dream only of the common achievements. This lasted but for a moment, but that moment was perhaps unexampled in the history of any other people.

The educated classes had nothing of that timorous and servile spirit which they have since inherited from revolutions. For some time past they had ceased to fear the power of the Crown, though they had not yet learned to tremble before the power of the people. The grandeur of their design made them intrepid. The love of well-being, which was one day to become the master of all of their other passions, was then but a subordinate and feeble predilection. That the new and inevitable reforms were bound to alter the condition of thousands of human beings was not considered at all. The uncertainty of the future had already damaged the course of trade and the exertions of industry, but neither privations nor suffering diminished the prevailing ardor. In view of the splendor of the common enterprise, these private calamities paled even to those who suffered by them.

The passions which had just disturbed so violently the various classes of society seemed suddenly to cool down in this hour when, for the first time in two centuries, these classes were about to act together: apart from a few skirmishes, everywhere a sudden and deceiving accord of spirits rose. All had demanded with equal fervor the restoration of the great Assembly, now reborn. Each of them saw in that reunion the means of realizing his fondest hopes. The Estates-General were to meet at last: a common joy filled those divided hearts and bound them together for an instant before they were to separate forever.

At that moment all minds were struck by the peril of disunion. A supreme effort was made to agree. Instead of trying to find the causes of difference, men wished to find only the common grounds of agreement: the destruction of arbitrary power, the self-government of the nation, the recognition of the rights of every citizen, liberty of the press, personal freedom, the mitigation of the law, a strengthening of justice, religious toleration, the abolition of commercial and industrial restrictions—these were the things demanded by everyone. Reiterations and mutual congratulations: the talk is of what unites them, while what might divide them is forgotten. Deep down there is very little agreement indeed; but people seek to persuade themselves that agreement is everywhere; they embrace, though they do not understand, each other.

I think that no epoch of history has ever witnessed so large a number so passionately devoted to the public good, so honestly forgetful of themselves, so absorbed in the contemplation of the common interest, so resolved to risk everything they cherished in their private lives, so willing to overcome the small sentiments of their hearts. This was the general source of that passion, courage, and patriotism from which all the great deeds of the French Revolution were to issue.

The spectacle was short, but it was one of incomparable grandeur. It will never be effaced from the memory of mankind. All foreign nations witnessed it, applauded it, were moved by it. There was no corner of Europe so distant and secluded that this glow of admiration and of hope did not reach it. In that immense mass of memoirs left to us by the contemporaries of the Revolution, I have found none in which the recollection of those first days of 1789 has not left imperishable traces; everywhere they reveal the clarity, the freshness, the vivacity of the impressions of youth.

I venture to say that there is but one people on this earth which could have staged such a spectacle. I know my nation—I know but too well her errors, her faults, her foibles, and her sins. But I also know of what she is capable. There are enterprises which only the French nation can conceive; there are magnanimous resolutions which this nation alone dares to take. She alone will suddenly embrace the common cause of humanity, willing to fight for it; and if she be subject to awful reverses, she has also sublime moments which sweep her to heights which no other people will ever reach.

NOTE I

[*On a separate sheet, entitled* Movements of public opinion, *Tocqueville defines the stages of its evolution on the eve of the Revolution*]

1. Above all, a powerful, general movement of reform; the passions of social classes are violent but at the same time formless, latent, aimless, without any clarity of consciousness, still drugged by the prevailing state of social and political immobility. This is the end of the old regime: here I stopped.

(The phenomenon of Illuminism really belongs here, between 1. and 2.; a transitory stage.)

2. But in 1787[3] this new spirit of opposition and of dis-

---

[3] (T) This transition is best marked by the correspondence of Madame de Staël with Gustav III, 1786 to 1789. (*Revue des Deux Mondes,* 1 November 1856.) The letters before '87 are

content assumes a definite form. From a state of vague opposition it turns into a spirit of struggle. It becomes involved with certain persons and things: the hatred of certain officials, the passionate accusations of certain figures; above all, war on the Court, a vague term embracing the entire old regime.

3. During the constitutional discussions before the Estates-General class hatred and jealousy suddenly crystallize and soon manifest a spirit of extreme violence. With these previously invisible emotions the true and fundamental character of the Revolution openly appears.

4. Then comes '89 and the *cahiers*. Before this great affair minds are temporarily calm and elevated. It is then that class hatreds and jealousies seem forgotten in view of the grand task ahead. They pale before the grandiose beauty of the future. It is then that, astonishingly enough, genuine altruism and mutual accord appear. Every hand is stretched out—but from afar and in the dark. Then the light rises, people suddenly see each other face to face and they rush at each other . . .

---

full of Court anecdotes, mostly frivolous ones, indicating the ideas and passions of the times but vaguely, a disgust with abuses, philanthropy. In 1787 the style suddenly changes. Political affairs have kept Paris so busy during the past six months, she writes, that other events of interest may have become rarer since persons may not wish to draw attention to themselves by unusual activities when these would be obscured by this universal preoccupation with politics.

BOOK TWO

[From Tocqueville's projected chapters
and notes on the Revolution]

CHAPTER I

*[From the Assembly of the Estates-General to
the Reduction of the Bastille]*

1. Jottings. I think that in the first phase of the history of
the Revolution, which is the phase about which most has
been written, one should be involved with as few facts and
details as possible. Otherwise I should be lost in their immensity. But what larger traits, what general problems to
select?

What place should be given to leading figures? They certainly played a great role in the beginning.

Louis XVI; above all, the Court. Mirabeau.

My mind gets entangled in details and it is as yet unable
to extract the main ideas.

I shall not be able to disentangle myself if I am going to
do a mere history, even though it may be a philosophical
history, of this first phase and if I attempt much beyond
certain considerations. But which ones?

Why did reform turn so rapidly into revolution?

Why was apparent, or even real, agreement followed by such a violent division? How could a mob riot make the Revolution? Paris. How did the people suddenly become so furious and how did they suddenly become the dominant power?

Why the impotence of leading figures? Why the impossibility of civil war?

First to be sketched is the period from the Estates-General to the Bastille and to the Constituent Assembly. From that moment on the Revolution is made.

Here lies the beginning and the most difficult part of the whole book. It is within this narrow space of time that I must concentrate my entire attention. I shall do nothing *a priori*, but perhaps from the details the general principles will emerge.

For this initial phase I must select the problems leading to the establishment of the Constituent Assembly.

From there judge the actions of that Assembly. Disentangle what was fundamentally true, great, and durable; then show how it nevertheless fades and weakens. This is a principal part of my work . . . Seeming unanimity; good dispositions; general love of liberty. This is the first portrait . . .

When I come to the analysis and to the judgment of the Constituent Assembly, the horizon brightens: to show the grandeur, the decency, and the attractiveness of its principles on one hand; on the other, its want of wisdom and of common sense, which will result in the disorganization of everything . . .

How the old regime suddenly collapsed into revolution.

Perhaps to ask this question first: Could the old regime have fallen without revolution? . . .

2. *The Constituent Assembly.* I. The disposition of the nation at the moment when the Estates-General meet. Characteristics: Where is there universal agreement? Good

intentions. A revolution begun with less ill will than any other. Symptoms thereof. How did this come about? How is it explainable at all? Try to penetrate deeply into the passions within each class. What had animated them: what they thought, demanded, wished and hoped for.

To find all these matters and truthfully paint them. Sources: first, the collections in the archives, *cahiers,* ministerial correspondence. Second, if there is any other contemporary official correspondence between the government and its agents.

II. To try to show how these excellent intentions and this apparent concord at their first contact with reality naturally developed into the deepest enmities and into terrible passions.

3. *About the election of the Constituent Assembly.* (This is very roughly sketched.)

Make it very clear how the attempt to restore the old estates resulted in the most dangerous kind of modern assembly that could be conceived.

Since under the pretext of separate chambers a body distinct from the great clerical and secular property owners was established, the third estate became reduced to nonproprietors and lawyers. And since the great property owners were discarded or appeared discredited, the result was that the lawmaking power fell almost exclusively into the hands of those who did not have that conservative spirit which comes from one's own possessions. A unique situation: nothing like this had happened before or has happened since.

If from the beginning the aim had been an Assembly to which everyone could be elected and for which everyone could vote, it is probable that in the country many aristocratic or ecclesiastic proprietors would have been chosen by the people. The result would have been a much less dangerous Assembly.

4. How the Constituent Assembly consisted of more lawyers than any other political body. This Assembly was elected to represent solely one class, but not a nation. Within this class there were as yet few property owners, and its political experience was purely urban. The rural classes were invisible there . . . Examine whether, proportionately, there is a similar excess of lawyers in the American political bodies which would indicate that an abundance of lawyers is a consequence of the constitutions of democratic societies more than of anything else.

5. Very important to know what happened in the counsels of King and Court between the opening of the Estates-General and the 14th of July. After that the outside movement dragged everything with it. But until then much depended on what was going on in the Court.

Is this side of the problem clarified at all? It should be in the memoirs, but in which ones? There must be many curious reminiscences on this decisive phase, M. Necker's, among others.

6. How and where to sketch the portraits of the principal figures? Mirabeau, for example (see what Mounier says). To depict him in full.

Perhaps I should do a chapter on the influence of persons; or, rather, on their impotence, once they no longer go with the tide, in the first phase of the Revolution . . . Of the part individuals played in the Revolution.

This cannot come in the first book: The Revolution is not yet fully *launched.*

7. Impotence of individuals and even of entire classes in the beginning of the Revolution and as long as its impulse remained strong. This is one of the main characteristics of the Revolution. Sketch its sources very sharply. A great and terrible spectacle.

8. The struggle of the estates before the 14th of July in

the correspondence of the provincial deputies of Anjou.[1] This is a collection of reports sent from time to time to Angers, where they were printed. Among the editor deputies were Larevellière-Lepeaux (who signed himself then M. de Lepeaux) and Volney.

The King more popular with the third than with the other orders. Upon the entry of the King at the *Te Deum* of Versailles on 4 May, "extraordinary acclamations of '*Vive le Roi*' by the commons alone," appears several times.

Embarrassment, inexperience of the third estate during the first sessions. Despite that harmony of sentiments which is the best guarantee of order in large assemblies, the inexperience and the novelty of their situation made the first sessions ludicrous and confusing. Everyone spoke at the same time; they argued without clear aims; they did not know the forms of address; they hardly knew each other; talented men have not yet taken the lead. Mounier is called M. Mounier Dauphinois; M. Malouet of the Auvergne; Barnave is written Barnabé; Robespierre, Robert-Pierre; he is already admired, but no one yet knows his name exactly. On the other hand, those who later lapse into permanent obscurity are making themselves known. The Anjou deputies and Mirabeau in the Provence dispatch speak about the great rhetorical talents and of the fine speeches of a M. Populus, whose name fails to appear in any subsequent biography.

Still, the sense of omnipotence already exists. Despite that confusion, the Assembly is already omnipotent through a feeling of unity and of the tide of public opinion, which it senses closely behind it.

The Oath of the Tennis Court in every mind: it appears six weeks before the actual event. Already on 9 May the Anjou deputies write home: in a few days "all means of

---

[1] (T) From the *Correspondance de MM. les députés des Communes de la province de l'Anjou avec leurs commettants*, ten volumes, April 1789–September 1791.

conciliation will be employed to bring the privileged orders to join the third. Once these efforts are spent a National Assembly will be constituted."

Thus it was not the emotion of the struggle which made people sweep beyond their original goals. They had announced them to the whole world beforehand.

There is something infantile and feeble in these early efforts of an Assembly without experience. But amidst all these vacillations they became grand, strong, and seemingly irresistible. For they may have been vacillating in their choice of approach but they did know where they wanted to go.

Their very isolation had made the third estate irresistible. This may seem paradoxical, and yet it is true. During this whole first phase the complete unity of the entire third estate appears. Their class interests and relationships, the similarity of their positions, their uniform grievances of the past, their corporative discipline kept them strongly united. This made very different people march together, the very ones who in the future were to disagree so violently on the course to be taken and the goals to be attained. In the beginning, persons had put their class opinions before their private ones. The isolation of the third would have been a source of weakness if the class they represented had also been weak. But in those circumstances and amidst those social changes it was an immense force.

Fashions. Futility of large and indolent assemblies. Mirabeau. In the midst of the most profound deliberations, on 25 May, there is a deputy who wants to address the Assembly on the important topic of proper costumes. Mirabeau hoots, hisses, and ridicules him.

Strange mixture of men before the crystallization of parties. As late as 10 July one finds such heterogeneous figures as Mirabeau, Robespierre, Barnave, Péthion, De Sèze, Tronchet within the commission chosen to present the famous threatening address to the King.

Rules obstructing the members of the nobility most disposed to the joint session. I see M. de Lafayette appear for the first time in the general assembly (at least I have not found his name among that minority of noblemen who met before the King's letter); he declares that his mandate does not permit him to take a deliberative role but that otherwise he is allowed to speak. Consequently he proposes the Declaration of Human Rights.

Orderly and disorderly characteristics of the Paris mob in revolt. The idea of their transformation. A mirage during every revolution. After the 14th of July one sees these traits emerging. "In the tumult the prisoners of common crimes escaped; the people opposed their release, declaring that criminals were not worthy to mix with the makers of liberty . . . If an armed man committed something vile he was immediately taken to prison by his comrades . . ." This is particularly French.

The Anjou deputies conclude: "Certain remarks made during these disorders might indicate that a change has taken place in that part of the people known under the name of populace, to the effect that their love of liberty begins to animate them more than their love of license." How well these contemporary words reflect the distrust of the lower classes felt by the upper ones; one senses the transition which will make that very people "known under the name of populace" the most respected power and authority all over France.

Lafayette obscure during the struggle for the verification of powers. Until 11 July the name of Lafayette does not appear. He had been sent to the Estates-General as a deputy of the nobility with a mandate to stand against the joint vote. [Yet] He does not appear to have been among the dissidents. His name does not appear on the protestations signed by the minority of the nobles. One does not even see his name among those nobles who meet before their invitation by the King. In the first sessions he is among those who declare that they are qualified to speak but not to vote. Only on 11 July does he suddenly appear, presenting a project, the Declaration of Human Rights, which suddenly puts him in the forefront. On the 15th he is chosen to head a delegation of forty members to Paris, bringing the good words of the King, to re-establish the public harmony. He speaks at the Hôtel de Ville in the name of this delegation and is elected colonel-general of the militia by acclamation.

How success and dizziness hid the horror of crimes. At first the Anjou deputies entitle their report about the murder of M. de Launay[2] "Dreadful News." Next day they laconically mention that there is a new Mayor, M. Bailly, whose predecessor, M. de Flesselles, was on the previous night "punished by death for his treasonable crime."

9. *Mirabeau.* (From the correspondence of the Anjou deputies.) Evidently his influence in the Assembly was not established at once. On 16 June a speech of Mirabeau's to the effect that the third estate should adopt the name of the People's Representatives is criticized as being too rhetorical. "Loud complaints and numerous interruptions were heard."

. . . .

[The Assembly is already becoming the sovereign government]
The nobles and the clergy declare their readiness to vote. 16 July.—All the members of the nobility and the clergy who have taken part in the sessions without voting now declare that they are ready to do so. Declaration followed by great applause.

Embarrassment and weakness of the Assembly in the face of anarchy and the crimes of the people—20 July and after. The victorious Assembly, having relied on the aid of the people, now finds itself singularly feeble and embarrassed

[2] The commander of the Bastille.

when it faces the crimes of this same people. One sees it wasting its time in petty details, receiving deputations and addresses, in debating questions of procedure while outside the mob is hanging men and cutting throats. Not even during the horrible butchery of Foulon and of Berthier de Sauvigny does the Assembly stir. It does not want to extinguish the fire but only to circumscribe the rules of incendiarism. "The impetuous spirits must be tempered without stifling their *salutary fermentation*." These instructions written by the deputies of Anjou reflect the very essence of what was going on.

Not until the 22nd does Lally-Tollendal propose to make a timid address to the people, recommending moderation. Many days pass without the Assembly putting it to vote. Its few vigorous words are meanwhile constantly retouched. Mirabeau and Barnave want to strike it from the record altogether . . .

On the 25th it is not yet acted upon. Here is the worst error, one may say, the grand crime of the Constituent Assembly: from this day onward it was destined to obey and not to command. The people of Paris have become the sovereign rulers. In a single moment power slipped from the Assembly to the mob. The Assembly still had immense moral authority; it seemed unanimous; it represented the entire nation; had it really known its own power and prestige it would have faced royalty as well as the mob and kept in its own hands the reins of the Revolution. The majority surely wished to do so, but it had no idea, on the one hand, what popular revolution meant and, on the other, it had none of that sureness of touch which political experience gives. Like the very classes it represented, it was devoid of organized and disciplined forces, very different from that English Parliament of 1688, which, while it deposed James II, also prevented the mob from interfering with problems before Parliament had done so, thus accomplishing a revolution and preventing its degeneration into mob revolt.

The assembly completes its own servitude in keeping silent about the crimes of the 6th of October.[3] Nothing is more shameful during the entire life of the Constituent Assembly than the cowardice with which this Assembly, greatly responsible for what was happening, and no less than the King humiliated by the violence of the mob, allowed itself to pass in silence over these crimes happening under its very eyes, crimes in part already directed against it.

CHAPTER II

[From the 14th of July to the End of the Constituent Assembly]

1. *Plan of the Chapter*

(A)	How, for the first time, it suddenly became clear that Paris was the master of all France	Storming of the Bastille
(B)	How the nobility suddenly discovered that it was a mere body of officers without an army	After the Bastille, popular risings in the provinces
(C)	What were the principles of '89	

[3] I transposed this single paragraph about the Assembly from Tocqueville's fragmentary notes on Chapter II. It is printed on p. 222 of the *Oeuvres Complètes* volume.

(A) Move rapidly through the quarrels of the estates, even though there exist details hardly known, to come to the storming of the Bastille, not to narrate it but to show what I summed up under (A). For contemporaries that was the victory of the Revolution in 1789. For us, from the distance of seventy years, it is the first manifestation of the Parisian dictatorship, already deeply entrenched in private and administrative habits; dictatorship and a source of future revolutions. To find in the official papers whatever there is about the *passivity* of the provinces until Paris had risen.

(B) Have all sorts of governmental detail on this point. But where and how? Things were becoming so disorganized in the government that I wonder who kept writing reports and to whom.

(C) An examination of the legal system of the Constituent Assembly to show the divergence between Liberalism and Democracy, which sadly reminds me of the present.

2. *Why the Revolution did not and could not engender civil war.* That this was not due to the small number or to the moral cowardice of those who opposed the Revolution. [But] no nuclei of resistance, neither around certain men nor around local authorities . . .

Why, on the contrary, the Revolution led to riots and how it was established by armed violence.

3. *To depict clearly this first Parisian revolution, this model to all others.* Same technique, same process: the middle classes agitate, excite, set the people in motion; they give it moral support and propel it much further than they wish it to go.

4. *How the moderates set things afire.* On 31 August 1789 the Abbé Fauchet, speaking to the workers of the Faubourg Saint-Antoine in the Church of Sainte-Marguerite, complains that they are distrustful of their leaders, of

Bailly and Lafayette. The obvious aim of this discourse is to persuade the workers to remain tranquil and to make them resort only to legal means. But in order to make himself better understood and liked, the speaker attacks the old regime with extraordinary fury and passion, without noticing that it is this fury and not at all his call for moderation which registers with his audience.

5. *The nobles did not see the catastrophe which would strike them after the Bastille* only because very shortly before that revolutionary explosion the submission of the people was still general and seemed natural.

6. *Emigration.* This new and extraordinary development, the emigration of an entire class, is explicable by a new and extraordinary development in history. A nobility, established for a thousand years, suddenly finds itself so uprooted that it cannot remain standing on its own feet; an entire upper class unable to find a force of resistance in any of the other classes of the nation which it could join; not one sentiment of sympathy, no common interests . . . it is the position of officers who suddenly find that the soldiers are firing at them.

This is their historic condemnation and, in this case, it is also their excuse.

This sort of thing is typical of France, where, apart from the general causes of events there is an emotional tendency which brings everyone together in the blind passions of the moment. It resulted in a universal hostility to the nobility which was even more intense than were the original grievances held against it.

7. *The nobles have been reproached for not having defended themselves;* at times they reproached each other. But how could they? For a long time they had lost their influence on the population; there was no contact between the two. Left to itself, an aristocracy is only a handful of men.

8. *Where are those Frenchmen today who would repeat the sublime folly of the night of 4 August?*[1] Let us not deprecate our ancestors; we do not have the right to do so.

9. *The principal ideas at the base of the new social and governmental system:*

Natural equality must be represented in all institutions.

All men have the same rights in civilian life. All have the same right to participate in government.

The institutions must be the same everywhere and for everyone.

The sovereign power resides in the nation. It is one and omnipotent. It is not from traditions, not from examples, not from precedents, not from the particular rights of certain bodies or classes, not from the rights achieved, not from established religions that these principles derive but from general reason, from the natural and primordial laws regulating the human species.

10. *Seventeen eighty-nine turned into a national tragedy not because of the improper way in which the new ideas were put into effect but because there were no ideas which could have been reasonably realized without revolution.* This moment of our national history is characterized by definite ideas and by inexperience at the same time. No trial-and-error mood, few hesitations: not even that murky dawning of vision with which people sense the existence of still invisible obstacles.

11. *The French Revolution was made by a system of general ideas,* forming a single body of doctrine, a kind of political gospel where every idea resembles a dogma.

[1] The night session of the assembly, during which the nobility and the clergy spontaneously rushed forward to renounce their privileges in an extraordinary transport of generous enthusiasm. It had the rare atmosphere of a revivalist meeting conducted by aristocrats. (Perhaps this is why Acton, who also regarded this 4 August as the key date of the Revolution, failed to see the generous spirit in that historic event.)

Its aims not only inspired enthusiasm but also proselytism and propaganda. Its secular doctrines were not only believed but ardently preached, an entirely new thing in history.[2]

12. Whenever I examine the laws of the Constituent Assembly, I find their dual character: *Liberalism, Democracy*—reminding me bitterly of the confusion of our own times . . .

13. *Democracy. — Democratic Institutions. — Divergent meaning of these words.—Resultant confusion.* Very much confusion is caused by the employment given to these words: *democracy, democratic institutions, democratic government.* Unless they are clearly defined and unless there is agreement about their definition, we shall live in an inextricable confusion of ideas, to the great advantage of demagogues and of despots:

They will say that a country governed by an absolute ruler is a *democracy* because he governs by such laws and maintains such institutions as are favorable to the great mass of the people. Such a government, it will be said, is *democratic, a democratic monarchy.*

But *democratic government, democratic monarchy* can mean only one thing in the true sense of these words: a government where the people more or less participate in their government. Its sense is intimately bound to the idea of political liberty. To give the democratic epithet to a government where there is no political liberty is a palpable absurdity, since this departs from the natural meaning of these words.

Such false or obscure expressions are adopted: (a) because of the wish to give the masses illusions, for the ex-

[2] One of the extremely rare recurrent errors of Tocqueville, who failed to recognize the totalitarian tendencies of the Puritan wing current during the English Civil War of the 1640s. See Introduction, above, pp. 23–24, note 5.

pression "democratic government" will always evoke a certain degree of appeal; (b) because of the embarrassing difficulty in finding a single term which would explain the complex system of an absolute government where the people do not at all participate in public affairs but where the upper classes have no privileges either and where legislation aims to provide as much material welfare as possible.

14. *Go through the rubbish[3] of my Chapter VII.* Put aside everything that indicates why in the beginning of this Revolution men wished to construct a society which would be not only democratic but free; not a military but a civilian society. Who among them would have predicted that, except for the institution of household slavery, their great revolutionary movement would end in a sort of Roman society in decadence, a minor copy of the gigantic and despicable Roman Empire. . . . To keep this for the chapter about what the proper name of the ideas of 1789 should be.

15. *In the midst of the Constituent Assembly, show the just character of its general views,* the grandeur of its aims, its generosity, its high sentiments, the occasional evidence of a joint and admirable taste for liberty and equality. . . .

And its awkward blunders, its lack of common sense with which so many good intentions and reasonable opinions lead to impossible government, to powerlessness, to administrative anarchy and, finally, to general disorder, from which rises the Terror.

16. *Centralization.* (Perhaps this should go to the 1789 chapter; perhaps to the Consulate.) In 1788 and 1789 all the pamphlets published, even those by the future revolutionaries themselves, are opposed to centralization and in favor of local rule. (See even Condorcet.) It is due to habits

[3] This "rubbish" which appears in the original ms. as "débris" does not refer to those large Tocqueville dossiers of general miscellany which their author consistently marked as "rubbish" or "rubish," in English.

and not to ideas that centralization remained strongly established.

[Notes about Paris after the 14th of July]

17. *On the morrow of the Bastille.* The Bastille taken, Paris spent a night amidst the greatest anxieties, without a government, believing that at any moment the royal army would attack the city. According to this pamphlet,[4] it was then that the idea of pulling up the pavement stones first arose.

Wednesday morning they find out about the withdrawal of the troops, the royal note to the Assembly, the deputation of the latter to Paris, led by Bailly and Lafayette. The mood changes to joy and confidence. Bailly is named Mayor and Lafayette captain-general by acclamation.

How, as so often thereafter, the cowardice of the defeated becomes visible. The Archbishop of Paris sings a *Te Deum* in Notre-Dame while the bodies of the massacred officers and lancers are still warm. The clergy always behaves in this fashion. It supports compromises and governments at the same time. When these fail, they sing the *Te Deum* for the new victors.

It is remarkable that though during this anarchy in Paris the parliament is still in existence it acts as if it were dead. It is not only doing nothing but no one thinks of it, not even of attacking it. It is dead.

18. *Organization of the provisional municipality of Paris, August 1789–August 1790.* After the 14th of July the municipal government consists of the bourgeois and of the moderates. The really powerful movements of popular sentiment do not pervade it at all: it neglects the important

---

[4] Some of the following Tocqueville extracted from a contemporary anonymous pamphlet, *Paris sauvé ou récit détaillé des événements qui ont eu lieu à Paris . . .* a pamphlet which he much admired.

question of subsidies and the very delicate matter of the police.

The spirit of that municipal body seems moderate, reflecting far more the spirit of the bourgeoisie who prepared the Revolution than that of the people who accomplished it. The upper classes are treated respectfully; so is religion (it is that formal respect which well-brought-up people pay even when they themselves no longer believe). Thus a chaplain in need of the income is maintained to say a Mass for this municipal body every Sunday. But after him the position is abolished. The same with the processions during Holy Week: the Mayor may authorize them, but only if the people wish them to be held, and a large part of the receipts must go to the poor. . . .

The proletariat remains the master. Among other instances, this is evident when it comes to the job of demolishing the Bastille. The city officials had given the job to contractors. The workers do not like this; they clamor. All right, say the minutes, mutiny must be avoided rather than suppressed . . . The city fathers grasp this pretext to cancel the contractors' bids, and they obey the workers.

[Tocqueville's notes on the provinces in 1789]

22. *Anarchy.* One sees the unceasing removal and replacement of local officials. Other municipal officials intercept and open the letters of the royal Intendants. Thousands of incidents provoked by one pretext or another. Grain troubles. Attacks on country houses and persons. No definite direction, but the tumultuous spasms of a disjointed society. The traditional powers are disregarded or destroyed. The traditional ruling classes are only partially armed; the new rulers are not yet firmly in power. The old regime is nearly uprooted, holding out at only a few points; the new one is not yet established.

To depict with sharp colors this first phase of the Revolution, when the Assembly had already actively or passively destroyed the existing administration without, however, putting anything in its place.

24. *Revolt in Lyon, 4 July 1789.* This revolt begins on 4 July on the arrival of the news about the Oath of the Tennis Court and, I think, about the joint session of the orders.

First, universal joy. Then disorder, almost always *opportunistic,* that is: the customs' barriers are burned, the title papers destroyed, wine and all sorts of commodities are brought in by force without paying the city tax. No garrison: a search is sent out for some soldiers in the neighboring garrisons, an appeal is made for volunteers. Twelve hundred young men present themselves. They are armed. They re-establish order. Seeing the bourgeois in arms against them, the mass is surprised, since it believed that it had to face the nobles only.

The disorder comes mostly from the outside; the peasants riot. Letters are sent to the village priests to read proclamations from the pulpit. From this it appears, first, how the countryside was left without administration and without political leadership; second, how people still kept thinking in the old ways, wishing to employ the forces of the old regime to calm the outburst against that very regime.

25. *Correspondence of the Anjou deputies: the feeling in the provinces on the 14th of July.* Evidently even before the news of the Parisian events protest began to appear in the provinces. It appears that in the different towns of Anjou, in Laval, Saumur, Angers, there were spontaneous town assemblies, formation of national guards. The people of Ponts-de-Cé occupy and guard the bridges. Two thousand workers join the patriots of Angers. At Grenoble on 15 July, before learning of the Parisian events, a general assembly: a revolutionary resolution is adopted, signed first

by the clergy, by the nobles, and then by three thousand others.

At Lyon, on the news of Necker's departure and amidst the indistinct tremors coming from Paris, a general assembly of all the orders takes place on 17 July. It is resolved to formally join the National Assembly; should the latter be dissolved, no taxes will be paid. This is signed, among others, by the loyal canons and by the Counts of Lyon.

Yet the greater part of these provincial agitations and movements do not begin until the outbreak and frequently not until the end of the Parisian insurrection. Emphasize this strongly.

Some of the privileged classes are still with the revolutionaries during this phase. In a letter written by the Anjou deputies (21 July): The people are satisfied to see men of quality mixing with the people in the patrols. Not merely humble bourgeois but men distinguished by title, rank, and birth demanded and accepted employment in the new militia.

Paint in detail this last, dying effort of the great movement of 1788, when the *entire* nation moved against royal despotism.

26. *Troubles in the provinces after the storming of the Bastille, 1789: a bourgeois struggle on two fronts.* The Intendant of the Champagne Province to M. Saint-Priest, the Minister of the Royal Household: "the extreme unrest in my province began at the moment the rumor about the revolt in Paris arrived. The rising is general in almost every town." . . . There follow numerous accounts of riots; all the customs' offices are sacked; the registries burned; the agents mistreated . . . "There remains, I think, but one means to prevent even worse misfortunes which I now foresee: it is the immediate establishment of a citizens' militia, to be composed of men of all the orders and from which workers and artisans should by all means be excluded."

From this and from other similar pieces one can see how, when the people rise, the bourgeois themselves are afraid. In this first phase of the Revolution the bourgeoisie tries to struggle simultaneously against the classes above and below it.

CHAPTER III

[Notes on the Convention, on the Terror, and on the Directory]

1. *Internal development of the Revolution. The Terror.—* Very typically French. A result of general causes which *local* conditions carried to extreme ends. Born of our habits, of our character, of our customs, of centralization, of the destruction of every kind of hierarchy . . .

Its means, its true face, its powerful organization, its tremendous force amidst all that disorder and anarchy.

To sketch the general characteristics of the periods that follow, the broad movement of the Revolution through the period of reaction, of disenchantment, of fatigue, of the bored indifference to assemblies and to liberty. The growing preponderance of military power; the increasing military character of the Revolution. . . .

3. *It must be described how, during revolutions, it is always a minority that rules.* Always true of revolutions: it is only the spiritual state of the majority which makes this tyranny by a minority possible.[1]

[1] (T) In the original ms. this follows a passage from A. C. Thibaudeau, *Mémoires sur la Convention et le Directoire,* 1824,

6. *Why Frenchmen so easily submitted to the hardships and to the miseries of the Revolution.* The French were not yet a manufacturing, a commercial, a proprietary people; their material interests did not yet coincide with the tranquillity of State. They had not yet fully acquired the taste for material comforts; they were more preoccupied with ideas and sentiments. Their habits were ruder and more rustic, simpler and manlier than those of the French of today . . .

7. *France, while becoming quite industrious, was not yet an industrial nation:* the great part of the population did not yet feel the overwhelming need for internal peace. However advanced in refinements and even in certain luxuries, France was not yet a nation in which everyone is accustomed to comfort. Life was ornate but there were only a few of those small comforts which today become the necessities of peoples and which frequently result in interior tranquillity *at any price.*

9. *Hatred of the old regime: this passion dominating all others.* This is indeed the *fundamental, essential, primordial* characteristic of the Revolution, *never* abandoned, *whatever* the circumstance. The revolutionary ideas, tastes, passions change in a thousand ways. This sentiment rests fixed amidst the swirling eddies of other passions. It even persists among those who suffered most from the Revolution. More, it even gains among the original enemies of the Revolution. And this sentiment will be shared by the very princes who in the end will find something good in the destruction of the old order.

I, 48: " . . . The majority of the Convention were no more terroristic than the majority of the nation. But they could not or dared not disapprove and kept somberly silent. The otherwise so heated sessions were, for the most part, becoming passive and cold, lasting seldom more than one or two hours. The Convention would not use its few remaining shreds of liberty save for subjects of little importance."

12. *The hatreds of the Terror are soon forgotten.* Nothing shows better the levity and the emotional fickleness of men than that, however malevolent some of them may have been and however inclined to hate more than to love, they abandoned their hatreds almost as rapidly as they had their friendships.

16. *The Revolution and the Church.* The causes of the violent hatred against priesthood and religion should be sought with much care. It is the most vivid and also the most persistent of the revolutionary passions. The suppression of the priests came last but their persecution lasted beyond that of all the others: so far as the priests are concerned, the Terror continues under the Directory. The hatred against them is more violent and more persistent even than the hatred against the émigrés, against the very Frenchmen who were fighting France with arms.

17. *Anti-religious fanaticism: a principal mark of the Revolution.* It is indeed a superficial view to hold (as does Burke)[2] that religious opinions are "the only cause of enthusiastic zeal and sectarian propagation. There is no doctrine whatever on which men are warm that is not capable of the very same effect . . . this fanatical atheism left out, we omit the principal feature of the French Revolution." This is the trait which confused all spectators and induced in so many minds a sort of magical horror, as if they were faced with a fiery comet from hell suddenly thrown in their midst. A party openly attacking every religious idea and the idea of life hereafter; a party dedicated to these very enervating principles with the ardor of proselytes and even of martyrs; a dedication which previously only religion could evoke, an almost inconceivable and a surely frightening spectacle, capable of misleading even the best of minds.

[2] See *Four notes on Burke,* pp. 163–65.

Never forget the ideological character of the French Revolution: its principal *characteristic*, though a *transitory* one.

18. *An III [autumn 1794–autumn 1795]*. Pamphlets not directly political. Many insignificant writings in this period. Many deal with speeches about opening of schools, education, etc. Two things are especially remarkable. First, the hatred which the Terror inspired among the learned. Second, that, while these detest the revolutionary crimes, they are still captivated by the anti-Christian mood of the Revolution. Their political reaction has not yet become an ideological reaction. The irreligious, Voltairian, Encyclopedist impulse still moves the writers and speakers, while it has already ceased among the masses, where a contrary movement is beginning. This is a frequent phenomenon during revolutions. Those who had helped to make the revolution with their phraseology continue to write and speak in the same manner for a long time while the majority has already silently begun to change.

Governments are overthrown with the help of certain phrases which incite the masses against them. This free and loud way of speech continues even after the Revolution. The noise drowns out the effects, and when the noisemakers are, in turn, overthrown we are surprised to find that their opinions are no longer shared by anyone.

20. *An V [autumn 1796–autumn 1797]*. Account of the bishops assembled in Paris by the Citizen Grégoire, Bishop of Blois, 8 December 1796. That part of the clergy which took the Oath to the Constitution is now in a very peculiar position. On the one hand, their position is made difficult by the continued malevolence and distrust of the government and by the Terrorist party, which is still playing a certain role and which is full of hatred for religion and especially for Catholicism in every form. On the other hand, there is the virulent anger and detestation of the "constitutional" priests by that part of the clergy which had refused

to take the oath; also by the faithful who trust only the latter.

The Abbé Grégoire is full of invective against the Terrorists. He is also bitterly recriminatory against his co-religionists who did not take the oath. Thus the spiritual poverty of that unfortunate schismatic clergy is revealed: its rootlessness, its sometimes undoubtedly honest effort of taking its mission seriously, its superficial successes, its martyrs.

Above all, the dreadful picture of demoralization that those two disputing factions present to the people: one group regarded *intruders,* protected by the State and still in possession of the external symbols of religion; against them the other group, the persecuted *faithful;* and around their quarrels a government and a ruling party proclaiming their antipathy and contempt for both, with the only difference that their antipathy is stronger for the second group while their contempt is worse for the first.

CHAPTER IV

[The Revolution Abroad]

1. *Enthusiasm in Europe in 1789.* Enthusiastic delight all over Europe after the fall of the Bastille and during the first period of the Constituent Assembly. Perhaps make a chapter out of this.

4. *What is so extraordinary in the French Revolution is not so much the procedures it employed and the ideas it conceived.* The new and astonishing thing is that so many

nations should arrive at a stage where such procedures could be so efficiently employed and such ideas so easily accepted.

6. (A great chapter whose place or arrangement I do not yet know.) *Development of the Revolution abroad.* Revolutionary wars. Causes of their success. Particular advantages of democratic armies in the era of democratic revolutions. The new world against the old. Victory snatched by surprise. Its new effects on war. There the novelty of the Revolution is more evident than anywhere else. Propaganda. Europe is ravaged but she aids those who ravage her. The senile imbecility of princes who are shattered before they understand what is going on.

7. *Why all coalitions failed before 1813 and why that of 1813 succeeded:*
First. The old diplomacy could not grasp the new character of a situation in which all interests had to be definitely subordinated to the necessary destruction of the common enemy.
Second. The zeal of the peoples dragged the kings along.
Third. The very victories of the Republic and Empire, which, by destroying many small states, concentrated all political power in the hands of two or three great powers.
Emphasize and make this *disunion* of Europe very tangibly evident. This, together with the *concentration* of French power, caused the victories of the latter.
Finish this chapter on the wars of the French Revolution with the picture of England defending herself by opposing the French with a similar force, a central government, a nation in arms. It is not the Channel which saves England; it is her spirit, her constitution, above all, her *liberty.* A grand spectacle: *liberty* alone capable of struggling successfully against *revolution.*
Where should this chapter go? It is large, and it could be very new or, at least, full of new details.

Before coming to Napoleon: the truly revolutionary wars peter out with the Directory.

8. *The military power* persists amidst governmental feebleness and internal distrust. Very evident during the Directory.

9. *The character of revolutionary conquests.* It has something in common with the early Islamic period, when the Arabs converted large portions of the earth while ravaging them at the same time.

10. *The French Revolution in Europe.* Audacious, violent, imprudent. A natural mark of revolutionary democracy, especially when French.

11. *A profound revolution in the art of warfare:* it is one of the great characteristics of the French Revolution. A large chapter about this.

12. One will be successful in enterprises which demand the qualities one possesses. But *one will not excel except in things where one's very faults work also to one's advantage.* This explains why the French are so much better waging war than in government and than in almost in any other civilian and moderate enterprise.

13. *The Consulate. The enthusiasm of propaganda is followed by the exploitation of Europe.*

14. *The old governments of Europe in the face of the French Revolution.* Their incapacity, their ancient routines, their old jealousies, their lack of concert, their slowness, their superficial and selfish views; they do not see the greatness and the new character of events; they fail to see that their very life is at stake. . . . Depict this old administrative Europe in the face of this revolutionary government. The Revolution exploded in the midst of this antique machinery like a cannon ball from nowhere, the crash and

surprise of the noise proving more frightening than its actual force.

Show also, in considering these existing antiquated governments, that the triumph of the Revolution could hardly have been avoided. Its success was, really, not particularly dependent on good fortune. Emphasize and elaborate on this.

15. *The German struggle against the French.* The spirit of the people moves the kings. The latter are tempted to see a revolutionary and subversive movement in noble and proud passions which in the end save them: trembling they let themselves be saved.

18. The year 1789 passed without having any great effect on the German constitutions. Yet, in 1803, *it was the princes who began to translate the revolutionary ideas into practices.* A very curious effect of the Revolution on Germany, fifteen years after the event.

21. *The greatest enemies of the Revolution willingly contribute to its effects.* Baron von Stein, the German aristocrat, the bitterest enemy of France and of French ideas in 1807, in order to make the Prussian people rise against France (the regular state armies had proved insufficient), introduces reforms flowing directly from the French revolutionary spirit: the law of 9 October 1807 destroying the landowning privileges of the aristocracy. Serfdom is abolished; the nobles are, in turn, allowed to enter into industry and commerce. Civic equality established. Appeals to the citizens to participate in politics. Municipal elections on the basis of limited suffrage, but without any distinction of birth or of religion. Army ranks are opened to everyone. A general tendency toward representative government.

22. *Fatal influence of the French Revolution.* In September 1848, M. Vogt in the Frankfurt parliament, proposing a break with the great German powers after the Armi-

stice of Malmö,[1] cried out: "If we reject the armistice, they will be afraid of us. We shall be in the situation the French were in in 1793: menaced from inside and outside, but depending on the people, they created a popular army; an army rose from the soil and Europe was conquered. This was done by convention: only a convention can reproduce such great things."

That Convention, whose follies caused so much harm to its contemporaries, continues to do harm through its image. It introduced the politics of the *impossible,* the theory of folly, the cult of blind audacity. People fail to see the specific circumstances of the 1790s which had helped to bring about the victory of the French revolutionary democratic government in 1792. They think that it is enough to repeat the performance and that thoughtless fury and blind audacity are sufficient to make it succeed.

[1] Between Prussia and Denmark.

BOOK THREE

[France before the Consulate]

CHAPTER I

How the Republic Was Ready to Accept a Master

One of the most extraordinary subjects of contemplation among the shifting scenes of human affairs is the internal life of the Republic before which all Europe trembled.

Her government, which had at its disposal the most formidable armies and perhaps the greatest generals who had appeared in the world since the downfall of Rome, tottered at every instant, steadying itself with difficulty, always nearly falling under the weight of its vices and its follies; it was devoured by innumerable diseases. In spite of its youth it was consumed by the nameless evil which attacks only old governments—a sort of general feebleness, of senile consumption, of which there can be no other definition than an inability to live. Attempts were no longer made to overturn it, but it seemed to have lost the power of standing upright.

After 18 Fructidor[1] more power was conferred on the

---

[1] On 18 Fructidor (4 September 1797) the Directorate and the troops of General Augereau struck against the emerging conservative majority in an unscrupulous and successful *coup d'état*.

Directory than had ever belonged to the kings whom the Revolution had overthrown. For it had in fact become an absolute sovereign; moreover, it succeeded a revolution which had destroyed all of those barriers with which laws and habits could formerly restrict the abuse, and sometimes the use, of power. The press was mute. France furnished the representatives designated by the government; local administrators who were not submissive had been superseded; the legislature, humbled and powerless, wished only to obey.

Still the Directory was incapable of governing. It occupied the helm of government, but it was unable to steer. It could never reintroduce regularity to the administration, order to the finances, or peace to the country. Its reign was nothing but anarchy tempered by force. It was not expected to endure by any one of its supporters. The parties never took it for an established government. They kept alive their hopes and, *above all*, their hatreds.

The government itself was only a party—always restless and violent, it was the least numerous and most contemptible party of all. It was a coterie of regicides, composed almost entirely of second-rate revolutionists who, by merely following in the wake of greater criminals or by committing only obscure crimes, had survived both the Reign of Terror and the reaction which followed Thermidor. These men looked upon the Republic as their refuge, yet in reality most of them cared for nothing but for the power and the pleasures which they enjoyed under it. Cynical and sensual, all that they had preserved of their former selves was their vigor. It is remarkable that almost all the men whose moral sense had been destroyed in the course of this long revolution still retained, in the midst of their acquired vices, some remnant of that disordered and wild courage which had enabled them to take part in making that revolution. Often, amidst their embarrassments and their dangers, they had contemplated and desired a return to the Reign of Terror.

They thought of it after Fructidor; they tried to restore it after Prairial, but in vain. This suggests certain reflections worth considering.

In the beginning of a violent revolution laws, regularly passed, are milder than public opinion, suddenly so harsh under the influence of new passions. But later laws become more stringent than public opinion, whose enervation begins to paralyze their execution. At first, terror reigns without the legislator's interference; afterwards he often spends his strength in endeavoring to create terror. The cruelest laws of 1793 are less barbarous than many of those passed in 1797, 1798, and 1799. The law which deported without trial representatives of the people and journalists to Guiana; the one which authorized the Directory to imprison or deport at will any priests whom it considered dangerous; the graduated income tax, which, under the name of forced loan, deprived the rich of all they had; and, finally, the infamous law of hostages show a perfection of legal terrorism which even the laws of the Convention did not have. And yet they did not reawaken the Terror. The men who proposed them were as bold, as unscrupulous, and perhaps even more intelligent in the devices of tyranny than were their predecessors; furthermore, these measures were voted almost without discussion and promulgated without resistance. While most of the laws that prepared and established the Terror had been heatedly debated and had excited the opposition of at least a part of the country, the laws of the Directory were silently accepted. Yet they could never be completely enforced. What is even more important, the very same cause aided their birth and deadened their effect. The Revolution had lasted so long that France, enervated and dispirited, had little astonishment or reprobation left to show when these violent and cruel laws were propounded. Yet this same moral enervation made their regular application difficult. Public opinion no longer lent its aid; it opposed to the virulence of the government a passive resistance of the masses whose very languor made this resistance elusive and almost invincible. The Directory thus wasted its efforts.

It is true that this government, so rich in its constant invention of revolutionary procedures, was strangely awkward and incapable of organization. It never learned to supply the absence of popular enthusiasm with an ably constituted administrative machinery. Its tyranny was always in want of instruments, and its victims escaped because of its want of agents. The Directory never understood that maxim of great despots, soon to become evident, that to command and to maintain obedience tyrannical laws capriciously followed are less efficient than milder ones regularly and equally enforced by an able administration. This deadness of the passions, this lassitude of public opinion existed not only in the application of revolutionary laws but also in the selection of punishments. For the scaffold deportation was substituted, a penalty often severer than death but the execution of which is not visible, so that while popular vengeance is satisfied the unpleasant sight of suffering is avoided.

Towards the end of the Directory the Jacobins reopened their club. They resumed their badges, their phrases, and their habits, for political parties seldom change, and it is worth remarking that they are more inflexible both in their ideas and in their practices than the individuals who compose them. The Jacobins then acted precisely as they had acted under the Reign of Terror, yet they were unable to bring it back. The only effect of the fear which they inspired was to make the nation even more inclined to surrender her freedom.

The Directory, after having governed without opposition and almost without any checks, having interfered with everything, having tried everything with the complete powers bestowed on it by the events of Fructidor, seemed gradually to expire of itself without an effort. (Especially after

June 1799; 30 Prairial, *an* VII.) The very legislative body
that it had decimated, in part replaced, and always treated
as its slave, regained mastery and resumed governing.
But soon the victors did not know what to do with their conquest. Hitherto the administrative machinery had worked
irregularly; now it seemed to stand still. It is evident
that assemblies, which are admirably suited at times to
strengthen and at other times to restrain governments, are
less capable than are the worst governments of directing
public affairs.

No sooner had power returned to the legislative body
than a sort of universal atrophy pervaded its administration
throughout the country. Anarchy spread from private individuals to public officials. There was no opposition, but
there was no obedience either. The general picture was that
of a disbanding army. The taxes, instead of being badly
paid, were not paid at all. Conscripts preferred highway
robbery to rejoining the army. At one time it seemed as if
not only civic order but civilization itself were collapsing.
Neither persons nor property, nor even the roads, were safe.
In those fragments of government correspondence which
still exist in the national archives a true impression of these
calamities may be found: for, as a minister of that time
noted, "The public accounts given to the nation should be
reassuring; but in those niches where the government de-
liberates unexposed to the public eye everything ought to
be told."

Here is one of those secret reports on the condition of the
country by the Minister of Police, dated 30 Fructidor, *an*
VII (16 September 1799). I gather from it that of the
eighty-six departments into which France (properly so
called, for I except the conquered provinces) was divided
at that time, forty-five were left to disorder and civil war.
Troops of brigands forced open the prisons, killed gendarmes, and set convicts at liberty; the receivers of taxes
were robbed, killed, or maimed; municipal officers mur-

dered, landowners imprisoned for ransom or taken as hostages; lands laid waste and stagecoaches held up. Bands of two hundred, of three hundred, of eight hundred men appeared all over the country. Armed gangs of conscripts resisted those whose duty it was to enroll them. The laws were disobeyed in every quarter, by some to follow the impulse of their passions, by others to follow the practices of their faith. Some profited by the state of affairs to rob travelers—others to ring the long-silent church bells, or to carry the symbols of the Catholic faith back to the desecrated cemeteries.

The means used to suppress disturbances were at once violent and efficient. We read in these reports that when a refractory conscript tried to escape from the soldiers they frequently killed him as an example. The private dwellings of citizens were continually exposed to public inspections. Moving columns of troops, almost as disorderly as the bands which they pursued, trampled through the countryside and extorted ransoms for want of pay or rations.

Paris was cowed but uneasy. She was disturbed by painful dreams. A thousand rumors of some terrible outbreak were circulating in the city. Some said that a great movement against the Directory, in favor of democracy, was in the making; others, that a royalist move was immediately due and that a huge fire was to give the signal. Men were heard to say that it is foolish to pay one's rent, for a blow will be struck that will settle every debt; blood will shortly be shed again. Such is the language of the reports. It is curious to observe the despair into which the sight of this universal confusion throws their reporters, the causes they assign, and the remedies they propose. The citizens are in absolute apathy, say some; the public spirit is utterly destroyed, say others. One asserts that brigands are harbored everywhere; another says that to the politicking of parties and to the impunity of crimes patriots are deplorably indifferent. Some ask for measures against the makers of fanaticism; many propose still more stringent laws against émigrés, priests, and nuns. The greater number are confused and find the situation incomprehensible. This secret disease, astonishing the agents of the Directory, this unknown and invisible atrophy was the state of minds and of hearts. France refused her own government.

During revolutions of long duration it is easy to mistake the signs indicating the approach of great turning points; for these signs vary with the different periods. They even change their character as the revolution advances.

In the beginning public opinion is excited, lively, intolerant, presumptuous, and mobile; at the end it is stolid and sad. After having tolerated nothing, there seems to be nothing it will not endure. But submission is accompanied by resentment, irritation increases, suspicion becomes more inveterate, and hatred grows in the midst of obedience. The nation has no longer, as in the beginning of the Revolution, sufficient energy to push a government towards the precipice; yet everyone enjoys the spectacle of its fall.

Such was the state of France in 1799. She distrusted and detested yet she obeyed her government.[2]

---

[2] (T) Tocqueville had eliminated here a long passage about which he noted: "This is good but should be conserved for use elsewhere. It interrupts the sequence of ideas." The passage follows: "This internal resistance of hearts sufficed to paralyze the power of a government which had no organic vitality. Often, in our own day, we have seen administrations survive governments. While the paramount powers of the State were expiring or overthrown, the subordinate powers still continued to function with regularity and firmness. These were times of revolution, but not of anarchy.

"The reason for this is that now in France the actual administration forms a special body with habits, rules, and instruments of its own, so that it is able for a certain period to present the phenomenon of a headless body still proceeding on its way. This was the work of Napoleon. We shall see how, by the construction of this powerful machine, he made our revolutions easier and less destructive at the same time.

At this time she presented a sad spectacle: everywhere France bore the traces of the sort of moral decay produced in the long run by the movements of revolutions.

All revolutions, even the most necessary ones, have had such an effect for a time. But I think that in our case it was stronger than in any other, and I do not know of another event in history that contributed more to the wellbeing of succeeding generations or more entirely demoralized the generation that brought it about. For this there are many reasons: first of all, the immense mass of property confiscated by those who gained from the Revolution. The French Revolution multiplied, to an extent never before seen in any civil war, the number of doubtful properties whose title rested on law but not with a secure conscience. The sellers of confiscated estates were not quite sure of their rights to dispose of them, nor the buyers of their rights to acquire them. Their idleness or ignorance frequently prevented them from having correct opinions on this central matter, and their interests kept most of them from looking too closely into it.

This gave millions of men a disturbed frame of mind.

During the great revolution which preceded the religious reformation of the sixteenth century—the only revolution that can be compared with the French Revolution—the property of the Church was confiscated, but it was not brought under the hammer; a few great nobles seized it. With us, on the other hand, not only the estates of the Church but those of almost all great landowners—not the

---

"Nothing similar existed at the time of which we are speaking. The old administrative authorities were overthrown without anything else yet taking their place. The administration was as incoherent and disorderly as the nation; as much without rules, without a hierarchy, and without traditions. The Terror had been able to hold this ill-made and ill-adjusted machinery together; but to return to the Terror had become impossible, and in the absence of public spirit the whole political machine fell into pieces."

property of a single corporation but the patrimonies of a hundred thousand families—were divided up. Note further that men grew rich not merely by the purchase of confiscated estates at absurd prices but also by the pretended reimbursement of enormous amounts of debts. The profits were legal and dishonest at the same time.

Following this comparison, I find that the revolution of the sixteenth century threw doubt upon only one part of human opinions and disturbed established habits only on some points. At that time that moral sense which in most men is founded less upon reason than upon custom and prejudice was merely shaken, whereas the French Revolution assailed at the same time political and religious beliefs, desired to reform the individual and the State, tried to change old customs, established opinions, and fixed habits on every subject simultaneously; all of this produced universal moral perturbation and consciences tottered everywhere.

But in long revolutions men are demoralized less by the faults and by the crimes that they commit in the heat of their convictions and passions than by the contempt that they finally acquire for these very convictions and passions. When tired, disenchanted, and deceived, they turn against themselves and consider their former hopes as having been childish—their enthusiasm and, above all, their devotion absurd. No one can conceive how often the resistance of even the strongest souls is broken during such a decline. Men thus crushed cannot only no longer attain great virtues, but they seem to have become almost incapable of great crimes.

Those who saw Frenchmen reduced to this state thought that in the future they would be incapable of any great moral effort. But they deceived themselves, for if our virtues never satisfy the moral philosopher our vices never leave him without hope; the truth is that we never tread either path so firmly as not to be able to leave it.

The French, after they had passionately loved—or after they had thought they loved—Liberty in 1789, loved her no longer in 1799, though no other love had filled their hearts. Having at one time bestowed on her a thousand imaginary charms, they now could not even see her true qualities; they saw only her bothersome and risky nature. It is true that for the last ten years they had found in her little else. In the strong words of a contemporary, the Republic had been nothing but agitated despotism. In what other period in history had the habits of men been so violently disturbed; when did tyranny enter so deeply into the details of private life? What sentiments and what actions had been left free? What habits and what customs had been respected? The simplest person was forced to change his days of work and rest, his calendar, his weights and measures, even his language. While obliged to take part in ceremonies which to him appeared ridiculous and profane, he was not allowed to worship God except in secret. He broke the laws whenever he followed his conscience or his taste. I do not know if anything similar could have been endured for so long by any other nation, but there are times when there is no limit to our patience and others again when there is none to our resistance.

Often during the course of the Revolution the French thought that they were on the point of finding a solution to this great crisis. At times they trusted in the constitution, at times in the Assembly, and at others in the executive power itself. Once or twice they even trusted in their own exertions, which is always the last thing they think of. All these hopes had been deceived; all these attempts had been in vain. The march of the Revolution was not arrested. It is true that it brought great changes no longer, but its continuous agitation went on. It was a wheel running empty but seeming to go round and round forever.

It is difficult to imagine even now that excess of fatigue, apathy, indifference or, rather, of contempt for politics into which such a long, terrible, and vain struggle had thrown so many minds. Many nations have presented a similar spectacle, but since every nation brings its own peculiar character into such situations, on this occasion the French appeared to abandon themselves to fate with a sort of passionate merriment. Despairing of escape from their misfortunes, they tried to forget them by substituting delights. The amusements in Paris, wrote a contemporary, were not interrupted for a single moment by either the crises of the present or the fear of the future. The theaters and public places had never been so crowded. At Tivoli you heard people say that things would soon be worse than ever; patriots are called idiots, and through it all we dance. One of the police reports this inscription placed on the pedestal of the statue of Liberty: "Our government resembles the Mass for the Dead: there is no Gloria, no Credo, a long Offertory, and in the end no Benediction." Fashion was never so extravagant nor so capricious. Amidst all this despair fashion strangely revived all the frivolity of the past. All it assumed were a few new features; it became eccentric, disproportionate, in fact, revolutionary; as in other, more serious matters, there remained few rules or limits.

Political institutions are like religions: in that observances for a long time survive faith. It was curious to see the government of a nation which no longer cared for liberty or for the Republic, in which all revolutionary zeal seemed to have expired, still obstinately persevering in all the revolutionary ceremonies. In May it attended solemnly the Fete of Popular Sovereignty; in the spring it was present at the Fete of Youth; in summer at the one in honor of Agriculture; in autumn at the Fete of Old Age. On 10 August all public functionaries were assembled round the Altar of the Nation to swear fidelity to the Constitution and hatred to tyrants.

François de Neufchâteau, Minister of the Interior in 1799, in the very days when France was threatened by foreign enemies abroad and devoured by anarchy within, was chiefly occupied in arranging these civic fetes; most of his circulars are on this subject. It is of course true that this was one of the most harebrained men of letters ever in politics. As no one would regard these ridiculous fetes in earnest, a law was passed (17 Thermidor, *an* VI) to force the shop-keepers, on pain of fine or imprisonment, to close their shops on fete days and on the *decadi,* and to forbid any work to be done on these days on the public roads or within the public view. As the appellation of "citizen" was now considered vulgar and had fallen out of use, the government posted up these words in large letters in every public office: "Here men proudly wear their title of citizen."

The governing revolutionary party kept up in its official language all the rhetoric of the Revolution. Likewise the last thing that a party will abandon is its phraseology, because among political parties, as elsewhere, the vulgar make the rules of language, and the vulgar abandon more easily the ideas instilled into them than the words that they have learned. When one reads the harangues of the time, it seems as if nothing could be expressed simply. Soldiers are called "warriors," wives "faithful companions," children "pawns of love." Duty is never mentioned, "virtue" always; no one ever promises less than to die for his country and for liberty.

The contemptible part is that most of the orators who delivered these speeches were themselves almost as wearied, as disgusted, and as cold as the rest; but it is a sad condition of great passions that long after they have lost all their influence over the hearts their marks on the language survive. From the newspapers one might have imagined that one lived in the midst of a nation passionately fond of liberty and most interested in public affairs. Never was their language more inflated, nor their assertions more clamorous than now when they were on the eve of a fifteen-year silence. To ascertain the real power of the press, attention should not be paid to what it says but to the way in which the public listens. The very vehemence of the press is sometimes a mark of its weakness and a forerunner of its demise; its clamor is often the proof of its own perils. It screams only because its audience is growing deaf, and this deafness of the public makes it safe to silence the press later.

Although the people were estranged from politics, it must not be thought that they were indifferent to their particular dangers. The very contrary was true. The French had never perhaps so dreaded the consequences of political events as when they were no longer directing them. In politics fear is a passion that frequently grows at the expense of all others. Everything is feared when nothing is any longer ardently desired. The French, besides, have a sort of lighthearted desperation which often deceives their rulers; they laugh at their own misery, but they feel it no less. At this time, though preoccupied with their own petty affairs and dissipated by pleasure, they were worn by political anxieties. An almost unbearable suspense, a terror that seems to us incredible, took possession of every soul.

Although the dangers of 1799 were, on the whole, infinitely less than those at the beginning of the Revolution, they inspired terror that was more intense and more general because the nation now had less energy, feebler passions, and more experience. All the evils that had overpowered the people for ten years had assembled in their fancy to form a picture of the future; after having contributed to the most terrible catastrophes, they now trembled at their own shadows. From the writings of the times it appears that the most opposite of things were simultaneously feared: some dreaded the abolition of private property, others the return of feudal rights. Often the same men, after fearing one of these evils, immediately turned to dread the other: in the morning a restoration, in the evening a return of the Terror. Many were afraid to show their fear, and it was not until after the crisis of 18 Brumaire that the extent of their relief and the excess of their joy revealed the depths of pusillanimity into which the Revolution had plunged these enervated souls.

Although experience ought to prepare us for any amount of human fickleness, still we may be surprised at the sight of so great a change in the disposition of a nation: so much selfishness after so much dedication; so much indifference after such vehemence; such fearfulness after so much heroism; much utter distrust of what they had desired so ardently and paid for so dearly.

Such a complete and sudden revolution cannot be so simply explained. The character of our nation is so peculiar that to understand it the study of human nature in general will not be sufficient. It constantly surprises those who study it: a nation more gifted than any other with a capacity to appreciate extraordinary things and even to accomplish them; able to scale the greatest heights in a single endeavor, yet unable to maintain herself at those heights for long because she acts upon impulse, not on principle; the most civilized people in the world and yet, in certain respects, retaining more of the savage than any other. For it is in the nature of savages to decide by the sudden impressions of the present, without recollection of the past or thought of the future.

CHAPTER II

*How the Nation, though Ceasing to Be Repub-
lican, Remained Revolutionary*

Seeing how disgusted the nation was with liberty, the
royalists fancied that she was anxious to return to the old
regime. This is the mistaken belief of parties whose day has
gone by: that they are wanted because their successors are
hated. They do not see how much easier it is for men to
remain constant in their antipathies than in their affections.
Though she no longer loved the Republic, France was still
profoundly attached to the Revolution. From this condition
such important consequences follow that they should be
considered at some length.

As time passed and the old regime faded in the distance,
the people grew more and more resolved not to return to
it. This was a remarkable phenomenon: the Revolution
seemed to become dear to the nation in proportion to the
suffering which it inflicted.

From the writings of the time it appears that, of all
things, this astonished the enemies of the Revolution most.
When they observed the evils produced by the Revolution
together with the attachment retained by the Revolution,
France to them seemed to have become raving mad.

These opposite effects, however, were due to the same
cause.

People suffered more from the Revolution the longer
its bad administration lasted; but this very duration entrenched new habits and increased the number and the va-

riety of the interests dependent on it. As time advanced, barrier after barrier rose behind, impeding a return.

Most Frenchmen had taken an active part in affairs since the beginning of the Revolution and had publicly attested their allegiance to it; they felt somewhat responsible themselves for the evils that had ensued. With the increase and duration of the evils this responsibility seemed to grow. Thus the Reign of Terror even gave to many of its own victims an unconquerable aversion to the re-establishment of masters who would certainly have many injuries to revenge.

Something like this has been witnessed in every revolution. Even the most oppressive governments make a return to a former state intolerable to the people, provided that these governments last long enough.

The French Revolution, besides, did not oppress the whole country in the same manner; some suffered little by it, and even among those who bore the burden many had found considerable advantages mixed with the evils. I believe that the comfort of the lower classes was much less disturbed than is commonly supposed. At least they had wide alleviations of their misfortunes.

As great numbers of workmen had volunteered or were enlisted, those who remained in France got much higher pay. Wages rose in spite of all public and private miseries, for the working class diminished more quickly than the demand for their services.[1]

One of the principal foes of the Revolution, M. Mallet du Pan, writes in 1796: "The working men earn more now than in 1790." Sir Francis d'Ivernois, who for ten years imposed on himself the task of convincing England every year that France, exhausted by misery, had no more than six months to live, acknowledges in his last pamphlet, written

---

[1] (T) Similar causes produced a similar phenomenon at the close of the Empire. The condition of the working classes improved in the midst of our disasters.

in 1799, that wages had risen everywhere since the Revolution and that the price of wheat had fallen.

As for the peasantry, I need not repeat that they were able to acquire much land at ludicrous prices. It is impossible to set their gains down in precise figures, but it was more than considerable.

Everyone knows that the Revolution abolished many heavy and vexatious taxes, such as tithes, feudal dues, compulsory labor, the salt tax, some of which were never restored and others only incompletely reimposed at a much later period. Today we can scarcely imagine how hateful many of those taxes were to the people, either because of their oppressiveness or the ideas with which they were connected.

When in the year 1831 in Canada, I was talking with farmers of French origin, I found that in their language the word *taille* was synonymous with misery and evil. They called any great misfortune "a real *taille*." The *taille*, I believe, never existed in Canada; at any rate, it had been abolished for more than half a century. No one remembered its real meaning; the name alone remained in the language as a lasting proof of the hatred that it had inspired.

Another gain, which has not sufficiently been noticed, was the indirect and irregular but no less great benefit conferred by the Revolution on a multitude of poor debtors. Their debts were not actually abolished, but they were practically reduced by the issue of paper money.

It is now known that in many French provinces the number of small proprietors was considerable even before 1789. There is reason for thinking (although it cannot be completely proved) that most of these small landowners were in debt, for at that time they bore the chief burdens of taxation. Even nowadays, with equal taxation, it is that class which is still most subject to debt.

The towns were full of the owners of small encumbered

estates; for France has always been a country where people have more pretensions and more vanity than wealth. We must also note that before the Revolution, as in our own day, independent farmers were numerous, because our farms are generally small.

The rapid depreciation of paper money was universal, as if all securities had been thrown away and rents reduced to nothing. General disorder and, still more, the weakness of the administration prevented even debts to the State from being regularly or fully paid. The financial records of the Republic show that the State could not collect more than one fourth of what was due either from the old taxes kept up or from the new ones imposed. The State was maintained by *assignats,* by payments in kind, and by the spoils of Europe. M. Thibaudeau said justly in his memoirs that "the discredit of the *assignats* ruined the great proprietors and bondholders while it enriched the peasants and farmers."

"The country," wrote the same Mallet du Pan, whom I quoted earlier, in 1795, "grows rich by the poverty of the towns; fabulous profits are made. A sack of flour pays the farmer's rent. The peasants have become calculators and speculators; they fight with each other for the lands of the émigrés and pay no taxes."

An intelligent foreign observer traveling in France at this time writes: "In France, today, the true aristocracy is that of the farmers and peasants."

It is true that the peasant was frequently subject to vexations, to the billeting of soldiers and requisitions in kind, but these partial and momentary evils did not ruin his appetite for the benefits produced by the Revolution. On the contrary, he became more and more attached to them, and he bore these annoyances as he bore storms and floods, for which good land is never abandoned though they make the owner long for a fair season that will enable him to turn it to his profit.

When one considers the means by which the makers of our first revolution succeeded in winning the agricultural classes, and with what substantial gifts they obtained the support of the small farmers and lower classes (that is, of the great mass of the nation) despite the general misery and desolation, one wonders at the simplicity of some radicals in our own day who thought that it would be easy to persuade a highly civilized people to submit patiently to the inevitable inconveniences of a great political change by merely offering them liberty instead of plunder and profit.

The middle class, and especially the town bourgeoisie who began the revolution, was, among the victors, the class that chiefly had to bear the burden. Its personal sufferings were greater, and its substantial losses almost as great as those of the nobles. Its trade was partially, its industries wholly destroyed. The small government jobs and many other privileges from which many of the bourgeois had profited were abolished. But what had ruined them also made them the governing class. The powers of the State passed to them immediately; a great part of the public wealth soon followed.

The greater part of the reforms suddenly produced by the violent and disorderly tyranny of the Revolution had been announced, extolled, and desired all through the eighteenth century. These reforms placated the minds and charmed the imaginations even of those with whose interest they interfered. The only fault found with these innovations was that they had cost too much. Yet the very price that had been paid made some of them still more precious. Much as people trembled and suffered, there was always one thing which seemed worse than the pain and anxiety of the present: a return to the old regime.

A royalist writes during the famine year of 1796: The people swear and curse at the Republic. But try to talk sense to them, tell them that they were happier before:

they respond that the aristocrats employ hunger and fear to make them cry out for the King, but they would rather eat cobblestones.

Certain ingenious writers of our days have tried to rehabilitate the old regime. I must say that it is small proof of the excellence of a government when men praise it only when they have ceased to believe in the possibility of its restoration. I myself have tried to judge it not from my own ideas but from the feelings which it inspired in those who endured and then destroyed it. All through the course of that cruel and tyrannical revolution I see the hatred of the old regime surpass all other hatreds in French hearts, so deeply entrenched as to survive its very object and to become a passion and, from a temporary passion, a permanent national instinct. I observe that during the worst vicissitudes of the last sixty years the fear of the return of the old regime has always extinguished every other fear in our restless and excitable minds. For me this is enough. The trial, in my opinion, is over; the judgment has been made.

This impossibility of making the French return to the old order of things was, moreover, evident almost immediately after they had emerged from it. Mirabeau declared this right away, and many among the greatest opponents of the new institutions discovered this soon. The following extract is from a little pamphlet published during the emigration by M. de Montlosier (in 1796), perhaps the most remarkable product of this vigorous and eccentric mind.

"The Monarchy," he said, "has sunk with the weight of our rights and privileges, which cling to it for salvation. We must sacrifice our rights and privileges to help it rise to the surface. We are assured that everyone curses the Revolution. Certainly! I believe it. I am only trying to find out if there is not some difference between cursing the Revolution and wishing to restore the old state of things. France wishes only to remain as she is, and to be at peace.

No one wants to lose the fruits of his talents or of recent events. Generals will not again be privates, judges do not choose again to be constables, the *maires* and *presidents* of the *départements* are not willing to be once more laborers or artisans; those who acquired our fortunes are not likely to give them up. The thing is done, the Revolution cursed by all France has spread over the whole of France. We must take this confusion as it is, find our places in it, and convince ourselves that we will not be valued at our former price."[2]

Most of the émigrés had quite different ideas. The folly of certain royalists abroad would seem inconceivable if we did not know that they were brought up with the illusory beliefs of an already powerless aristocracy and that they had long lived in exile.

The pains of exile are especially cruel in this respect, that while they inflict suffering they teach nothing.[3] They *immobilize*, in a way, the minds of their victims, fix in them the notions acquired in childhood, or those that were in vogue when they were exiled. For them the new events that occur, the new habits that are established in their country, do not exist. They stand like the hands of a watch at the hour when it stopped. This is said to be an infirmity peculiar to the minds of certain exiles. I believe that it is the common malady of exile; few are able to escape it.

[2] (T) In a report on the debts of the émigrés, made in 1798 by the head of the "Bureau de Liquidation," Bergerat, we read that the debts of the émigrés from the Department of the Seine alone equaled all the debts left by the émigrés in the other departments, because all the great landowners of France lived in Paris. Nothing shows better that the nobles had ceased to be a political aristocracy and had become merely a select society; that they had exchanged real power for court favors.

[3] (T) Another marginal note by Tocqueville: "Exile had taught them the virtues of resignation and industriousness amidst poverty; but it failed to give them political common sense. It even took away the common sense of those who had originally had some."

The émigrés, thus, lived in the imaginary enjoyment of their privileges long after these had been lost to them forever. They were always dreaming of what they would do when they would be reinstated in the possession of their estates and of their vassals, without remembering how those vassals now made Europe tremble. Their chief anxiety was not that the Republic might last but that the monarchy should not be restored exactly in the way it had been before its fall. They hated the liberal constitutionalists even more than they hated the radical terrorists;[4] they talked only of the just severity that they would exercise when they returned to power; in the meantime they devoured each other; in short, they did everything to maintain the hatred felt for them, and they succeeded in impressing France with the image of an old regime even more odious than the real one which had been destroyed.

Between fear of the royalists and of the Jacobins, the majority of the nation sought an escape. The Revolution was dear, but the Republic was feared lest it should result in the return of one or the other. One might even say that each of these passions nourished the other; it was because the French found precious certain benefits assured them by the Revolution that they feared all the more keenly a government which might interfere with these profits. Of all the privileges that they had won or obtained during the last ten years, the only one that they were disposed to surrender was liberty. They were ready to give up the liberty which the Revolution had merely promised, in order to finally enjoy the profits that it had brought.

The parties themselves, decimated, apathetic, and weary, longed to rest for a time during a dictatorship of any kind, provided only that it was exercised by an out-

[4] See Gobineau, p. 301; also Introduction, p. 17 ff., about those new "radical conservatives" who preferred Gobineau to Tocqueville.

sider and that it weighed upon their rivals as much as on themselves. This feature completes the picture. When great political parties begin to cool in their attachments without softening their hatreds, and at last reach the point of wishing less to succeed than to prevent the success of their opponents, one should prepare for servitude—the master is near.

It was easy to see that this master could rise only from the army.

It is interesting to follow through the different phases of this long revolution the gradual advance of the army toward power. In the beginning the army was dispersed by an unarmed populace or, rather, it disappeared amidst the rapid movements of public opinion. For a long time it was a stranger to all internal affairs; the populace of Paris alone usurped the power of making and unmaking the rulers of France. Meanwhile the Revolution goes on. The enthusiasm which it had inspired fades; the able men who had directed it in the Assembly retire or die; its government weakens; its stern habits become enervated; anarchy spreads in every direction. During this time the army pulls together; it acquires experience and fame; great generals emerge. It preserves a common goal and common passions while the nation has them no more. In short, the military and the civilians grow into two entirely different societies within the same period and within the same nation. The ties that bind the one together are drawn closer, while those that unite the other relax their hold.

On 13 Vendémiaire in 1795 the army, for the first time since 1789, took a part in internal affairs. It caused the victory of the Convention and defeated the bourgeois of Paris. On 18 Fructidor in 1797 it helped the Directory overcome not only Paris but the legislative body, and the whole country by whom that body had been chosen. On 30 Prairial in 1799, it refused to support these same Directors, whom it held responsible for its own reverses; they fell before the Assembly.

After 13 Vendémiaire there could be no government without the army. Soon after that there could be no government except through the army. Having reached this point, the army wished to govern. One step induced another. Long before they were really masters, the soldiers adopted the tone and habits of command. A German Swiss, a great partisan of the Revolution and a friend of the Republic, traveling in France in 1798, remarks regretfully that, to judge from the military parades, from the arrogance and the insolence with which the soldiers treated the public at the public fetes, one would think that in no royal festival had so little respect been shown to the people.

The friends of the Republic, who saw this growing influence of the army, kept telling themselves that the military had always shown its ultra-republican sentiments; they repeated this even when these sentiments had ceased to affect the entire nation.

What the republican partisans took for love of the Republic was chiefly a love of the Revolution. In fact, the army was the only class in France in which every member, without exception, had gained by the Revolution and had a personal interest in supporting it. To it every officer owed his rank, and every soldier his chance of becoming an officer. The army was, in truth, the standing Revolution in arms. If it still fiercely exclaimed: "Long live the Republic!" this was really a challenge to the old regime, whose friends cried: "Long live the King!" Deep down the army cared nothing for civic liberties. Hatred of foreigners and a love of his native land are generally the only elements of the soldier's patriotism even in free nations; still more must this have been the case at that time in France. The army, like almost every other army in the world, could make nothing of the slow and complicated gyrations of a representative government; it detested and despised the Assembly, because it understood only powers that were strong and simple; all it wanted was national independence and victories.

Everything was, then, ready for a new revolution; and yet it must not be supposed that people had a clear idea of what was coming. There are moments when the world resembles one of our theaters before the curtain rises. We know that we shall see a new play. We already hear the preparations on the stage; the actors are close to us, but we cannot see them, and we do not know what the piece is to be. In this manner, toward the end of 1799, the approach of a revolution was felt everywhere though no one knew whence it was to come. It seemed impossible that the existing state of things would continue; but it seemed equally impossible to escape from it.[5] In every correspondence of the time the thought that "things cannot remain as they are" appears—nothing more is added. Even imagination was exhausted; men were tired of hoping and predicting. The nation abandoned herself to her fate; full of dread, but also of languor, she turned her eyes nonchalantly from side to side to see if no one would come to her aid. It was evident that this deliverer must rise from the army. Who will it be? Some thought of Pichegru, some of Moreau, others about Bernadotte.

Retired to the country, in the heart of the Champagne, M. Fiévée wrote in his memoirs: "One single observation

[5] (T) Towards the end the approach of a catastrophe became so evident that even the amusements of Paris were interrupted. At the end of Fructidor, about two months before 18 Brumaire, we find in a literary journal of fashion, among various attempts at poetry, this note reflecting the frivolity, the anxieties, and the ludicrous taste of the time: "We shall publish no new fashions until this crisis is over. Until then fear and anxiety appear to have usurped the domain over the amiable hearts of our countrymen."

only recalled politics to me; every peasant whom I met in the fields, in the vineyards, or the forest stopped me to ask if there was any news of General Bonaparte and why he did not return to France; no one ever asked me anything about the Directory."

BOOK FOUR

[From Tocqueville's projected chapters
and notes on the Consulate
and the Empire]

CHAPTER I

[Tocqueville's Plan]

1. *Sorrento, December 1850—Napoleon.* What I want to paint is not so much the events themselves, however surprising or important they may have been, as the spirit of these events; less the different acts in the life of Napoleon than Napoleon himself, that singular, incomplete, but really *marvelous* person. It is not possible to study his period without feeling that one is confronted by one of the most extraordinary historical spectacles.

I should like to show what factors in his fabulous enterprises were due to his own genius and what were furnished to him by the contemporary spirit and by the state of the nation. I should like to describe how this truculent nation so suddenly decided to servilely follow a master; his incomparable ability to discover the most demagogic features of the Revolution, and to profit therefrom. On the interior scene I wish to consider the achievements of this almost supernatural intellect and its gross employment in suppressing liberty; this perfect and lucid use of force, which only the greatest genius of a most enlightened and civilized century could have conceived. And I must show society suppressed and stifled under this intelligent machinery: the increasing intellectual sterility of minds, the mental lassitude, the spiritual seclusion, the gradual disappearance of great personalities, the slow unfolding of an immense, flat human landscape in which very little was to stand out except for the colossal figure of the Emperor himself.

And when I come to his foreign policies and conquests, I must sketch the violent course of his fortunes across nations and kingdoms. I want to describe how here too the singular grandeur of his military genius was assisted by the curiously disordered grandeur of his times. What an extraordinary picture, if one could only paint it! Power and weakness, as they appear together within this impatient and mobile genius: as he ceaselessly constructs and destroys his own works, as he keeps rearranging and replacing the burdens of empires, throwing nations and their rulers into despair not so much by the sufferings he imposes on them as by the endless uncertainty in which he leaves them about their future.

I should, finally, like to propose through what course of excesses and errors he himself precipitated his fall. And despite these errors and excesses I must pursue the immense traces he left behind him in this world, not only memories but lasting influences and deeds: I want to describe what it is that died with him and what it is that endures.

And, in the end, to show what the Empire meant for the French Revolution, the place which this singular phase occupies within that strange drama whose end is not yet in sight.

Those are the great objects that I glimpse: but how to seize them? . . .

The memories; silence.

2. *To relate and judge at the same time* . . . To relate, first of all, the way in which Napoleon seized power. This extraordinary outcome of the Revolution. The facilities the Revolution provided him. The form and the constitution which, in turn, he gives to the Revolution. Picture of his prodigious nature and mental activity when applied to matters of administration, even before a sketch of the institutions he created. Changes which develop within the very personality of the Emperor while his fortunes increase and while his powers seem to become irresistible: how he loses the otherwise so salutary safeguard of fear . . .

[There follows Tocqueville's brief outline of ten planned chapters. The last batch of these notes reads *Another chapter:*] How his fortunes drew him beyond his original plans and made him mix old materials with new ones in his constructions.

The comic, charlatan, petty, even vulgar side of this great man. His characteristics of someone newly rich, of a parvenu. His taste for tinsel, for false grandeur, for the inflated, the gigantic.

The incoherence, the absence of any clear plan, the fickleness of his foreign policies. . . . The great cause of his fall: Europe was so vanquished, its rulers so broken and so mediocre that they would have submitted to the worst enormities if they only knew their fixed and precise limits. They were reduced to despair less by their sufferings than by their perpetual uncertainty about their future, by the fearful expectation of ever worse things to come . . .

Oppression of the defeated, while improving their conditions and laws. Partly resulting from the manner in which Napoleon waged war, partly caused by the wrong idea of making war attractive to the army by the prospect of loot. Result that those peoples who had the least love for their own institutions and who prospered most by the new Napoleonic laws were the very ones who turned most furiously against him . . .

His conquests are different from those of other conquerors: he is propagandist as well as conqueror, continuing thus at least in part the ideological character of the wars of the Republic. Violence mixed with philosophy and enlightenment. There we have Napoleon and the nineteenth century together.

Daring, self-contradictory, unprecedented enterprises of this Emperor and of his genius, coming not merely from his nature but from those extraordinary times of upheaval and innovations within which he lived; from the unforeseen, curious, unprecedented turn that human affairs have taken.

―――

CHAPTER II

[Bonaparte—the Consulate]

1. *The personality of Bonaparte.* This man who alone filled the immense stage which the Revolution had opened.

2. *Everything that may throw a light on the first appearance of Bonaparte should be explored:* his early opinions, his first writings, his character before his coming to power, how he really behaved on 13 Vendémiaire, on 18 Fructidor, in Egypt—in one word, his whole career before 18 Brumaire.

3. *Buonaparte.* It may be said that he impressed the

world even before his name became known. During the first Italian campaign his name is spelled and pronounced in a variety of forms; among others, an ode in his praise in 1796, entitled *Vers sur les premières victoires de Buonaparté:*

> Et toi, Postérité,
> Comble de tes honneurs l'heureux *Buonaparté* . . .

4. *His reception on his return from Italy.* The loquacity of Barras. Bonaparte's style: curt but very obscure; he says that the organic laws of the Republic should be established, that the era of representative governments should begin.

He observes the parties and appears to embrace none. He has ties with the Thermidorists, Barras, Tallien (who have become moderates compared to Sieyès). The Jacobins, who have a marvelous instinct for scenting their enemies, attack him (even though he had often assisted them); his Corsican compatriot Arena says that Bonaparte is the man most dangerous for liberty (which is precisely what his reputation needs, since during revolutions public opinion is often ahead of politicians, and what the latter consider defamatory is often admired by the public). Public opinion, favorably inclined, lets Bonaparte dare anything. People are tired of a confusion whose end is not in sight. For the sake of rest and order the nation throws herself into the arms of a man who is believed sufficiently strong to arrest the Revolution and sufficiently generous to consolidate its gains.

Public opinion, first impressed by the reserve of Bonaparte, now rings with his name everywhere. The Directory, fretful of his presence, seeks every occasion to remove him from Paris. He plays the role of a disinterested and lazy man; he seems as if he wished nothing but to rest. He silently watches the political scene.

He and the Directory become two rival powers; they must clash or separate. During the Italian campaign the

Egyptian idea frequently appears in his letters. He is given full powers to prepare the Egyptian expedition.

5. *The Italian or, at least, the Mediterranean side of Napoleon's genius.*

6. *The old regime leaves indestructible impressions on his otherwise so revolutionary mind.*

7. *Bonaparte irritated by the hostility of the salons.* His taste for them. Amidst all his personal glory the habits of the old regime impress this parvenu. On this point Lafayette is superior to him, for Lafayette has been an aristocrat; his hatred of the old regime is not mixed with the attractions of envy.

8. *His insistence on pomp and on the externals of power.* This is rare in great men; still, it is one of the most deeply rooted passions of Bonaparte. I think that this inclination reflects the cheaper side of his character.

9. *Bonaparte's conversations with Lafayette.* "You may dislike my government; you may think I am a despot, but you will see, you will see one day whether I work for myself or for posterity . . . but at least I am in control, I, whom the Revolution, whom you, whom all the patriots have brought to where I am now; if I were to call the émigré princes back, all of you would be delivered to their vengeance." Lafayette says that these sentiments were expressed so nobly and that Bonaparte spoke so well about the glory of France that Lafayette was moved and grasped his hand. Here, on one hand, is that filial sentiment which Napoleon preserved for the Revolution; on the other, the self-interest of all those who, having been responsible for this Revolution, wished to maintain it if only as a barrier to prevent the return of the monarchy. . . .

11. *The most extraordinary quality that I find in this extraordinary man is his suppleness* or, in other words, the

flexibility of his genius, which permitted him to easily comprehend the great affairs of the world and immediately afterwards to concentrate on the pettiest matters.

12. *Napoleon treated his generals like the hunter treats certain favorite dogs,* letting them devour some of the animals killed, for the sake of giving them the taste of pursuit . . .[1]

13. *Napoleon. His character. Judgments about him.* A speech by Pitt in 1800, cited by Villemain (in his eighteenth-century literature course) in which Pitt brilliantly analyzes Bonaparte's situation and character, predicting that he will be endlessly driven from war to war: I must read this speech . . . Same place where Villemain relates that Fox, after the Peace of Amiens, went to see the First Consul and reported the impression of a man satisfied, thinking of little else beyond a glorious rest on his laurels, a reasonable young person full of philosophic ideas about the future friendship of the white and black races. (Try to find the source of this curious episode. Is it in the letters of Fox? . . .)

True and profound is the judgment which Villemain delivers on the character of Napoleonic government. "His habitual weapon was not violence." The maintenance of order, the regular application of laws, the abolition of all unnecessary cruelty, even a certain taste for justice were characteristic of his government. Yet his suppression of free thought, the destruction of social responsibility together with *the exaltation of martial courage* were the main principles of that government.

I underscored the previous phrase. Notice that Napoleon

[1] Compare this with Hitler, who in his *Table Conversations* said that he was disappointed with the German generals: "In the beginning I thought that they were bloodhounds and I had to keep them back; I know now that the opposite is true. They want to keep *me* back."

wanted not to proscribe but to direct enthusiasm; he wanted to suppress every great passion of the human heart for the sake of one, that one which makes people die in battle. This great man understood that some kind of high passion is always needed to revivify the human spirit, which otherwise decays and rots. It would have never occurred to him to make hearts and spirits concentrate merely on their individual welfare.

14. *The clamor for Bonaparte appears even abroad.* Mounier in *De l'influence attribuée aux philosophes* recounts that since the early Directory the German Wieland, writing about the Jacobins, contended that in order to end the troubles of France all power should be concentrated in the hands of a single person, and that this person should be Bonaparte.

15. *The 18th Brumaire.* An event for which there was no precedent and no sign in the history of the Revolution. . . . By and large, one of the worst conceived *coups d'état;* its execution unbelievably poor. It succeeded only because of the tremendous force of the general causes which led to it: the state of public opinion and the inclinations of the army, the first cause perhaps even more than the second . . .

[The Consulate]

20. *There are times when not even a giant is strong enough to arrest the course of a revolution, but there are others when a dwarf suffices.* Early in the French Revolution people thought that this or that person would bring it to an end any day. Toward its end the Revolution was believed to be irresistible; it seemed that it would destroy every obstacle in its way. A double error.

21. *How the very same conditions seem alternately sup-*

*portable and insupportable to the very same people, de-
pendent on the prevailing current of public opinion.* When
he came to power, Bonaparte increased taxes by one quarter. Nobody said a thing. The people did not turn against
him: everything he did was popular. In 1848 the provisional government did exactly the same; it was violently
attacked. Bonaparte did with the revolution what the people had wanted; they did not want the same thing when it
was done by the Revolution of 1848 . . .

22. *Eighteen hundred. This should go into the chapter
on the Consulate and Empire.* Whenever a despot rises, one
may be sure that soon legalists will appear ready to prove
that violence is lawful and that the defeated have been
guilty.

23. *The administrative facilities he had found. This
should go into the chapter about Bonaparte's reconstruction
of the governmental machinery.* (Probably at the end of
the book.) Positions were one of the means with which the
kings of France had raised money. In the foreword of the
bound volume of the *Moniteur* published in 1795 one
reads: "Toward the end of the last royal regime M. Quinaut
was directed to list all the positions that had been created
for financial reasons. They amounted to more than three
hundred thousand."

Almost all of these were bought by the bourgeois, by
the lower ranks of the nobility, by the new rich. Thus these
positions were at least as numerous at the end of the old
regime as they are today. The taste for them had been
generated by the kings themselves. Yet the effects of that
appetite had been different. They had rendered honor
rather than income. Instead of having made their new hold-
ers servile, they actually increased their independence, since
these positions were usually permanent and independent of
the central power. The Revolution and Bonaparte merely
changed the character, but not the essence of this practice.

Thereafter it resulted in increasing servility. These positions remained the principal means of distinction for most citizens; these appointments, now given gratuitously, became the most desirable sources of revenue for families; having been permanent appointments within a fixed system of rank subordinated to governmental centralization, they brought everyone appointed under the central power and by every day their dependence on the central government grew.

It is curious to watch the old French customs, ideas, and habits as they disappear in the vortex of the Revolution; to see them lost and then to see them reappear, merely modified during the Consulate and the Empire, like the flow of the Rhône, where the eye detects a bluish stream here, a yellow one there, and the merger of both a little farther downstream. The original colors may have been different; the river remains the same.[2]

24. *The influence of administrative practices on the destiny of a people should not be exaggerated.* The principal sources of these (political) vices and virtues are always to be found in the original ideas. This truth was very evident at that time. (Perhaps this should go to the place about the resumption of centralization.)

25. *The perfection of the administrative machine built by Bonaparte is proved by the ease with which it has kept running even when the central motor was shut off.* Just as today, the administration continues to function in the hands of mediocre weaklings almost as well as if it were run by the best of minds. The machine is hardly dependent on the worth of the men running it. This was obvious at that

[2] (T) It should never be overlooked that, beyond everything else, the increasing number of official positions and the growth of the public appetite for them are a general and permanent consequence of social democracy and of the bourgeois state.

time; the governmental wheels obeyed the first comer who pulled the lever.

26. *Bonaparte's policy toward the Church.* His precautionary measures against the spirit of the eighteenth century. His policy was to humiliate the Church and to win it at the same time. To involve it against the old regime and to compromise it with his own despotism. Alliance with the Church against the spirit of the Enlightenment, their mutual enemy. To Lafayette he said: "You shouldn't complain. I am taking the clergy down a rung from where you left them, so that a bishop will feel honored if a prefect invites him to dine. You don't care a damn about the holy phial[3] and all that stuff; neither do I. But believe me that it is important to make the Pope and all his people commit themselves against the legitimacy of the Bourbons. Every day I am damned to find that the dioceses of France are still ruled by bishops in the pay of our enemies."

He forces the clergy to share Bonapartean ideals; not only to subject them but to make them sing praises to their tyrant. Bonaparte's bitter tirade to Lafayette, ending in these famous words: "With my prefects, my gendarmes, and my priests I should be able to accomplish anything I want."

27. *This should go into the chapter after the re-establishment of religion under the Consulate.* The new position of the clergy (the nation Catholic), zealous in their religious duties, more faithful, more ultramontane, more independent of the government in religious affairs; more servile, however, in civil matters, quite lacking in public virtues, abstaining from the passions and interests of the nation, not really *citizens.* All of this due to the same cause: the priest ceased to be *proprietor;* and as he was not the head of a family, the personal ties that would bind him to the political interests of society did not exist.

[3] Religious symbol of French coronations.

A very important idea, to be put either at the end of the book or at the beginning when I say that the Revolution was not directed against faith. Describe clearly how religion regains its influence in each class when that class becomes imperiled by revolution—first the upper classes turn to religion in 1793, then the middle classes in 1848, a time when even the lower classes, or at least those who possess some things, are led to respect and esteem religion because of their material anxieties.

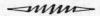

CHAPTER III

[Notes on the Empire]

1. *When I get to the Empire, analyze this structure: the despotism of a single person resting on a democratic basis.* This was the combination most suitable for those times: most suitable for limitless despotism, sustained by the appearances of legality and of national honor; supported by the greatest number and at the same time by the least responsible of people. The extraordinary character of a government which pretends that its mandate originated in a popular election; what is true in this claim.

Here a comparison. Recall the Roman Empire. To study and sum up the character of that government, its causes, its structure: where it resembles the idea conceived by Napoleon and further realized by his nephew.

Bring in examples here; how scholars establish legal theories and philosophies for this power created by violence and by force; the policy of these time-servers.

Because of the wide prevalence of the study of Roman law in every European nation despots find legal spokesmen even more easily than henchmen. These two sorts abound under the rule of a tyrant; even a mediocre usurper will easily find legal advisers to prove that Terror is Law, that Tyranny equals Order, that Servitude means Progress.

2. *Roman Empire. Its analogies with the French Empire: products of revolutions.* Democratic characteristics of the Roman Empire. Notes on the principles and sources of the imperial idea. (To utilize this in the chapter on the early Napoleonic Empire.) Differences and resemblances between these different revolutions which in France and in Rome led from liberty to despotism . . .

Exploitation of democratic passions and ideas by both. The same procedures: to govern in the name of the people but without the people; to represent the masses and to govern with the enlightened classes. Satisfaction given to the masses by affirming their representation through the abolition of all those intermediary orders of society which had humiliated them; thus satisfaction is given to the passions of envy and to the sentiments of equality in their grossest forms (i.e., everyone reduced to the same level of servitude). At the same time satisfaction given to the rich by assuring them material order, the tranquil possession of their goods, by continued well-being and opportunities of enrichment through official positions . . .

Difference: The Roman Revolution tried to attach itself to the past, preserving the forms of that past even though their content was destroyed. The French Revolution boasted of doing everything over, and the despotism that followed kept this pretension *in part*. From here grow all subsequent differences. (To develop this further.)

In Rome it was liberty that had been habitual, in France despotism. Augustus took away the substance of republican government but he felt obliged to maintain the shell: Bonaparte did not. The one had to change national habits; the other had to reintroduce them . . .

Very interesting in the book by Merivale [*A History of the Romans under the Empire*] how Augustus and his first successors portrayed themselves as representatives of the Roman people (and, which is more complex) as champions of democracy while, on the other hand, they governed exclusively with the aid of the aristocracy (though it is true that this aristocracy was, in part, their creation and, at any rate, wholly dependent on them). These Emperors left some place for popular action. They left quite a large place to the Senate, which not only helped them to govern but, under Augustus, did indeed govern some of the provinces (though only those peaceful ones where there was no army). Thus the Emperor appeared as a protector of order rather than as a destroyer of the aristocracy.

It should also be noted that Augustus maintained the semblances of electoral procedure and of popular government while in reality he made them illusory and impotent. He also substituted *paid* positions for the formerly merely honorary positions of the Republic, and he increased their number. He created permanent military forces, some of which were garrisoned for the first time in Rome. The powers of a lifelong Emperor gave him full control over the army; at the same time he maintained a semblance of aristocracy as well as of democracy. His tribunal powers rendered him invulnerable, though the fears about his vulnerability no longer existed. His censorial powers allowed him to name senators. His pontifical powers put him at the head of the state religion. In the end, all the functions that republican Rome had kept separated in order to avoid the omnipotence of state power were now permanently united and incarnated in a single man.

More care and more precautions taken by Augustus than by Napoleon and than are taken today—in order to cloak the full establishment of despotism and to manage the transition.

The democratic physiognomy of the Roman Empire. Trajan did not want to permit the associations of workers, for, as Pliny records (*Epist.* Book X:), *"neque enim secundum est nostri seculi morem."*[1] Trajan himself, the great and virtuous Trajan, after a century of unchallenged imperial government, fears the self-help associations of workers. He sticks to the maxim that the sovereign is the sole representative of the Roman people and that thus there should be none but isolated individuals!

To study this democratic monarchy of Rome. A great analogy: common servitude replacing common liberties; the complacency of satisfied envy replaces the enjoyable privileges of liberty. Social equality dearer to the low and vulgar than equality before the law; yet permanent social inequalities continue and the existence of the law makes tyranny respectable.

Roman government: not really one of the forms of democracy, as is vulgarly or stupidly believed by people who ignore the meaning of words or who wish to ignore them. It is merely one of the forms to which democratic equality will easily lead. It is a structure which those cheap sentiments and ignoble instincts that are the products of equality will make people accept and even love . . .

Villemain[2] during his literary lectures of 1830 remarked that Cicero in one of his letters (I must look up which) recounts how astonished he was to find that in the country all of the peasants were for Caesar. He finds this out talking with them. One might imagine him as well in France! . . .

In a scholarly study I now read that when Roman liberty succumbed under the force of the Emperors the republican forms were conserved and authority passed into imperial hands without a subversion of the ancient constitution

[1] "Since they are not in accord with our present customs."
[2] See Note 2, page 307.

(Tacitus, *Annales*, I. 2); the supreme power, at least in theory, rested with the people. When Ulpian and Gaius say that the wish of the ruler is law, they suggest the idea behind this law, which appears at the beginning of every new rule. By this law the Senate transferred to the prince every one of the rights of the people (*quum omne ius suum populus in principem transferat.* Tacitus, *Hist.* IV. 3).

BOOK FIVE

[General notes on the French Revolution]

CHAPTER I

[*The Peculiar French Physiognomy of the Revolution*]

1. *To depict the character of France during this revolutionary epoch of history; how this revolution was affected by the French national character.* A new view, were I only able to approach it with a fresh mind, of which perhaps now I might be capable, removed as I am from politics; now when I have no passions which would make me embellish or blur things; I have no passion aside from finding out what is true and trying to record it.

2. *French character. Different traits.* The Frenchman needs a little license in everything, even in servitude. He likes to go beyond his original commands; when in servitude, he exceeds in that too.

3. The French love liberty, but only as the least of their possessions; they are often ready to convince themselves to abandon her in moments of peril.

4. The upper classes distrustful of liberty, the lower classes inclined to license: that is France.

5. The French peasant has never understood the working of free institutions. The deputy he helps to elect has always been to him an object of jealousy, a busybody neighbor who unjustifiably succeeds in wangling a government post. . . .

11. In France there is more genius than common sense and more heroism than virtue.

CHAPTER II

[*The True Characteristics of the Revolution*]

1. *Similarities and differences between the Revolutions of 1640 and of 1789.*[1]

2. *The real character of the Revolution.* When one sees how easily Frenchmen succumbed during that great revolution to a despotic government as long as it represented neither the old regime nor equality, it is easy to discern that the real object of the Revolution was less a new form of government than a new form of society; less the achievement of political rights than the destruction of privileges.

3. Even today marvelous effects are attributed to what some call "our liberation of the soil"; there are many among us who will gladly overlook the servitude of the inhabitants as long as they believe that the soil is free . . .

4. How did such a cruel revolution issue from such a mild, human, benevolent climate? Gentleness prevailed on

[1] See Introduction, Note 5, page 23; also Note 2, page 102.

the top; violence came from below. The gentle classes suffered the Revolution while the rough classes made it. Nowhere else was there a greater contrast: a high society, civilized, softened, sweetened by civilization, and the lower classes uncouth to an extreme degree.[2]

5. A new and terrible thing has come into the world, an immense new sort of revolution whose toughest agents are the least literate and most vulgar classes, while they are incited and their laws written by intellectuals.

6. *That violent and persistent class hatreds are not merely the products of unjust social conditions but of the struggles that upset these.* Other nations had aristocracies as vain, as irritating, as wrong as that of France. Yet the hatred these others had inspired was so much less bitter, less violent, less vivid than with us. This may seem astonishing to certain people. But they do not note that what inflames, embitters, exasperates people and what makes the hatred of an aristocracy enduring is not only the extent of these abuses but the duration and the sharpness of the struggle over them. A very abusive aristocracy which gradually weakens with time or which falls at one stroke will provoke less hatred and rancor and will leave after it a milder aftermath than another and much less harmful aristocracy which collapses after a long civil struggle. Thus it is not only the abuses that should be considered but the way in which they are modified or abolished.

This is an important idea, but should be expressed more briefly, in a shorter, more staccato and direct manner to avoid giving it the air of a commonplace, which it is not.

7. The religious revolution of the sixteenth century was

[2] (T) The coexistence of a civilized aristocracy with the barbaric habits of the lower classes has, of course, existed elsewhere and in other times. But then the upper classes were not only cultured: they had real power.

made by the materialist appetites of the upper classes, who employed the spiritual enthusiasm of the lower ones.

The French Revolution was made by the unselfish enthusiasm of the upper classes assisted by the appetites and passions of the lower ones.

Thus the enlightened classes of the eighteenth century were worth more than those of the sixteenth.

To employ this idea, a valid one, in order to restore attention to certain virtuous traits of our fathers (above all, to their civic virtues).

8. Why in America similar principles and political theories led to a change of government while in France they led to a total overthrow of the social order. (This could take up much space, but I do not know where to put it.)

9. . . . *A new type of revolutionary.* True, we have seen issuing from the French Revolution a new kind of revolutionary, a turbulent and destructive type, always ready to demolish and unable to construct. He, however, is not merely violent; he scorns individual rights and persecutes minorities but, what is entirely new, he professes to justify all this. The idea that there are no individual rights but only a mass of people to whom everything is permitted is now elevated to a doctrine.

Similar things happened after all great revolutions. But here there are particular causes: First, the democratic character of our Revolution, leading to a distrust of individual rights, to violence, since the people have become the main agents of the Revolution. Second, its ideological character, constantly in need of a theoretical justification of violence. Third, a revolution not limited to a short period of time but which has now been evolving for sixty years. Only the scene changes, so that this race of revolutionaries is always renewed. During the last sixty years some great revolutionary laboratory was always open in some part of the world where shiftless minds and irresponsible embezzlers may repair in search of instruction.

10. *Four notes on Burke.*

[On the margin of a pamphlet entitled: "Substance of Mr. Burke's Speech in the Debate on the Army Estimates" (1790): ("The French have shown themselves the ablest architects of ruin that had hitherto existed in the world . . . They have done their business for us as rivals, in a way in which twenty Ramillies or Blenheims could never have done it.")] There is no foresight here of the fury which was not only destructive within France but which pushed the nation abroad and which multiplied its original savagery a hundredfold.

[About Burke's "Reflections on the Revolution in France and on the proceeding of certain Societies in London relative to that event" (1790)]: Altogether this is the work of a powerful mind, full of that practical wisdom which in a free nation some men acquire almost instinctively. His superiority is evident here to a high degree. His insight into new institutions and into their immediate effects is masterful. So was the common sense of Young, that gentleman farmer so much superior to an impractical genius like Mirabeau. Thus Burke is admirable when he analyzes in detail the new institutions, their immediate effects, the numberless and growing errors rising from the ideological presumptions and from the inexperience of the new reformers. He perceives some of the great future dangers. But the general characteristics, the universality, the portents of the Revolution, then beginning, completely escape him. He lives, confined in England, within the old world, and he does not comprehend the new and universal meaning of what is happening. He sees in the Revolution a French episode; he sees only its French characteristics. In this work his violent anger against our reformers (for he senses that it is the traditional world which is being assailed, without yet saying that it is on the way to succumbing) is mixed with a supreme disgust not only at their crimes but at their stupidity, their ignorance, their impotence. Later, as his anger increases, elements of fear begin to appear, with that sort of respect which men have when they are confronted by great accomplishments even though devoted to wrong causes. "They are rascals," he says in 1792, "but the most terrible rascals the world has ever known."

[On the margin of a fragment of "An Appeal from the new to the old Whigs" (1791)]: For Burke the Revolution was not the product of a long development but the sudden outburst of a perfidious emotion.

All of Burke's picture is full of true touches, and yet it is a false picture altogether. It is very true that almost until the outbreak of the Revolution the spiritual state of the people was indeed different from what was to follow. It is very, very true that the spirit of liberty had not yet taken root among the lower classes (it never did). People still lived on the ideas of another century, like a vehicle still moving with the motor shut off. But it is very wrong to say that the habits and even the ideas of the Revolution were not introduced well beforehand by society. It was not a sudden achievement. There was the obvious feebleness of the nobility, the jealousies and the vanities of the middle classes, the miseries and wounds of the lower classes, their ignorance: all of these were powerful and organic seeds which needed only to be fertilized . . .

In traditionally free nations the symptoms of coming revolutions may not be visible from afar. In an old and unreformed society, where sentiments and ideas have no ways of appearing on the surface, the revolutionary tendencies may not be visible but remains latent until the outbreak.

[About the "Remarks on the policy of the Allies with respect to France" (1793)]: The aim of this pamphlet is to oppose the policy which attacks France as if she were a *foreign* nation and not a nation within which there exist internal allies in a civil war. Burke attacks the old viewpoint of national interests, since it fails to see that the main aim of the war should be the complete destruction of the French Revolution and that this destruction cannot be achieved except by aiding the counterrevolutionary party of the old regime and only this party (he cannot imagine the possibility of a compromise), which should be treated as the legitimate portion of the French people and which should be allowed to direct the interior affairs of France.

Here Burke was quite out of step with the English government itself. As he himself tells us, at Toulon the gate held by the British (unlike the other gate occupied by the Spanish) remained closed to the royalists.

CHAPTER III

[*Diverse Reflections*]

1. *The pendular motion of our revolutions is illusory*. It will not withstand close examination.

In the beginning always a movement toward decentralization: 1787, 1828, 1848. In the end a further extension of centralization.

In the beginning people follow some logic; in the end, they stumblingly follow their habits, their passions, power.

To sum up, the last word always rests with centralization, which grows deeper even when it seems less apparent on the surface, since the social movement, the *atomization*, and the *isolation* of social elements, always continues during such times. (Re-examine this.)

2. *What is the natural form of government of the new society created by the Revolution?* (This should perhaps go at the end, when I say that when I stop it is not because the Revolution has come to an end, nor because we definitely know yet where it is still going to lead.)

Those who saw the First Republic have told me . . . and I myself, without having yet reached the ordinary span of human life, have already heard it said on four occasions that this new society made by the Revolution has now finally found its natural and permanent form. Four times events afterwards proved that people were wrong. When I was a child, people assured themselves that the Empire was exactly the government most suited to France. (Why? Explain.) Later it was said that in a society such as ours despotism was a mere accident; that anarchy logically leads to despotism and that a moderated political liberty was the most natural state for France . . . Thus spoke the publicists and statesmen whom I heard in my youth. Soon afterwards I saw the Restoration disappear. Again I heard the new victors say that . . . etc. *Their* reasons. They kept repeating these things until the new revolution in 1848 destroyed *their* achievements.

The Republic followed; it again had its own philosophers who explained why it had to endure. Its end, in turn . . .

Every government gives rise to its own sophists who, during the very time of its own mortal illness, are busily proving that it is immortal.

3. *That the main fruits of liberty are not so much its practical advantages as an instinctive taste that freedom gives to people.*

The hatred which free men and those worthy of the name of men nourish against absolute power is intellectual and instinctive at the same time.

They have learned and found that in the long run arbitrary rule will never fail to endanger public prosperity; that it frequently leads to oppression and to war; and that it does not even guarantee that standard of well-being for which personal greediness and national degeneracy so often forsake liberty. Thus free men reject arbitrary rule. Yet this courageous rejection results from a taste for independence, which taste, to some extent, is selfless, instinctive, and unconscious. It is the manly and noble pleasure to be able to speak, to act, and to breathe without restraints; it is the sense of one's not being dependent on any man, but on God and on law.

Revolutions and misery might teach even the greediest and the most cowardly of people that despotism is wrong. But where will people get their real taste for liberty if they do not know it or if they have lost it? Who will teach them these noble pleasures? Who can make them love liberty if that love has not been originally planted in their hearts? Who will even pretend to make them understand those pleasures of liberty which men can no longer even imagine once they have lost their habitual experience?

Do you want to know whether a people is free? Do you want to know the prospects of its liberties? Then examine closely the essence of the ties which it attaches to liberty . . . What, then, is the assurance that it will preserve its liberties? The very taste of freedom; the very wish to be free.

You will see tranquil and prosperous peoples amidst free institutions. They grow, they become rich, they shine. Do not then believe that their independence will endure if it is only these material goods which attach them to liberty. For they may be deprived of these goods in a moment; on the other hand, despotism may procure these goods at least for a time . . . Material interest will never be sufficiently permanent and tangible to maintain the love of liberty in the hearts of men unless their taste for it exists . . .

There is, thus, an intellectual interest in liberty, the main source of which is the tangible benefices which it provides. And there is an instinctive tendency, irresistible and hardly conscious, born out of the mysterious sources of all great human passions. Never forget that in your thoughts. It is a taste which, it is true, all men have in some way or another; but its primacy exists only in the hearts of very few . . . It is the common source not only of political liberty but of all of the high and manly virtues . . . It is not so much the material advantages provided but the enjoyment of freedom which attaches free people strongly and jealously to their rights.

4. *That the destruction of political liberties will not lead to a revival of literature.* It would seem that civilized people, when restrained from political action, should turn with that much more interest to the literary pleasures. Yet nothing of the sort happens. Literature remains as insensitive and fruitless as politics. Those who believe that by making people withdraw from greater objects they will devote more energy to those activities that are still allowed to them treat the human mind along false and mechanical laws. In a steam engine or a hydraulic machine smaller wheels will turn smoother and quicker as power to them is diverted from the larger wheels. But such mechanical rules do not apply to the human spirit. Almost all of the great works of the human mind were produced during centuries of liberty. It does not seem to be true that the spirit of literature and of the arts is recharged or that they attain high perfection when liberty is destroyed. Looking closely at what happened then, we will see that certain absolute governments inherited certain forms, certain intellectual practices, and the liberty of imagination which free habits and free institutions had created before them. The despots then contributed the sole benefit of absolutism: a degree of tranquillity was added to the continued usage of those intellectual treasures acquired from the previous governments they had destroyed. It might, therefore, seem that certain absolute governments were spiritually fruitful ones. But this is a false semblance which quickly pales with the passing

of time: soon the true face and the true tendency of these absolute governments appears.

This explains Augustus, the Medicis, and Louis XIV. The Roman Republic, Florentine democracy, that feudal liberty which still existed amidst the religious and civil wars of the Fronde had produced those various grounds from which sprang the great men who illuminated what were called the times of Augustus, of Leo X, of Louis XIV. And the proof of all this is that as these new absolute regimes became entrenched these pretended beneficial effects began to disappear. In turn, their true nature, the silence and the sterility of despotism, reappeared.

5. *Why patriotism is justifiable.* From a general, higher viewpoint patriotism, despite its great impulses and deeds, would seem a false and narrow passion. The great efforts suggested by patriotism are, in reality, due to humanity and not to those small fragments of the human race within particular limits called peoples or nations. It would seem, at first sight, that those Christian moralists especially who are inclined to care more for humanity than for their fatherland are right. Yet this is but a *detour*, at the end of which we will find that they are wrong.

Man has been created by God (I do not know why) in such a way that the larger the object of his love the less directly attached he is to it. His heart needs particular passions; he needs limited objects for his affections to keep these firm and enduring. There are but few who will burn with ardent love for the entire human species. The way in which Providence lets most people work for the good of humanity seems to divide this great object into many smaller parts, making each of these fragments worthy objects of love to those who compose them. If everyone fulfills his duties in that way (and within these limits such duties are not beyond anyone's natural capacities if properly directed by morals and reason), the general good of humanity would be produced by the many, despite the absence of more direct efforts except by a few. I am convinced that the interests of the human race are better served by giving every man a particular fatherland than by trying to inflame his passions for the whole of humanity. The latter, whatever one may do, the common man will perceive only from a viewpoint that is distant, aloof, uncertain, and cold. (A good idea, which could be fruitful, though badly sketched here.)

6. Human laws and institutions are ordinarily so imperfect that they can be destroyed by merely drawing all the consequences from their principles.

7. *That local liberties may exist without national liberties.* Local liberties may exist for some time without general liberties when such local liberties are traditional, habitual, customary, rooted in memories; or, on the other hand, when despotism is relatively new. But it is senseless to believe that while general liberties are suppressed such local liberties can be voluntarily created. This is the dream of some among us, pure dream.

8. People complain of the Catholic clergy having instincts of domination. This might be true, but it is not worthy of remark.

A political body is like a man: individual human passions are reflected within a human association. If such a body is egotistical and willful, this suggests that its structure is strong and that it resembles a man. Whenever the Catholic clergy wants above all to rule as a body, this will reflect traits of individual egotism; yet these traits are not specifically Catholic traits, but merely those of human willfulness. Preserve any association and change its purposes: you will arrive at the same results.

9. I believe that civilized men are by nature more disposed to exempt their individual reason from the authority of the Faith in times of equality and democracy than at other times. But I am far from believing that this tendency

is irresistible. Whatever the force exercised by the state of society and by the political circumstances of a period on the ideas of its contemporaries, these ideas will not be able to prevail for long against that need of hope and of belief which is one of the most profound and powerful instincts of human nature.

10. Yet I also believe that our times are as blind and as stupid in their systematic and absolute denigration of what is called the thought of the eighteenth century as were the men of that century in their blind infatuation with it . . .

11. There is certainly something in the revolutionary illness of our times which should not be confounded with the similar evils engendered by all other revolutions. Ours may have more durable traits because what I call the revolutionary sickness of our days, though accidental, still seems to have certain very strong roots in the new permanent society, in the habits, ideas, and lasting customs founded by the Revolution.

First, what *seems* unique is its *doctrinal* character. This is not merely a habit, a tendency of minds and hearts; it is a theory, a philosophy, if it may be called so, deriving from three sources:

(a) The democratic character of this revolution. It deprived tradition of its power, deprived morality of its stable force, deprived the person and his rights of that instinctive respect which even during revolutions prevails in aristocratic societies. This democratic revolution created a social power which, by its nature, has few scruples and meets with few obstacles of resistance.

(b) The triumphant example of the first French Revolution which thoughtlessly and by the mere employment of violence, energy, and recklessness overthrew the monarchy and conquered Europe. It led superficial minds that had not paid attention to particular causes to believe that all that is needed to gain power is violence, energy, and recklessness.

(c) The essentially ideological character of this revolution, which led to the general practice of justifying violence through some sort of philosophy, and which suggests the need of this practice to the usurpers themselves.

These unique symptoms explain, at least in part, the endurance of the revolutionary illness in our times. Its characteristics derive in part from the particular essentials of the society created by the Revolution. Thus some of its features will remain even after the revolutionary era is finally behind us. These are: a certain restlessness, chronic instability, and a permanent inclination to fall back into revolutionary habits.

All of these ideas ought to be indicated somewhere, but where? At this point? Or, rather, at the end of the book, when I shall try to paint the *permanent* features achieved by the Revolution? I am inclined to the latter. Look into this again, as well as many of the chapters which are now only first sketches, the initial efforts of my thought seeking to engage itself on paper.

12. Generally speaking, people are not very ardent or indomitable or energetic in their affairs when their personal passions are not engaged. Yet their personal passions, however vivid they may be, do not propel them either very far or very high unless these passions keep growing before their eyes, unless they seem to justify themselves by being related to some greater cause for the service of mankind.

It is due to our human sense of honor that we should be in need of this stimulant. Add to passions born of self-interest the aim to change the face of the world and to regenerate the human race: only then will you see what men are really capable of.

That is the history of the French Revolution.

Its narrow-minded and selfish nature led to violence and darkness; its generous and selfless elements made its impulse powerful and great.

Comparative Table of the Tocqueville Papers about
"The Revolution"

(See Introduction, p. 10)

LETTERS EXCHANGED
WITH GOBINEAU

A Note on Gobineau

This is the first publication in English of the letters exchanged between Alexis de Tocqueville and Arthur de Gobineau during the sixteen years from 1843 to 1859. Some of these letters appeared first in the *Revue des deux mondes* in 1907; a book edition was published by Plon in 1908; some letters were reproduced in German, and an Italian edition with a thoughtful introduction and with excellent annotations by Signor Luigi Michelini-Tocci saw the light in 1947. Though the overwhelming part of Tocqueville's letters remain unpublished, there is some reason to believe that his published correspondence with Gobineau, at least for the years 1843–44, 1849–51, and 1852–59 is nearly complete, and that the errors in the original Schemann transcription are relatively minor ones. Our edition includes a newly found important Gobineau letter, published by J. P. Mayer in the April 1955 issue of the *Nouvelle nouvelle revue française,* which appears in this book as No. III., due to Mr. Mayer's generous courtesy. Here I also wish to record my indebtedness to the American Philosophical Society, whose speedy generosity in the form of a minor purse allowed me to devote the larger part of the summer of 1955 to the study of this correspondence together with additional Gobineau letters.

Save for the middle period of the correspondents' relationship—the letters exchanged between January 1850 and

April 1852 which are of somewhat less importance than the others since they mostly comprise Gobineau's lengthy accounts about Switzerland—all hitherto (1956) available letters are included in this volume.

Gobineau was eleven years younger than Tocqueville, and he survived his mentor by twenty-three years. He was born on the 14th of July, and against the ideas symbolized by the *Quatorze Juillet* he fought during most of his life. He died in 1882, a bitter little black man, having suffered a sudden heart attack in a trolley car; he passed away in a lonely hotel room on a quiet October afternoon in Turin. Fifty years later, during the Mussolinian era, a small tomb was erected to honor his memory in the cemetery of Turin, inscribed to the great "Prescient Thinker": *Presago Pensatore*. Like many other inscriptions of the era of Mussolini, this suggests a half-truth; Gobineau was often a great thinker, while he was by no means very prescient.

He was certainly one of the most extraordinary personalities among the crowded scene of thinkers in that large and transitory drawing room which the nineteenth century represents in the intellectual history of Western civilization. His life illustrates the nowadays obscured principle that the most decisive marks on the character of men are almost always established in the parental circle during adolescent years. Like Tocqueville, Gobineau came from an old regime family. Unlike the Tocquevilles, the Gobineaux represented a caricature of some of the vices of the last court aristocracy of the Bourbons. Tocqueville did not share some of his father's political views but he remained a respectful and loving child of an excellent father, of an admirable head of a Christian family. Gobineau, in the long run, shared most of the prejudices of his reactionary, shiftless, Gallican father, while his family relationships were often shot through with hatred; regrettably enough, this was expressed in some of his letters. Tocqueville's mother was a mild, sad, sweet woman. The Comtesse de Gobineau was irresponsible: she and her husband separated after ugly quarrels. Gobineau, having inherited the perverse and insubstantial affectations of his parents, often lived beyond his means. Tocqueville married an unattractive wife, without money or social standing, and his letters reflect a high standard of conjugal love and dedication; Gobineau's wife was attractive but he left her, nonetheless, to live with the Comtesse de la Tour.

Perhaps the most revealing contrast is the one between the ways in which Tocqueville and Gobineau regarded their respective family traditions. The family of the first was far the better one: the Norman baronial name of Clérel de Tocqueville appears in a document from the very court of William the Conqueror. There is no such evidence in the case of Gobineau, who nevertheless wrote a long, interesting, and somewhat fantastic book in which he claimed descendance from an Ottar Jarl, a Viking pirate raiding Normandy in the ninth century. Tocqueville showed no desire to refer to the illustrious Clérel ancestry; and in one of his noblest letters, to Madame Swetchine, he explained why he did not particularly care to use his proper title of count.

It was Chateaubriand, Tocqueville's uncle by marriage, who said that aristocracies usually go through three historic phases: the Phase of Duties, followed by that of Privileges and ending in the Phase of Vanities. It would not be too much to suggest that, in the penultimate hour, during the dusk of the French aristocracy, Gobineau had arrived at the third, while Tocqueville instinctively pointed the way back to the first phase. Because of his conceited and querulous nature, Gobineau's acute intelligence served him not too well during his diplomatic career. His conceit appears in some of the letters printed here, but also elsewhere: in a letter he wrote about his *Essay on the Races,* that "it will give an electric shock to historical science and completely upset it." He claimed to have preceded Darwin. He traveled a great deal; he was a most prolific writer. He wrote more than thirty volumes. He started a political magazine which soon folded. His most famous book, the *Essai sur l'inégalité des races humaines,* was written with scientific pretensions; there is a more scientific book on Persia, and several archaeological works, including one on cuneiform texts whose many inadequacies were, however, soon pointed out by Rawlinson, the archaeologist. As with Tocqueville, most revealing and important are Gobineau's unpublished or posthumously published writings; above all his correspondence, in part published: with Tocqueville; with a very intelligent Russian, Khanikov; with Mérimée (pub. 1902); with the Austrian orientalist and diplomatist Count Prokesch-Osten (pub. 1933); with the German Professor von Keller (pub. 1911); with two charming Athenian lady friends (pub. 1937); most important, with his sister, Mère Bénédicte, a nun (pub. 1958).

One senses some of the curious undercurrents of the human heart as one meets his own racialist beliefs, his love for the Nordic races, his feelings for Germany. In 1830 the erratic Mme. de Gobineau suddenly left her equally fickle husband, dragging her children and a train of dwindling servants to German Switzerland, where they set up a transitory household in the eerie castle of Inzlingen, near the German border, where Arthur had the formidable misfortune of being impressed with the dankest impressions of black-Gothick romanticism by a deadly earnest young German tutor. The tutor then became the lover of Gobineau's mother. Yet the intellectual impressions endured, perhaps comparable in depth with those left on his contemporary Ruskin by many generations of persevering Scottish Presbyterian ancestors.

It has been suggested that the impressive emphasis on

nobility and race in Disraeli's *Coningsby* was responsible for the awakening of Gobineau's racial interests. Yet it is overlooked that he showed little sympathy for Disraeli and for all that that extraordinary statesman had come to represent, while his attraction to Teutonism endured. "Not even a thickheaded Prussian professor," Tocqueville told him, "would speak about France the way you do." There is a letter of 1866 in which Gobineau admits to one of his German professor friends that he had come to regard Germany as his second (if not his real) homeland; that he preferred to publish in German rather than in French. By that time he was a lonely and bitter middle-aged man. Ten years of diplomatic service followed; he was Minister of France to Greece, Brazil, Sweden. The Brazilian Emperor, Dom Pedro I, introduced him to Nietzsche. He met Wagner.

Except for Renan and Sorel, Gobineau enjoyed little reputation in France. Not so in Germany. As Tocqueville had predicted, the Germans regarded Gobineau as their own. Within a year of his death, the first eulogistic article was published by a German anti-Catholic ultranationalist; after von Wolzogen came Kretzer and, above all, Gobineau's intellectual epigone, the earnest racialist Professor Schemann. An official, frock-coated *Gobineau-Vereinigung* assembled in 1894; Wagner's widow was the first inscribed member. Six thousand volumes on race, together with the Gobineau manuscripts, were collected in the Gobineau Library of the University of Strassburg, which was opened on 14 July 1906, on the ninetieth anniversary of the race prophet's birth. Schemann remained the *Spiritus Rektor* and the *Kurator* of these Gobineau materials, and it is to him that we are indebted for the most exhaustive Gobineau biography.[1]

[1] There are others by Faure-Biguet, Gigli, Lange, Spring, Rowbotham. The last two are Americans.

Another Tocqueville prediction was fulfilled when it was by way of Germany that Gobineau's reputation reappeared in France. There a wartime article by Ernest Seillière (pub. 1916) was followed by an interesting little magazine, *Europe*, whose issue of October 1923 was devoted to Gobineau, including one of the few articles that compare Tocqueville and Gobineau, by no other than Romain Rolland.[2] In February 1934 an accolade to Gobineau was offered by the *Nouvelle revue française*. Thereafter the perverse wing of that magazine, represented by Drieu de la Rochelle, Abel Bonnard, and Clément Serpeille, Gobineau's descendant, began to resuscitate Arthur in the service of what they considered "the New Europe" and what, in practice, amounted to anti-Semitism, to an uneasy sycophancy of Fascism and, by some, even of Hitler. Thus did a misreading of Gobineau contribute to the unattractive spectacle of some of these right-wing mandarins trying to extract intellectual profit from Hitler's Teutonic victory over France and Europe.

Yet it is a mistake to regard Gobineau a precursor of Hitlerism. That he was not altogether unattractive will appear from his occasional boyish honesty, from his fervent loyalty in his letters to Tocqueville. And also from elsewhere. During the Prussian invasion of France in 1870, this Germanophile and anti-republican aristocrat decided to represent and protect the village in which he lived. With courage he defended the inhabitants from military depredations, earning the respect of villagers and of Prussian uhlans alike. Though he had foreseen and criticized the folly of the war, he did not recriminate. "We have to save what is possible," he said haltingly. "We should not recrimi-

---

[2] See above, p. 27. The others were written by Schemann (1911), Seillière (1916), Thibaudet (1934), Michelini-Tocci (1947), Salomon (1935), Wach (1951), Richter (1958). The last three are Americans.

nate now." Not thus spoke Bonnard, Bardèche, or Brasillach, friends of his grandson, during that far greater national catastrophe seventy years later.

But, of course, by 1940 the last days of the old European aristocracy had passed. There is an essential difference between Gobineau's propositions on race and the sus-
picious sentimentalism evident in *Mein Kampf,* between
Gobineau's haughty affirmations of natural nobility and the
lower-middle-class political logic of Hitler. This difference
was hardly noted until an intelligent and conservative
Frenchman in exile wrote a fine article on Gobineau for a
small French magazine published in New York during the
war.[3] "I cannot imagine Gobineau in Germany today," M.
Étiemble wrote, "except as an inmate in Dachau; I can
imagine his grandson, his self-named disciple, Clément
Serpeille de Gobineau, among his guards."

Gobineau, moreover, was a great writer. He was respected not only by Sorel and Renan; his style was admired
by Proust. Léon Bloy said that his romantic style and his
romantic references to the past would belong "to a language of the near future." If Rawlinson dismissed some of
his scientific speculations, such a great Persian scholar as
Lord Curzon regarded Gobineau's book on Persia as indispensable. Gobineau wrote a number of lucid novels, of
which two, *Mademoiselle Irnois* and *Les Pléiades,* have
good English translations. It is unjust to dismiss him altogether because of his essay on race (which, incidentally, is
not devoid of profound insights); there is also the erratic
brilliance of *The Renaissance.*

True, he was seldom a great *presago.* He wrongly predicted the union of Austria and Switzerland, the defeat of
Prussia by Austria and Russia, the ruin of England by India, the impossibility of building a canal at Suez; he believed that the victory of Asia over Europe was inevitable;

[3] M. René Étiemble. "Gobineau—Juge du Fascisme," in *Renaissance,* October 1943.

he said that modern Greece would not endure; like certain Spaniards, he said that Columbus was a miserable fool for having discovered America; he also thought that the American union would inevitably collapse. Yet he was a great *pensatore:* and perhaps his best political writings are his posthumously published fragments, *Ce qui est arrivé à la France en 1870* (pub. 1923), his *Memoir sur les diverses manifestations de la vie individuelle* (pub. 1935), and an unpublished but fascinating essay on Europe and Russia. He was also a passably good poet and an amateur sculptor.

Unlike other racialists, Gobineau was not an anti-Semite;[4] he admired Heine; he hated centralization; he deplored mass wars; like Balzac, he was among the early handful who recognized the talent of Stendhal. Nor did he find anything inspiring in the "liberating forces of technological advance"; and he called the idea of the modern Fatherland "a wooden and beastly idea." All this is very unlike Hitler. And, unlike a string of modern proletarians from Spanish Falangists to Russian ex-Communists, Gobineau found little that was admirable in the new bourgeois Germany. It is amusing to see his follower Schemann struggling with that side of Gobineau, which sometimes (as in certain passages of the *Carnaval de Venise*) is mercilessly sarcastic about German bourgeois heaviness. Unlike his idol, Schemann possessed an overload of pedantry which was not lightened by any traceable sense of humor. In the end, Schemann felt compelled to concede with a grotesque phrase: unfortunately enough, Gobineau did not comprehend "some of the particularly worthy traits of our German character" (*"manchen eigenartig wertvollen Zug deutsches Wesens."*)

[4] Like his friend Nietzsche, who called himself an anti-anti-Semite (on "anti-anti" see Introduction, p. 22). Another curious coincidence: Nietzsche collapsed in Turin, in 1899 (in the year Hitler was born), in the city where Gobineau had died (nine months before Mussolini was born).

There is a remarkable letter by Gobineau to his German friend Professor Keller, written in 1866. Now that Germany will be united, Gobineau asks, "will you be happy? Is it really what the character of your people needs? Are you quite sure that in this striving there is nothing artificial, only to prove empty later, perhaps to become a source of future sufferings?" He repeated these sentiments six years later. "Perhaps," he wrote, "Germany paid too high a price for unity." And in one of his finest writings, in his posthumously published essay about 1870, he was, for once, chillingly prescient:

It is from above that inspiration and direction are fated to descend to the people; and when in these spheres of authority there no longer is any belief, no more confidence, no more will, no striving for the good and for the better, one may state with all the certainty of a mathematical proposition that power will fall to the first corporal who, in passing, will seize it.

That corporal was to be Hitler, who may justly be called the Sorcerer's Apprentice, which is a story with more symbolic meaning to the West than is the Germanic and bourgeois and essentially sentimental story of Faust about the intellectual who sold his soul to the Devil. Like Spengler, who, in his *Decline of the West,* inflated Faust into a fake heroic symbol of "Western man," there were many after Gobineau who predicted the inevitable collapse of Western Christendom. They were (and still are) wrong; but this Tocqueville knew.

PART ONE

Letters exchanged in 1843 and 1844

I

Tocqueville about their projected work[1]

Tocqueville,[2] 8 August 1843

You need not thank me, monsieur, for the interest I have shown in you. First of all, my interest is selfish; I am among those who are delighted when they find someone to praise. I am, really, obliged to the person who provides me with this kind of pleasure. And you are just the person to evoke such an interest. You have a broad knowledge, high intelligence, the best of manners—a thing that one cannot fail to observe, however democratic one might be. There is another, less flattering source of my interest. It is that I wonder what will become of all of these fine qualities: will the contagious diseases of this century affect them as they so often affect others of your generation? In this way you are interesting for what you could be, and also for what

[1] See above, Introduction, p. 14.
[2] Tocqueville took possession of his then partially dilapidated ancestral castle in 1836. He set to repair it forthwith and gradually came to regard it as a source of strength and of serenity.

one fears you might become. I hope I do not offend you by saying this. What else can I say? In you I see the image of youth, of that youth which, for me, has already begun to pass, and the least rational dreams of which are still worth more than the mature realism of old age. The older I grow the more I like the young. Were I to live in another age and in another country this might not be so. But this atmosphere chills me. Warmth and vitality seem to lessen with each day, and one hardly finds any fire in the minds and hearts of men of my own generation. I can still see a few sparks in the souls of those twenty-five years old and in those of sixty; the former still have their hopes, and the latter their memories. Yet the great majority of men of my own age merely want to get on with their small affairs, and that with the least possible trouble.

I should not conclude this letter without saying something about *philosophy*. Yet I do not quite know what to say on that subject. I confess to you that, since our meeting, I haven't thought about it at all. I lacked time and perhaps even taste for it. One follows the other: interest lags about matters when there is not enough time to do them well. You may now help pull me out from this kind of torpor through my obligation to write you. Yet it does not seem that you are much better off than I am. Well then, rise! I tell you that from now on I shall charge you with the entire responsibility for my own laziness. I shall deflect the fulminations of my friend Mignet,[3] who will leave me alone so long as he has you for a target. Seriously, my dear Gobineau, I ask you to try very much to go ahead with our discussion before the summer passes. If I return to Paris without getting into this to the point where I can see the main lines developing, I think I should renounce this endeavor altogether.

[3] François Auguste-Marie Mignet (1796–1884), the historian, Permanent Secretary of the *Académie des sciences morales et politiques*.

Mme. de Tocqueville has your greetings, and she asked me to thank you. On my part, I ask you to believe the expression of my vivid and sincere affections.

II

Tocqueville about the new social morality of our age

Tocqueville, 5 September 1843

Your letter, monsieur, arrived the day I left for the *conseil général*.[1] I found it upon my return. I want to answer you at once.

I shall ask you now to put all your books aside for a moment and to make a rapid mental survey of your recent readings and of your earlier studies, so as to answer this question in conversational form: What is there really *new* in the works or in the discoveries of the modern moral philosophers? By *modern* I mean not merely those of the last fifty years but those who immediately preceded them, those who belong to that generation which had decisively broken with the Middle Ages. Did they really see the obligations of mankind in such a new light? Did they really discover new motives for human actions? Did they really establish new foundations, or even new explanations, for human duties? Have they placed the sanctions of moral laws elsewhere? Through the darkness all I think I can rec-

---

[1] A sort of County Council for the Department of La Manche. Cf. E. L'Hommédé, *Un département français sous la monarchie de juillet. Le conseil général de La Manche et Alexis de Tocqueville*. Paris, 1933. (Unpublished correspondence.)

ognize is this: to me it is Christianity that seems to have accomplished the revolution—you may prefer the word change—in all the ideas that concern duties and rights; ideas which, after all, are the basic matter of all moral knowledge.

Christianity did not exactly create new duties or, to put it in other terms, it did not establish entirely new virtues; but it changed their relative position. Certain rude and half-savage virtues had been on the top of the list; Christianity put them on the bottom. The milder virtues, such as neighborly love, pity, leniency, the forgetfulness even of injuries had been on the bottom of the antique list; Christianity placed them above all others. Here was the first change.

The realm of duties had been limited. Christianity broadened it. It had been limited to certain citizenries; Christianity extended it to all men. It had been restricted and confirmed the position of masters; Christianity gave it to the slaves. Thus Christianity put in grand evidence the equality, the unity, the fraternity of all men. Here was the second change.

The sanction of moral laws had existed for this world rather than for the other. Christianity put the ultimate aim of human life beyond this world; it gave thus a finer, purer, less material, less interested, and higher character to morality. Here was the last change.

All of these things had been seen, shown, and preached before it came. But Christianity alone bound them together, making this new morality into a religion, and the minds of men were absorbed therewith.

We have lived with the rule of this morality for a long chain of centuries. Have we added much to it that is essential? This is what I do not see clearly. We may have put a few shades into the colors of the picture, but I do not see that we have added really new colors. The morality of our own time—the way I see it revealed through words and through action and through the ceaseless patter of our loquacious society—our modern morality (and I am leaving aside what is being printed in fat volumes about this subject) may have reverted in some of its facets to the notions of the antiques, yet for the most part it has merely developed and expanded the consequences of Christian morality without affecting the essential principles of the latter. Our society is much more alienated from the theology than it is from the philosophy of Christianity. As our religious beliefs have become less strong and our view of the life hereafter less clear, morality has become more concerned with the legitimacy of material needs and pleasures. This is the idea that I think the followers of Saint-Simon expressed by saying that *the flesh must be rehabilitated.* It is probably the same tendency that, for some time now, appears in the writings and in the doctrines of our moral philosophers.

For this reason some people have now felt the urge to find the sanctions of moral laws in this life. They could no longer place them with absolute certainty in the life thereafter. From this came the doctrine of benevolent interest, about honesty paying dividends and vice leading to misery. The English Utilitarians are upholders of this new trend of ideas, ideas rather unfamiliar to the Christian moralists of the past.

Christianity and consequently its morality went beyond all political powers and nationalities. Its grand achievement is to have formed a human community beyond national societies. The duties of men among themselves as well as in their capacity of *citizens,* the duties of citizens to their fatherland, in brief, the public virtues seem to me to have been inadequately defined and considerably neglected within the moral system of Christianity. This seems to me the only weak facet of that admirable moral system, just as this seems the only strong facet of the moral system of the antique nations. Though the Christian idea of human brotherhood may seem to dominate contemporary minds, those public virtues have also advanced in the meantime; and I am convinced that the moralists of the past hundred years are preoccupied with it far more than were their predecessors. This is due to the resurgence of political passions. They are, at the same time, causes and effects of the great changes we are now witnessing. Thus the modern world re-established a part of antique morality and inserted it within the moral principles of Christianity.

But the most noteworthy innovation of our modern moral teaching, to me, consists in the tremendous development and in the new form that is now given to two principles which Christianity had first put in grand evidence: the equal rights of every man to the goods of this world, and the duty of those who have more to help those who have less. The revolutions that displaced the old European ruling class, the general extension of wealth and education which has made individuals more and more alike have given an immense and unexpected impetus to the principle of equality, which Christianity had established in the spiritual rather than in the tangible material sphere. The idea that *all* men have a right to certain goods, to certain pleasures, and that our primary moral duty is to procure these for them—this idea, as I said above, has now gained immense breadth, and it now appears in an endless variety of aspects. This first innovation led to another. Christianity made charity a personal virtue. Every day now we are making a social duty, a political obligation, a public virtue out of it. And the growing number of those who must be supported, the variety of needs which we are growing accustomed to provide for, the disappearance of great personalities to whom previously one could turn with these problems of succor, now makes every eye turn to the State. Governments now are compelled to redress certain inequalities, to mollify certain hardships, to offer support to all the luckless and helpless. Thus a new kind of social and political morality is being established, a kind which the antique peoples hardly knew but which is, in reality, a combination of some of their political ideas with the moral principles of Christianity.

Here, my dear Gobineau, is all that I can now distinguish through the fog that surrounds me. You see that I speak only of what I see in the habits of people; I am unable to say whether the same signs are registered in books or whether they reappear elsewhere. These reflections of mine are not supposed to give you a foundation or a basic framework, but rather an example of what I think we should search for. We have to find whatever new concepts of morality may exist. I have tried hard, while attempting to keep close to realities. Do my propositions strike you as true? Do you have others to propose? Do these modern moral theories justify them? My own mental habit has made me look exclusively for these newer things which might directly influence the actions of our contemporaries. But I cannot afford to neglect those different moralistic innovations, the new theses, new concepts, new explications which I might be permitted to call sterile fantasies, were it not for my academic affiliation[2] that obliges me to term them "interesting products of the human intellect."

Only after we shall have *outlined* whatever there is new in the moral doctrines and tendencies of our age will we begin to follow the consequences of these primary data in some detail. We should ascertain them before all. So, my dear collaborator, put your head in your hands and think about the above. What I ask from you is no longer the work of a student but of a master, yet I am certain that this does not surpass your powers. Once we have this foundation the rest of the work will be easier and at the same time much more interesting.

Should you have something to send me, dispatch it by stagecoach mails to Valognes, Hôtel de Louvre.

[2] A reference to his membership not in the French Academy but in the *Académie des sciences morales et politiques*.

Farewell, monsieur. Please trust the expression of my very genuine affection.

P.S. Don't destroy this letter, as I might wish to reread it someday when I finally get down to writing.

III

Gobineau about the passing of the "mediocre" concept of Christian morality

Paris, 8 September 1843

Monsieur,

You honored me with a letter which I received this morning. I have been now thinking hard about your somewhat arduous questions, and I believe that with their impressions vivid in my mind it will be easier for me to answer now rather than later. Besides, you want my answer to be talkative, which means that you will excuse rambling and even imperfection.

I believe that there most certainly is a new morality in Europe since the last years of the eighteenth century. But one should agree on what this means. The new morality to me is not a solid body of vigorous doctrines which coheres to a central principle as does Christian morality, for example. It is, rather, a still somewhat incoherent compilation of conclusions drawn from principles still largely undefined. This does not mean that it should be disregarded or that it is only in the stage of abstract theory. No; to the contrary, it seems to me more visible in facts than in books.

This new morality undoubtedly springs from the bosom of Christianity, but only in the way in which Christian morality refers back to Socrates, whose ideas, in their turn, had their source in the maxims of an even older wisdom. The defenders of the Church in the very beginning felt a deep sympathy for the ideas of meekness and of social justice because they themselves had come from suppressed classes and because they had known the evil effects of despotic rule. They were glad to defend themselves against violence by proclaiming the obligations of love and gentleness. Surrounded by daily miseries, by woes of every kind afflicting the poor, how could these simple artisans refrain from the desire to restrict the powerful? Was it not the simplest policy to win people by offering them a gentler rule? Here was the point of departure, the basis of Christian morality: personal interest, instinct, sentiment rather than a contemplated and rational conviction of what ought to be.

The great problem was the faith: pagans, philosophers, Christians at all costs had to believe in a body of religious doctrines. The only important thing in life was to know the fate of man after death. The sectarians of Jupiter were no less possessed with this notion than were the Epicureans or those who listened to the Apostles. The entire moral performance of man was summarized in a principle alien to his life on this earth. Still, it cannot be denied that Christianity made great concessions to terrestrial humanity in one sense. It did not seek to destroy men before their time, since it forbade suicide, which the pagan doctrines condemned but feebly. Emulating the Jewish law, Christianity even proposed certain maxims which, like Mosaic hygiene, tended to conserve human life. Finally, through its exhortation to the gentler virtues, Christianity tried to make the fate of humanity more tolerable than it had ever been before. This was an effort, an improvement, but even this is inconsequential when one looks at the facts from this more general viewpoint.

"Suffering is holy"—this axiom the new doctrine proclaimed in a high, strong voice. We were certainly moved by this very sentiment. Yet its consequences were lethal, since it completely justified the existence of suffering. Why would a government try to destroy it? At the most, individual charity sought to attenuate it: establishment of a hospital, some relief to prisoners perfectly satisfied this not very exacting moral ideal. To be good, to be kind towards one's neighbor, was indeed a minor duty compared to the one of belief. What am I saying! The man who did not believe could not possess any virtue. Here, monsieur, lies to me the vast element of mediocrity in the moral principle of Christianity. Making everything rest on faith, all the other spiritual and mental powers were dismissed as relatively insignificant; deprived of their absolute importance, lost among the brilliance attributed to faith alone, they were easily forgotten or, rather, misused. The great concern has been salvation, and salvation could not be gained anywhere but in cavernous retreats where, without temptations and without social duties, there were few opportunities to be helpful to one's fellow men. I think it could be said finally with much justice that Christian morality restricts itself more or less to the avoidance of doing harm and that it hardly exceeds this limit. Of course, truly generous institutions will find in the Christian maxims all the possible reasons for their own benevolent acts; but here I am concerned only with the basic factors.

Once these facts are admitted (though they may be found too harsh, or too mild, I think that it is difficult to deny the kernel of truth which they contain) one can no longer doubt that our contemporaries will regard moral problems quite differently than do the founders of Christianity. "Morality today," the majority will say, "does not belong either to Catholicism or to Protestantism. A Moslem, a pagan may have a moral character as high as the most religious Christian hermit." You will agree, monsieur, that this now so widespread opinion is very remarkable since it just about completely dislodges those foundations on which morality has been established since the earliest of historical times. It begins by disconnecting the chain which unites men through their beliefs. It sends the creed of the most diverse dogmas back to the closed sanctuary of private conscience; it is through this that it gives incontestable sanction to the freedom of religion. As a matter of fact, the different religions never pleaded against each other before the secular power except with mutual accusations to the effect that the doctrines of their adversaries were immoral or dangerous to the social order. As soon as one's beliefs in a future life are recognized as being wholly inconsequential to one's actions or duties in this life it becomes difficult for a magistrate to find a pretext to intervene in the quarrels of sects. Here we have already a great and fortunate innovation due to the spirit of our age. It is doubly interesting to contemplate it, first because of the effects I mentioned above, and also because it is something quite new in the history of the world. I do not think that it is even comparable to the semi-tolerance of the ancients towards the different cults. In those times the Pantheon could easily welcome a new god, but today people respect only what they see and what they can touch. They have learned by experience and through the long clash of ideas that virtues are not the patrimony of one religion to the detriment of others.

This is not the only change in our ideas. As people have become less preoccupied with their future lives they have been thinking more of their present ones. To be exclusively preoccupied with this earthly life used to be the mark of men of levity or of passionate and vehement ambitions. Any soul blessed with gentleness turned towards matters of worship, and this earth was thus forsaken by the minds of those who were most capable of serving it usefully. Of course many of the economists of the last century and many of those utopian philosophers who preceded or succeeded Rousseau border on the ridiculous. Nevertheless, one cannot deny that these often so unduly exalted thinkers have marked their usefulness in history by having helped to establish that clearer order of ideas by which we live today. It was about the middle of the eighteenth century, under the influence of Voltairian ideas, that men began to ask whether it was not possible to give something more than poorhouses to the lower classes. For the first time they studied the exact nature of charity, its eventual purpose and its attainments. Thereafter came those often more enthusiastic than judicious studies about agriculture, about money, about financial circulation, about the nature of wealth, about the sources of its decrease or increase. These early efforts lost much popular esteem since many of the theories were silly, foolish, and pretentious. Yet we ought not forget that they marked the beginning of a new order of things in the world and that a Florian[1] was perhaps necessary to help us arrive at the heights of a Goethe. Since the early reign of Louis XVI one could feel the influence of these new ideas. To the different duties already imposed on the government another one was to be added, a more august one, never mentioned before. The State was to look after the poor.

One can understand what Christian ideas would have made out of this. Sloth would have been glad to pay a bribe to charity; the gentle faith of the believers, a little help to neighbors would have dispensed them from further tiresome sacrifices. But this is no longer what people meant by charity. They cared no longer for men, nor was their

[1] Jean-Pierre Claris de Florian (1755–1794), a French writer of moral fables, the La Fontaine of the eighteenth century. Note Gobineau's early suggestion about the superiority of German over French thought.

concern with their particular sufferings. Those external circumstances which evoke pity were passed over; in one sentence, people no longer felt compassionate to Man; they were concerned with Humanity. Seen from this viewpoint, suffering is no longer holy. Like the plague, like every scourge, it must be extirpated. I shall no longer be moved by the sight of a beggar and give him some help in passing. I shall, as a modern citizen, help put the government in a position to destroy misery and to restore the social usefulness of a worker who, in his capacity of a human being, must not remain idle. That is the theory.

Everyone has an equal right to work. Is this not a new maxim, quite different from that of Christ, who said, after Moses: *Man is condemned to work?* What used to be a painful duty becomes a right, a prerogative in the name of which each member of the social body has the right not to suffer from misery and destitution. The power and dignity which morality has gained by this principle are beyond question. The relation of work to virtue had been sensed by the ancients and confirmed even by Christianity, but this mutual affirmation meant a barren state of inaction. To put into practice this almost transcendental truth was a role reserved for sages and saints. There is more to this. The ancients considered spiritual labor alone to be capable of serving morality. Here the comparison with our new theories is striking; it favors the latter. The manual occupations are no longer excluded; by now it is recognized how, in more than one way, they may be equal to the sublimest efforts of the intellect. Today Plutarch would be ill advised to repeat what he said, I think, in his *Life of Camillus,* that an exalted soul may admire Phidias's Jupiter but would not desire to be its author. Indeed, Art is a sort of mediator between Science and Matter, say the Saint-Simonians, and this truth, nowadays generally accepted, puts craftsmen in a much more elevated position than the ancient world had. From this new perception of the occupations of the lower classes results a principle, not entirely unknown to Christianity but one to which our times are giving a much broader and greater application: the right of the poor to education. The necessity to enlighten the masses is today hardly contested at all. And not only the basic principles of religion are to be taught them, but they are to be introduced to scientific and literary progress as far as possible; in brief, they are called forth to share all the fruits of the human intellect.

People have now gone even further in this extension of human welfare. They are concerned with prisoners. It is being said with Voltaire that a man hanged is good for nothing, and people are trying to find a way to make criminals good for something. In this difficult endeavor people have again been led by the strong desire to better the lot of humanity on this earth. The result has been more moral, more kind, more merciful than Christians could ever have been. What have the writers concerned with prison reform done in the last forty years? What they did was to consider and compare the rights of society to punish and the rights of the criminals to be spared. The *rights* of the criminal! Here is certainly a modern employment of the term *rights*. Formerly the convicted criminal faced a thousand additional tortures beyond his legal condemnation, sufferings from which no one thought of delivering him and which were regarded the natural consequences of his fault. Nowadays it is thought that a matter as serious as the life of a man, big or small, deserves a more mature consideration. Surely this is an innovation which, though often exaggerated by misguided philanthropists, very favorably proves the progressive nature of morality.

It is easy to conclude from all of the preceding that at the bottom of these new ideas lies self-interest. But, to be sure, this is no longer that self-interest which was the answer of the reformers of the last century to the mocking questions of those who asked them whether virtue did pay.

Self-interest, at that time, meant the individual. It told him: Do not steal, for you will be imprisoned; do not kill, for you will be broken upon the wheel; work, for you will reap gains. These fragile arguments were rather vulnerable. If a man found satisfaction in an imperious passion, or if he was certain of impunity, he was suddenly above this principle of self-interest from which all morality was supposed to derive. Today the doctrine of interest has taken a different character. It is no longer limited to the enjoyments, to the material fruits of virtue. Its primary source is enlightened psychology and its scope is not the individual but all of humanity. And there is yet one more decisive factor.

Christianity severely restrained the passions. The present concept of morality is indulgent towards them; it does not renounce the hope to rationalize them since it believes that many of these passions are potentially useful. Thus the love of luxury and of material enjoyments is no longer an evil. To the contrary, if a man works more because he desires to raise his well-being, the urge of well-being in this case becomes a commendable virtue in itself. One may go further to say that any kind of reasonable satisfaction that does, in fact, involve no inconvenience to others is in no way opposed to the morality adopted by our age. Thus you will see, monsieur, how this doctrine of interest is confronted with considerably lesser difficulties now. Anyone motivated by common ideas and living more or less like most people will indeed find it much easier to conform to this morality, which is more indulgent to his natural inclinations than in the past. But we must admit that this new morality is nonetheless severe to everything that would injure someone's peaceful and normal relations with the other members of the social body.

This, I think, is about what strikes me as new in the type of morality developed by our times. I do not dare to venture too far. I bypass the specialized and, one might say, the rash opinions of the Fourierists and of socialists of every kind. The opinions held by these different sects derive more or less from the common base to which I have just referred. Ideas on marriage, on property, on education, on the proper guidance of individual tastes and passions have been fiercely debated by these philosophical camps. Still, I do not think that they are worth much notice. These very advanced doctrines have few partisans and none of their programs would seem to be able to attract many more followers in the future. I think that if we keep the different points which I have indicated at least for principal landmarks we could advance more safely within the bounds of the now generally admitted concepts of morality.

I must take a few steps backward. I said that self-interest seemed to me to be still at the bottom of everything. I added that philosophical motives now expanded and ennobled this self-interest. To clarify this I must also add that it is unfortunately at this basic point that the present system is weak. It is evident that the ancient religions found it easy to dignify morality by establishing it under the aegis of divinity. Now it has been brought down to earth, and it has not yet been possible to discover its sources. Moreover, many minds do not realize clearly enough that this morality belongs no longer to Christianity, and they still connect it with Protestantism or with Catholicism. Others link it to the narrow principle of pure Voltairianism. For others again it becomes a sort of philanthropy, sentimental rather than reasonable, the kind which easily goes astray. Here is a summary of the contemporary history of morality: an immensely difficult critical study of mankind about itself. On one hand, as you have so justly remarked, the new morality rehabilitates the flesh; on the other hand, it prevents the spirit from suffering in this rehabilitation and from withering once again. The results are evident, and I think we may be rather satisfied. But, as with everything new, its achievements and prospects have not yet been adequately defined. This is a land in the process of being cleared, the limits of which are unknown, its center not yet discovered but which already yields a harvest. You may perhaps conclude from this that the hurried writing of the history of such an endeavor still in its beginning might not be opportune at all, especially since we are to stop at 1830, at a moment when these ideas take such an extraordinary surge forward. But, monsieur, this is the concern of the *Académie;* and a history for not being complete is nonetheless interesting . . .

IV

Tocqueville about the endurance of Christian morality

Tocqueville, 2 October 1843

I had received, monsieur, your papers on Priestley and Bentham. They are very good papers, and they seem to fit the purposes of our planned work better than any of the previous ones you have done for me. I have thought that, beyond his big book on punishments and rewards,[1] Bentham may have written something more explicit and more philosophical about his utilitarian doctrines. Am I wrong in this?

I turn now to the long letter which you wrote me three weeks ago. I cannot answer it point by point. A book would be needed for that. I merely wish to point out the problems

[1] Reference to Bentham's *Rationale of Punishments and Rewards.*

that now exist between us and to try to direct our work accordingly.

I must tell you that my opinions about Christianity are absolutely opposite to yours. Christianity, to me, is vastly different from what it seems to you. It is vastly different from what had preceded it, and we are much less removed from it than you say. Whenever I read the Gospels I cannot help being overcome by the deepest emotions. Many of its doctrines, and the most important ones, have always struck me as if they were absolutely new, and all of it is something entirely different from that body of philosophical and moral ideas which had previously governed humanity. I cannot understand how, when you read these admirable books, your spirit does not breathe with that superior sense of inner freedom which their pure and grand atmosphere evokes in my own. If one wishes to be critical of Christianity, it is better to keep always two things in mind.

The first is this: Christianity has come to our generation through centuries marked by much rudeness, ignorance, social inequality, and political oppression, during which time it was often a weapon in the hands of kings and of priests. We must consider Christianity itself and separate it from the historic vehicles in which it was often forced to travel toward us. Almost all of those exaggerations and abuses for which you—and often quite properly—reproach Christianity should be attributed to these secondary circumstances—this I could easily prove—and not to the code of Christian morality whose first principle is this simple maxim: love God with all your heart, and love your neighbor like yourself—and remember that every one of its laws and prophecies rests thereon.

The second thing that one should always remember is that Christianity is not a philosophy but a religion. There are, of course, certain doctrines that are necessarily part and parcel of certain religions, and which are not the exclusive attributes of any one of them. Such are the *virtue attributed to faith, the utility of faith, the necessity of faith, the inadequacy of deeds without faith*—and their consequence is that certain amount of intolerance with the contemporary absence of which you seem so satisfied. These doctrines are inherent in all religions . . . and they are necessarily inseparable from all the good they bring us. Yet I am convinced that the eventual damage to human morality thereby caused is far less than what would result from moral systems that have emancipated themselves from religion altogether. The longer I live the less I think that the peoples of the world can ever separate themselves from a positive religion; and this growing conviction makes me less concerned with these inconveniences that are eventually inherent in every religion, including the best.

Most of those symptoms in which you claim to recognize a new morality seem to me only symptoms that have always accompanied the weakening of religious faith.

When there is no more faith in religion, it is logical that little attention should be paid to its moral precepts and that it will be judged merely by its external acts and forms. When the vision of the next world becomes obscure, it is again natural that people who are still unable to live without moral sanctions will try to find them on this earth and that they will thus create all these systems which may be different but which are all concerned with the doctrine of human interest.

And when the vision of eventual heavenly rewards is accordingly lost, it is again logical that people should be more and more attached to the only prospects that remain before them, to the benefits of this world.

I think that something similar may have happened during the decline of paganism, and that it is typical of the decline of all religions. The mass then comes forth and reveals its instincts, and it will find philosophers who will make doctrines to fit them.

I further tell you that I am not surprised at what is now called the *rehabilitation of the flesh*. It is possible that Christianity may have pushed the glorification of the spirit to excessive lengths. But this very tendency was a wonderful reaction against the Roman habits and forms of paganism. Don't you see the incomparable beauty of that rare, open struggle of the spirit against the ruling flesh? Even if Christianity was swept to spiritual excesses, entranced as it may have been by the grandeur of its own doctrines, I do not think that this is a very great danger. The inclinations of the majority of men pull them in a converse direction; they rehabilitate their own flesh without the need of philosophers.

As I am hastily jotting these different thoughts down, I must say that my aim is not to convince you but merely to make you understand where I differ from you. Most of the things that to you seem new apparitions of morality to me seem the natural and logical consequences of a weakened religious faith and of widespread doubts about the existence of the other world. I believe that similar circumstances in the past resulted in similar consequences.

Among these really new apparitions (and I think there may be a few attractive ones among them) the majority seem to derive directly from Christianity. They are only the applications of Christianity to a larger sphere, to other political forms, and to a very different social state. They are, briefly, the new consequences of an old principle.

You, then, consider the revolution of our times more original and more beneficent than I do. But you do see it, and this is the most important thing for the work we are trying to do. Most of the symptoms that you detect I see, too. Thus I think that this sort of epistolary conversation could lead to rather satisfactory results, as it should determine the direction of your future studies and the main characteristics of the books that are noteworthy for our purposes. Christianity is the great source of modern morality. Everything that to you may seem contrary or even different from Christianity in our laws, customs, ideas, philosophies you should put in evidence. This is the first rule. For what I have to present is not contemporary morality but its eventual divergences from the principles of the past. This limited subject is, thus, immensely and desperately large. What, after all, does it *not* include? To describe the various manifestations may be even more difficult than to demonstrate the new principles themselves. One of these definite manifestations, the changes of civil and criminal justice in the last fifty years, alone could be described in a heavy book. Sometimes I feel that I should curse either the *Académie des sciences morales* for having confided this work to me or politics for keeping me from its eventual completion.

To come back to you. You say you are going ahead with your study of the British writers. Very good; as I told you earlier, your last studies on these writers seemed excellent. After them I think you would do well to return to your Germanies. In the first place there is a field where my efforts cannot ever equal yours, as I don't know German. In the second place I must say that I am not yet satisfied with the results in that field as they seem inconclusive for my main purpose, which is, above all, to find and show what there is really *new* and divorced from Christianity in these modern moral systems. Kant seems to me beyond, rather than within, Christianity. Are the more recent German authors different? I should ask you to inform me positively on this subject. I may not ask you to do the French writers as I know the writings which I need most and I can obtain them more easily.

What I need is less information about new ideas than about their different manifestations and applications, especially abroad, for they are often difficult for me to know. Let me take your own ideas for example.

You are right when you say that it is typical of our times to be interested in acts apart from beliefs. This is evident in the modern laws which confirmed equal rights and equal duties to all Christian sects. In France this has been now extended to the Jews. Legislation abroad must surely show less visible but, at any rate, considerable symptoms of the same tendency.

You say that charity has become public instead of private, and that thus it has become more enlightened and less directly involved. I may agree with you in part, but I do not deduce the same consequences therefrom. I see therein less a new principle than a more modern, civil, bureaucratic, and democratic manifestation of Christian doctrine. Evidence thereof lies in the modern practice of governments in accumulating funds to administer to the needs of various miseries, to extend, briefly, the necessary administrations of Christian charity. This charity is legal and *direct*. Anything similar in Germany should be observed and registered carefully.

Then there is a legal charity that is indirect and consists in offering to the poor facilities to help themselves. Such are savings funds,[2] asylums, and other institutions of this kind. The eventual existence of similar institutions abroad is material of capital importance for me.

The efforts of governments to extend more universal education; the obligations imposed for this purpose; consequently, the laws and regulations that aim to multiply the number of schools and their pupils, and give instruction of a more democratic nature; the books that influenced and pushed governments in that direction particularly belong to our subject.

[2] Note that the establishment of savings funds, the idea of facilitating thrift was still considered a charitable rather than a business enterprise in the early nineteenth century.

I am leaving prisons and penal laws aside; I should be able to do that myself.[3]

You say that the right to work is a new principle of our times (and I must interrupt to say that it emphasizes the idea of work less than did the Christian doctrine about *all men* being condemned, in one way or another, to work on this earth). Which are the modern books, French or foreign, where this idea stands formulated? Has there been any legislative attempt to make this idea into a law?

I could go on much longer about this subject. But it would serve no purpose now when you are not yet through with your study of the contemporary philosophers. When you conclude that, and I hope as soon as possible, we will revert to these more practical subjects. Even if you were to feel you could not enter into them in great detail, your collection of ideas and sources should alone be of great help to me.

I conclude this interminable letter by asking you to trust my indeed sincere affections.

V

Tocqueville about the superiority of Christianity

Tocqueville, 22 October 1843

My dear Gobineau, you are an amiable, intelligent, and unorthodox adversary with whom I do not want to battle. It

[3] Reference to his own studies on the penal system which had led to his American journey.

is typical of philosophical debates that neither of the participants emerges dissuaded from his original opinions. Thus it is best not to dispute; it saves effort. Particularly useless are philosophical battles waged by the pen. The possibilities of misunderstanding then actually increase. Thus your letter attributes to me ideas that are not mine, a misunderstanding which I could have immediately clarified during a personal conversation. For example: I am supposed to have said that Christianity was absolutely different from everything that had preceded it. I have never thought that and I don't think I said it. Some of its maxims certainly existed, scattered and inert, in Greek and Oriental books. The other day I found some even in the Laws of Manu, and others probably exist elsewhere. But Christianity chose, developed, ordered, bound together certain maxims and ideas, some part of which had been presented earlier in an isolated or obscure fashion, and made out of the whole an absolutely new regimen of morality. This is the line of my thought.

Another example: that there is nothing new in modern morality. Again you wrongly attribute an idea to me. I only believe that almost all that we call modern principles should be considered as new consequences drawn from the old Christian principles because of our present political and social conditions. I do not deny their existence; I merely contest the extent of their meaning. You will see here, my dear colleague, that my ideas ought not to discourage you. The only difference between you and me is that you have more ambition than I have. I limit myself to finding new consequences where you wish to discover absolutely new principles. You want to change the face of the world, nothing less. I am more modest.

Unfortunately there also exist more profound divisions between ourselves. You seem to contest the social function of religions. Here we assume truly antithetical positions. You say that the fear of God does not stop people from murder. Even if this were true—and I doubt whether it is really true—what is the conclusion? Whether secular or religious, the function of law is not to eliminate crime (which is usually the product of deranged instincts and of such violent passions as will not be halted by the mere existence of laws). The efficacy of laws consists in their impact on society, in their regulation of matters of daily life, and in setting the general temper of habits and ideas. Laws, and especially religious laws, are thus so necessary that there never has been a people of any importance that could do without them. I know that there are many who now think that one day they may be able to do without this regimen, and every morning they keep looking eagerly for this new day. I think they are looking in vain. I should even be more inclined to believe in the coming of some new religion than in the continuation of the prosperity and greatness of modern societies without religion . . .

A last argument. While you are so severe with the religion which, after all, did so much to establish our leadership among the human race, it seems that you have a certain weakness for Islamism. This makes me think of another friend whom I met in Africa, where he had become converted to the Mohammedan religion. I was not impressed by this spectacle. I often studied the Koran when concerned with our relations with the Moslem populations of Algiers and the Orient. I must say that I emerged convinced that there are in the entire world few religions with such morbid consequences as that of Mohammed. To me it is the primary cause of the now visible decadence of the Islamic world, and though it may be less absurd than the polytheism of the antiques and its political and social tendencies are more to be feared, in my opinion, I still regard it as decadent compared to antique paganism. Here is something that I could easily prove if you were ever to entertain the painful thought of having yourself circumcised.

Forgive, my dear Gobineau, this useless banter. I wanted

to be very brief, and I am now beginning my fifth page. It was the pleasure of conversing with you rather than a desire to convince you that made me talk so much though I remain grieved about our disagreements. I like you too much to be indifferent as to whether you share some of my beliefs. Yet I find consolation in the knowledge that in the realm of finer sentiments we are and shall remain on the same side.

You ask me whether you should analyze Bentham on usury.[1] I do not need a detailed analysis. I think I know his essential thesis, which he pushes to unreasonable extremes, as is the habit of this type of person, though I do agree with some points. It would be enough to indicate briefly his principal premises and conclusions. I don't see the need to occupy yourself with his book on legislation.[2] I can do this easier as I am rather well acquainted with it. I am eagerly awaiting your analysis of the other British writers you mention.

Farewell, monsieur, and believe in my sincere and affectionate sentiments.

[1] Reference to the *Defence of Usury showing the Impolicy of the Present Legal Restraints on the Terms of Pecuniary Bargains.*
[2] Reference to the *Treatise of Civil and Penal Legislation.*

VI

*Tocqueville about their suggested method of
study*

28 November 1843

Dear monsieur de Gobineau,

The papers announced by your letter I received only the
day before yesterday. I read with great interest your manuscript, which is not in the least affected by the strains of
your illness and of the horrors of having had to move. As
you say, not all that glitters about Gudin[1] is gold. Yet I
think that you extracted what is best, and it is not your
fault that the primary material is of such mediocre value.

You ask for my instructions: it seems best to continue
the work which you began with Jacobi.[2] After that do those
studies with the help of the German librarian you mention.
If he will indicate to you the books that are noteworthy
and available in the public libraries, it would be best to
begin with them. If they are not available there, it would
be best to wait until I return: I shall easily obtain them
through the *Institut*.

I shall not say more today as I think that within three
weeks I shall have the pleasure of seeing and talking with
you again, something that I much prefer to writing letters.

[1] Paul-Philippe Gudin de la Brenellerie (1738–1812), a brilliant monarchist writer and a now seldom recognized forerunner
of romanticism.

[2] Friedrich Jacobi (1743–1819), a storm-and-stress thinker;
see also p. 34, above.

I hope that we shall meet often this winter; you are always welcome in our house, not only in your capacity as a philosopher but, what counts more, as a likable and intelligent man for whom I profess a sincere friendship.

P.S. I always forget to ask you to put a little biographical notice at the top of your study of each author.

VII

Tocqueville writes a hasty note during the county council session

Saint-Lô, 27 August 1844

I must confess that I left your earlier letter unanswered since I never thought that your youthful impetuosity could result in such unfortunate consequences. The savants are most reluctant to be dragged into battle; I know their habits. So I did not worry. It would perhaps have been better had you turned to the *Académie* instead of involving yourself in a polemic battle which could only lead to difficulties in your relations with the library. But it is water over the dam now, so let us forget about it. I wish, however, that you would find it possible soon to return to our morality studies. It was so often I who prevented speedy progress that I must forgive you when, for once, you are being upheld.

You may undoubtedly complain about the tardiness of my answer. But you would forgive me immediately if you saw the many petty domestic and electoral annoyances that weigh me down when I get back home. Right at the moment of this writing I am in the *conseil général*. Thus does the petty comedy of politics surround our great dramatic dialogue! Please attribute the eventual silliness of this letter to those who are now talking around me and whose words I may automatically record. Let me, therefore, end here, but not without telling you that we should be delighted if an autumnal excursion would bring you to these regions and we could receive you at Tocqueville. Tell me if and when you could come, for in September I must make a trip and I should like to arrange to be at home when you could be here. Farewell, monsieur; trust my best regards and affections.

VIII

Tocqueville advises Gobineau on writing

4 October 1844

Do not, my dear Gobineau, send me your moral studies. I shall be in Paris toward the end of the month, and you will give them to me in person. Furthermore, you have reason to believe that I accused you of laziness. Between ourselves, I still do. I think that you are bored with what we are doing, and I easily forgive you. I can see that it is difficult to devote oneself with pleasure to studies with indefinite limits and to the preparation of materials which may not be used at all. However, I ask you to make a last serious effort to help us complete at least the preliminaries. I shall be well satisfied to have the exact list of the relevant books and possible sources. This at least should help if, in the future, I should decide to set myself effectively to this work. If you would be able to produce this sort of an analytical catalogue, I shall ask nothing more from you, at least for the time being. I know how it is to be tied down with these examinatory labors without being guided every day by what exactly one should extract from the material. It is a labor that, at times, may seem unattractive as well as sterile.

I read in the *Commerce* your two essays on M. de Musset even before I received your eventual request to do so. I found there what I find in all of your writings, that is, a high intelligence. Yet I have some serious criticisms to make. First, your choice of the subject. You depicted M. de Musset without any consideration of perspective. If you devote your eighteen columns of small print on De Musset, your literary history must be longer than the one by Laharpe.[1] I find some charming qualities in the genius of M. de Musset; but, after all, as you yourself say, the whole impression is that of a second-rate genius. M. Musset is not extremely well known outside the Parisian literary world. He does not evoke vivid curiosity and interest such as would make the subscriber of a newspaper gladly read a long analysis of his work, even if the analysis were as intelligent as yours. Thus I reproach you for not having chosen a more popular or a more spectacular author, speaking as I am from the viewpoint of newspapers.

I shall criticize you also for feeling you had to describe your author in such detail. This again belongs in a *book*, but not in a newspaper. You forget that you are faced with a hurried and rather ignorant readership who are not interested in knowing anything well but rather in a sketch of the author's main literary habits or in his own story. They want a few vivid and decisive colors rather than a careful,

[1] Jean-François de Laharpe (1739–1803) had written an enormous *Lycée, ou cours de littérature ancienne et moderne* in nineteen volumes.

subtle, and detailed picture. You have treated the readership of the *Commerce* as if they were literary men. That
they are not, nor is any newspaper subscriber, at least when
he is reading his paper. Look at what Sainte-Beuve is doing:
he depicts at the most one or two features of his subject,
and he mixes his literary judgments, his anecdotes, and such
arguments therein so as to arouse the lazy minds of his
readers. I do not say that this is a good example for a literature course; but, I repeat, you are writing for a newspaper.

We were very sorry that you did not come to see us at
the time I had suggested. We had here a delightful old
English lord with his lovely daughter. My wife claimed that
you would fall in love with this young lady, and I contested that skeptical philosophers are not easily inflamed.
Why didn't you come to prove which one of us was right?
You may even have rehabilitated Voltaire and the eighteenth century in my mind.

I hope you will come next year. In anticipation do trust
my feelings of high regard and friendship.

PART TWO

Letters exchanged from 1852
until Tocqueville's death

IX

Gobineau about German sources of thought

Berne, 29 April 1852

Monsieur,

How many thanks I owe you! M. Flourens's answer finally relieves me; fortunately enough, I have advanced in
his eyes and I shall no longer get into trouble because of
my ideas. But I accept your proposal with great pleasure.
I should be indebted if you would not find it too boring
to read the chapter on the unity of mankind in Flourens's
Histoire des travaux et des idées de Buffon and to com-
municate their substance to me. Would you be kind enough
to jot down the proper title of the edition, the number of
this volume and of the respective pages?

The following occurred to me about your query. I think
I shall search Germany for the source of modern ideas in
the fields of philosophy, theology, and general scholarship.
It is noticeable that while in the rest of the world these

have served the progress of thought, in Germany progress has been more directly related to practice, as their universities have played a greater social role than have ours—except for the Middle Ages.

With this in mind I think it useful to go through the polemic literature of Luther and of some of his contemporaries, among them the extraordinary pamphlets by Ulrich von Hutten (*Epistolae aliquot obscurorum virorum* —I am not quite sure of the exact title). For the seventeenth century there should be something in the writings of Leibniz, who, *ultraconservative* as they would say today, by fighting against the progress of ideas unwittingly proved that this progress exists. In the eighteenth century Moses Mendelssohn enters with his Jewish ideas of reaction. A great mind. Lessing is a revolutionary; literary criticism and the drama were his weapons; there must exist at least partial translations of these writers, especially of Lessing, among others of his very modern drama, *Emilia Galotti.*

The biographies of Schiller and of Goethe but, above all, of the former, ought to be very informative, and they offer many insights into the state of German society. I recall that Pierre Leroux in his Introduction to *Werther*[1] said something about the revolutionary character, suggesting that Goethe described the prototype of the restless and discontented hero.

I offer you the above in the form of a program, an outline. Will you be kind enough to tell me what, to you, are the most important points which deserve deeper study, and I shall try to work on them at once. In the meantime I shall search for other important—or, rather, clearly outstanding—points.

Farewell, monsieur, and thank you indeed once more. Pray tell Mme. de Tocqueville that I remain her obedient

---

[1] Leroux (1797–1871), a utopian though moderate socialist, translated and introduced, together with George Sand, a new and famous French edition of *Werther* in 1845.

servant. Mme. de Gobineau joins in my sentiments. Trust my very devoted and respectful affections.

The Conservatives won in Berne. But I have unfortunately little trust in the future stability of Switzerland. Meanwhile I am submerged in my four volumes.

X

Tocqueville refutes early theories about race

Paris, 15 May 1852

My dear friend, I am late with this letter; my excuse is that the last ten days were taken up with the inconveniences of moving. However, I took time to read that chapter by Flourens which I had found in the second edition of his book, entitled *Histoire des travaux et des idées de Buffon,* in duodecimo; 1850, Chapter XIV, page 199. What I have to tell you about it is briefly this: Buffon and, after him, Flourens believe in the diversity of *races* but in the unity of the human *species.* The only reason they seem to give is the continuous procreation of the races among themselves, which, for natural scientists, should be complete and incontrovertible proof, since it is difficult to believe that God would have amused Himself by creating two physically almost similar species but then permitting their confusion through the effacement of His original line of demarcation. Without this clear separation a mixture of species would, in time, have produced common offspring which would sooner or later have replaced their original progenitors.

Flourens rightly notes that this secret faculty of reproduction demonstrates the fundamental unity of animaldom beyond their greatest physical differences while, at the same time, their greatest similarities mean nothing when the reproducing faculty is missing. Thus, despite their very different forms, bulldogs and lap dogs successfully mate, while horses and donkeys, similar to the point of potential visual confusion, are unable to produce but the seedless mule.

Mankind thus belongs to a singular species and, according to Buffon and Flourens, human variations are products of three secondary and external causes: of climate, of food, and of the manner of life.

The only thing that seems original to me in this chapter by Flourens is a discussion about that black subcutaneous substance which is supposed to exist under the skin of Negroes and about which Voltaire wrote, "Will our systematic mania confuse our minds to the point where we claim that a Swede and a Nubian belong to the same species when we see before our eyes the completely black *reticulum mucosum* of Negroes, the obvious cause of their inherent and specific blackness?"

Well, it now seems from the observations of Flourens that this same matter which he calls *pigmentary stratum* exists, in colors of varying intensity, in the American Indian and in a less pronounced but still very visible version in the Kabyl, in the Moor, and in the Arab, who belong to the white race, and that traces thereof exist even in Europeans.

Thank you for the interesting details about Germany. Because of my domestic revolution of the past few days I could not yet inquire about the existence of translations. Without translations all these works are dead letters to me. Let me know if you have other ideas or if you recall other books about the same theme. Please consider that I am less interested in the causes of the revolutionary spirit in Germany toward the end of the last century than in the breadth and in the character of that spirit, in its symptoms and in the principal places of its appearance. Even mediocre German books should contain such information. Books written about Germany by foreigners during that period, travel books, even the evidences in public laws and in private memoirs, should be further enlightening for my purposes.

I shall leave here in fifteen days and return home to Normandy. After that please address your letters to Tocqueville, through Saint-Pierre-Église (Manche). I shall be there all summer. A thousand cordial greetings.

Do not fail to remember us to Mme. de Gobineau.

XI

Tocqueville about the spiritual state of France

Saint-Cyr, par Tours (Indre-et-Loire), 11 October 1853

My dear friend,

Through an extraordinary coincidence I received today your book together with the letter you sent to Tocqueville six days ago.[1] My father brought the book from Paris; the letter was forwarded from Normandy. We did not spend the summer there. I don't now have a house in Paris, and the janitor of our former place must have been a jealous guardian of your book, for he did not let me know about it. Then, I no longer read the French newspapers since they are of less use even than are censored ones (from which one at least gets an insight into what the government does not want to see printed); I only get foreign newspapers

---

[1] Probably permanently lost.

here; the result is that I did not even know that your work had been published, and I was tempted any day to write you asking what may have happened to it.

In this letter I shall not say much about your book save that I am reading it very carefully, not in order to give you a detailed appreciation of its contents—from what I can see from your table of contents, it is the product of profound researches about parts of the history of mankind with which I am quite unfamiliar—but at least to let you know my general impression with full sincerity. And this is all that, I think, you may expect from me. I never concealed from you that I am greatly prejudiced against what seems to be your principal idea, which, I must confess, to me seems to belong to the group of materialistic theories. Moreover, it is one of its most dangerous members, for it applies fatalism not merely to individuals but to those perennial conglomerations of individuals called races. If, on one hand, I am a reader much inclined to regard your book favorably because of the vivid friendship which binds me to you, on the other hand, I am also drawn into battle by my pre-existent ideas on this subject. Thus I am in no sense an impartial—by which I mean good—judge. But I shall, after all, do my best. I am also concerned whether the present state of public opinion is at all propitious for the success of a book such as yours. For, even though people are every day becoming more subservient to materialism through their tastes and habits, and through the increasing mediocrity of political and moral doctrines, they become at the same time extreme spiritualists in their philosophy. The socialists have produced, and are still producing, so much fear that even the corner grocer does not want to hear anything discussed that is unorthodox; he keeps repeating that the people should be kept within bounds to impede the abolition of Property and Family, and to prevent them from ransacking his grocery. There is now little taste for freedom of thought; it is enough for an idea to seem dangerous and a sort of universal silence is drawn around it. There is not enough faith, not enough passion, not enough vitality to combat such ideas; instead they are shunned, passed over in silence, neither rejected nor recognized. Therefore, if you don't immediately reap the success which a vast and profound piece of work such as yours always deserves, you should not be discouraged. The cause will not be in the book but in the times during which it is being published.

I shall now explain to you why I am writing from Tours and not from Tocqueville, where I would like to, and also *should* be. My severe illness of last winter was caused, as I had told you, by rheumatism, or at least so I think. And the doctors counseled me not to stay close to the sea this year as the climate there aggravates rheumatic pains. So I rented a house a mile and a half from Tours. I like it quite well; after the excitements of the past few years it is tranquillity that I am enjoying here; I am so glad to evade the sterile ill will of those who now count for nothing and the triumphant baseness of those who have now become something that I have decided to make my winter quarters here. I have books sent down; now and then a true friend by chance remembers that I am still alive and comes to spend a few days with me. My health is appreciably better. My illness is cured, though I am still suffering from the medicaments which disordered my stomach. Mme. de Tocqueville finds herself quite well. Finally, the only thing missing to make me really happy is for me to be able to work a bit more. I am sad and shocked to have produced so little during these last four months. The horizon gradually opens as I progress with my work; and, though I feel able to keep my scope within well-defined boundaries, I am not yet certain how I shall be able to definitely limit my preparatory reading.[2]

[2] One of the first references to his projected work on *The Old Regime and the Revolution*.

I understand that you now wish to leave Berne. I too sincerely wish it for you; the time passed and services rendered there should facilitate your transfer. Yet the assigning of diplomatists has always depended on caprice, even in times when the role of caprice was otherwise limited. Imagine, then, the role it plays today!

Farewell, my dear friend. Remember us very specially when you write to Mme. de Gobineau and trust always in my vivid and sincere friendship.

XII

*Tocqueville about the monstrous fatalism of
racial theories*[1]

Saint-Cyr, près Tours, 17 November 1853

I owe you a number of excuses, my dear friend, for not having written you immediately and for having left your last letter unanswered for ten or twelve days despite my best intentions. My first failure resulted from certain embarrassments caused in my mind by the reading of your book and by my confused sentiments of criticism and praise. My fortnightly silence was, moreover, a consequence of my obligation to read a number of books I had borrowed from the Paris libraries which had to be re-

---

[1] Because of its central importance I decided, in this translation, to break the long arguments of this letter by more paragraphs. Elsewhere in this book paragraphing strictly accords with the original letters and texts.

turned. And now to the point. I shall proceed differently from others: I begin with the criticisms.

They relate directly to your principal idea. I must frankly tell you that you have not convinced me. Every one of my objections persists. You may, nonetheless, be right in defending yourself from the charge of materialism. Your doctrine is rather a sort of fatalism, of predestination if you wish but, at any rate, very different from that of St. Augustine, from the Jansenists, and from the Calvinists (the very last are closest to your doctrines), since you tie predestination and matter closely together. You continually speak about races regenerating or degenerating, losing or acquiring through an infusion of new blood social capacities which they have not previously had. (I think these are your own words.) I must frankly say that, to me, this sort of predestination is a close relative of the purest materialism.

And be assured that should the masses, whose reasoning always follows the most beaten tracks, accept your doctrines, it would lead them straight from races to individuals and from social capacities to all sorts of potentialities.

Whether the element of fatality should be introduced into the material order of things, or whether God willed to make different kinds of men so that He imposed special burdens of race on some, withholding from them a capacity for certain feelings, for certain thoughts, for certain habits, for certain qualities—all this has nothing to do with my own concern with the practical consequences of these philosophical doctrines. The consequence of both theories is that of a vast limitation, if not a complete abolition, of human liberty. Thus I confess that after having read your book I remain, as before, opposed in the extreme to your doctrines. I believe that they are probably quite false; I know that they are certainly very pernicious.

Surely among the different families which compose the human race there exist certain tendencies, certain proper aptitudes resulting from thousands of different causes. But that these tendencies, that these capacities should be insuperable has not only never been proved but no one will ever be able to prove it since to do so one would need to know not only the past but also the future. I am sure that Julius Caesar, had he had the time, would have willingly written a book to prove that the savages he had met in Britain did not belong to the same race as the Romans, and that the latter were destined thus by nature to rule the world while the former were destined to vegetate in one of its corners. *Tu regere imperio populos, Romane, memento,* said our old acquaintance Virgil. If your doctrine were to relate merely to the *externally* recognizable differences of human families and through these enduring characteristics assign them to differences in creation, it would still be far from convincing to me but at least it would be less fantastic and easier to understand. But when one applies it within one of these great families, for example, within the white race, then the thread of reasoning becomes entangled and loses itself. What, in this whole world, is more difficult to find than the place, the time, and the composite elements that produced men who by now possess no visible traces of their mixed origins? Those events took place in remote and barbaric times, leaving us nothing but vague myths or written fragments.

Do you really believe that by tracing the destiny of peoples along these lines you can truly clarify history? And that our knowledge about humans becomes more certain as we abandon the practice followed since the beginning of time by the many great minds who have searched to find the cause of human events in the influence of certain men, of certain emotions, of certain thoughts, and of certain beliefs?

If only your doctrine, without being better established than theirs, could serve mankind better! But evidently the contrary is true. What purpose does it serve to persuade lesser peoples living in abject conditions of barbarism or slavery that, such being their racial nature, they can do nothing to better themselves, to change their habits, or to ameliorate their status? Don't you see how inherent in your doctrine are all the evils produced by permanent inequality: pride, violence, the scorn of one's fellow men, tyranny and abjection in every one of their forms? How can you speak to me, my dear friend, about distinctions between *the qualities that make moral truths operative* and what you call *social aptitude?* What difference is there between the two? After, for some time, one has observed the way in which public affairs are conducted, do you think one can avoid the impression that their effects are the results of the same causes which make for success in private life; that courage, energy, honesty, farsightedness, and common sense are the real reasons behind the prosperity of empires as well as behind the prosperity of private families; and that, in one word, the destiny of men, whether of individuals or of nations, depends on what they want to be?

I stop here: let me, please, rest at this point. There is an entire world between our beliefs. I much prefer to turn to what I may praise without reserve. Though I am no less vividly impressed with this than with what I expressed earlier, I must unfortunately be much shorter here as I cannot enter in detail into everything that I do approve in your book. Briefly I shall say that this book is far the most remarkable of your writings; that, to me at least, very great erudition is manifested by your researches and that there is great talent and extraordinary insight in the way you have employed their results. Those who approve your fundamental thesis or those who wish it to be true (and, in our days, after the wear and tear of sixty years of revolution, there are many in France who may want to believe in something similar) must read it with great enthusiasm since your book is well constructed; it proceeds straight to its conclusion, and it is argued most intelligently. I proved my sincerity in my strictures; please believe equally in the sincerity of my praises. Your work has real and great value, and it certainly establishes you at the head of those who have proposed similar doctrines.

Having now written very rapidly and with a kind of *furia francese* (a racial quality, you would say), my hand is tired and I must ask you to let me stop here. At any rate, this is not a subject which can be easily treated in a letter. It is too complex and too vast, but we shall talk about it *abundantly* when we see each other. Tell me only: has the press mentioned your book yet? I get here an English and a German newspaper (I have audaciously put myself to learning German), but I economize at the cost of French newspapers, which, as I think I told you before, seem to have solved a problem held hitherto insolvable: there is less in them than if they were censored. I know of their contents only by hearsay. It seems that the *Débats* should be willing to review such an important book.

We shall be staying here until May. I should much like to see you in Paris at that time. They are leaving you buried too long in your Alps. I am grieved without being able to help. I am very well. I work much, and the days seem to fly. Farewell. Do believe in my sincere friendship.

P.S. Please do not fail to remember us to Mme. de Gobineau.

XIII

Tocqueville about the potential dangers of
Gobineau's thesis

Saint-Cyr, près Tours, 20 December 1853

I received your second letter, my dear friend, and I regret not having answered your first. I have not answered it because, as I told you, I do not wish to discuss this subject with you except in person. If, as they say, discussion so often only confirms previous prejudices, what then results from a written debate? It is waste or, at least, poor use made of time. You may perhaps be right, but you chose precisely the thesis which, to me, has always seemed the most dangerous one for our times. That, in addition, I persist in believing how false your principle is in its extreme applications should convince you that you will not be able to convert me, and certainly not from a distance. The last century had an exaggerated and somewhat childish trust in the control which men and peoples were supposed to have of their own destinies. It was the error of those times; a noble error, after all; it may have led to many follies, but it also produced great things, compared to which we shall seem quite small in the eyes of posterity. The weary aftermath of revolutions, the weakening of passions, the miscarriage of so many generous ideas and of so many great hopes have now led us to the opposite extreme. After having felt ourselves capable of transforming ourselves, we now feel incapable of reforming ourselves; after having had ex-

cessive pride, we have now fallen into excessive self-pity;
we thought we could do everything, and now we think we
can do nothing; we like to think that struggle and effort are
henceforth useless and that our blood, muscles, and nerves
will always be stronger than our will power and courage.
This is really the great sickness of our age; it is very different from that of our parents. Irrespective of your argument, your book supports these tendencies: despite yourself, it promotes the spiritual lassitude of your already
weakening contemporaries. All this does not keep me from
seeing what is truly remarkable in your book, and even to
be greatly interested in it, as one is in those bad children
whose parents are one's best friends and who, as it often
happens with bad children, are talented enough to please.
However, by studying German I have not yet become
enough of a German to be captivated so much by the
novelty or by the philosophical merits of an idea as to overlook its moral or political effects. I still would require your
spoken eloquence to convince me.

About the *Académie des sciences morales et politiques*
I need not tell you how heartily I agree with the idea of
Rémusat.[1] Where does he want to promote your candidacy? I imagine it must be in the section of philosophical
and general history. There Rémusat has considerable influence, since Thiers, Mignet, Guizot are the three principal
members, whom he may well impress in your favor. If I
were in Paris, I should gladly join my own efforts; but, as
I wrote you, I shall not return there until May. From a
distance one can do nothing in these matters since there is
no voting by proxy. Do you know whether there is a vacancy in that section? For the number of corresponding
members is fixed. The proper time for the official promo-
tion of your candidacy will very much depend on the echoes
of your book, which I cannot ascertain from this distance.

[1] Tocqueville's close friend and fellow academician (1797–
1875).

A preliminary step would be to arrange for your book to be offered to the *Académie* by a member who would then attract attention to it. Rémusat could easily do this for you. Whatever I can do, let me know; I hardly need tell you that you should count on my very sincere friendship. I may not like your book but I like its author, which counts more, though it may not entirely please you. I assure you that you may also count on Beaumont.[2]

You didn't tell me about your diplomatic advancement, which interests me as much as does your academic progress. I presume that during your stay in Paris you will try to find a way not to have to return to Berne. You should let me know if anything develops. We continue living here quite agreeably; more difficult to believe and yet true, we like it more and more in spite of the winter and of the solitude. Farewell. Remember us very particularly to Mme. de Gobineau, and trust in my unchangeable affection.

XIV

Gobineau about his academic and diplomatic prospects

Paris, 3 January 1854

Monsieur,

Before I answer your kind and generous letter I must tell you something about its effects. I showed it to M. de Rémusat, who was much impressed and congratulated me.

[2] 1802–1866, one of Tocqueville's closest friends, his companion to America, and the devoted, though imprecise, editor of his posthumous writings.

Your letter may have made him persevere further with his good intentions. As you had suggested, I sent my two volumes to M. Mignet for their eventual proposition to the *Académie*. This took place during the session when M. de Rémusat introduced me to him. He too was at once very benevolent and asked *my very sponsor* to give an oral account to the learned assembly. This was fixed for one of the forthcoming Saturdays. I also sent my book to M. Guizot and, before him, to M. de Beaumont. I think, therefore, that I did my part. About the newspapers, the *Débats* will, I think, publish an article toward the end of this month, and M. de Rémusat is looking for a competent person to write another for the *Revue des deux mondes*. But there are difficulties concerning competence. There are physiologists and there are historians, and perhaps even some philologists, though this latter species is rarely found on the latitude of Paris, but to find someone who is all of these is rather difficult. I am quite preoccupied about this problem,[1] though, after all, something is much better than nothing. After that I sincerely believe, monsieur, that the rest is in your, in Rémusat's, and in God's hands. I shall not say much about the lively criticisms of my sponsor, which are very similar to yours; I defend myself as well as I can. With him, as with you, I find myself in a position where I do not know whether I should weep for not having pleased men whom I admire or whether I should be delighted that their dislike of my thesis is overcome by their personal interest in me. I may have to weep and laugh at the same time.

And now about my diplomatic career. I am here by the order of the Minister[2] since M. de Fénelon,[3] with whom I never even had a word of dispute, wrote that he cannot

---

[1] See below, p. 331, note 3.

[2] Édouard Drouyn de Lhuys (1805–1881), several times Foreign Minister of France.

[3] Minister of France to Switzerland.

bear me and requested that they send me elsewhere. They brought me here and assured me that there are no complaints against me, and that they are, on the contrary, quite satisfied with my work, but I may *probably* have behaved in a way to exasperate Fénelon without having given grounds for quarrel and that, consequently, as I have requested transfer for some time, I shall be sent elsewhere in a couple of months and in the meantime I should stay put. I am thus here, with my regular salary being paid and in sight of the long-awaited transfer. I have no reason to complain.

M. Drouyn de Lhuys[4] has praised me to everyone. The underlying reason of the Fénelon business was the latter's dislike of the Department's benevolent attitude to me; his own lunacy did the rest. What made Drouyn de Lhuys act I do not know. But I am altogether satisfied. I wish you were also satisfied with me in every possible way; the thought vexes me. Both of us send our respects to Mme. de Tocqueville, and in this new year, as in all others, I hope that you will remember the devotion of your very affectionate servant.

4 See above, note 2.

Gobineau about his career

Paris, 9 February 1854

Monsieur,

I have good news about my career. I shall not return to
Berne. The Minister is sending me to Frankfurt.[1] It is a
transfer and not an advancement, but I leave Switzerland,
where I have felt hemmed in and petrified; I leave a detestable climate for a better one; I shall be present at
greater events of increasing political importance; and what
is more important, I hope to have a Chief of Mission who
has enough self-confidence not to be afraid of me. M. de
Reinhard and M. de Fénelon vexed me enough, and I assure you that even with the latter, who is mad enough to
be tied, I have made lately some noticeable advances. So
I am going to Frankfurt, and I am quite satisfied; I am
stoic about not having advanced in grade, and I should be
glad to know how you feel about this. I thought of asking
your permission to come to spend a few hours with you as
I cannot resign myself to being back in France without
seeing you. I have thousands of things to ask and tell you.
But I dare not request this now since I am leaving around
the 20th and until that time I know I have to make many
assiduous calls to promote my book, not to speak of my

---

[1] Then seat of the Federal German Diet.

uncle,[2] whose affectionate nature is such as not to let me get out of his sight.

I wanted to talk to you especially about my book as I am afraid of that large and dangerous gulf of objections in which I may well drown. It does not seem to disappear upon reflection; it deepens instead. Please help me to avoid these greater dangers; I appeal to your friendship. Be assured that I shall answer in detail. But I must keep my present course unless I receive new admonitions.

I had the honor of meeting M. Guizot. He was very kind to me, which is a favor attributable to Caesar, that is, to M. de Rémusat. M. de Beaumont also honored me with a letter in which I found many of your thoughts reflected. In a few days in the *Débats* a probably favorable article will appear by M. Alloury.[3] However, he already told me that he regretted having assumed the task of this review, for he feels he is getting lost in the subject. Many others have told me the same. The philologists shun the philosophical parts, and the naturalists steer clear of history.

Farewell, monsieur. Mme. de Gobineau sends her best wishes to Mme. de Tocqueville, and I ask you to share with her the affectionate wishes of your most devoted servant.

[2] Théobald Joseph de Gobineau, a tetchy, rhapsodic, and somewhat mad partisan of the Bourbons, whose relationship with his nephew varied from threats of strangulation to emotional embraces.

[3] Editor of the *Journal des débats*, a moderate conservative.

XVI

Tocqueville gives some diplomatic advice

Saint-Cyr, 19 February 1854

My dear friend, I read your letter with very great pleasure. It brought the excellent news of your nomination to Frankfurt. For someone like you who knows how to navigate in the inkbottle of German thought, it should be good sailing ahead. But, seriously, I think this development very fortunate for you. I feared a long period of inaction, and the consequently more or less unfavorable impression it would leave on the record of a recalled and not immediately transferred diplomatist. You must certainly know Tallenay[1] as well as I do. You will, I think, find him as little disposed to let his first secretaries write his dispatches as to invite them to dine. You should not be too eager about the first if you don't want to see the Berne affair repeated in Frankfurt. Even if he ignores you for a few weeks, I advise you to be very modest and inactive during that time. You ought to remember every day that you don't have to prove your talents but your *sociability*. Write books, but don't write either memoirs or dispatches unless you wish to reach rapidly a point where there remain no superiors willing to work with you. At least this is the unsolicited advice of an old friend.

You may be sure that upon my return to Paris I shall look into your academic affairs, and if something remains

[1] Minister of France to the Federal German Diet.

to be done on the spot, I shall do it. I believe that my neighbor Beaumont is well disposed toward you. I have not spoken with him, as I have not seen him, but he wrote me and spoke with considerable esteem about your book, even though he objects to the same things I do. But what do you expect? Two stubborn old men, obstinately stuck with our idea of liberty, as Courier stuck with his *Charte*,[2] said about himself, without ever being able to do without it.

If, as I imagine, you were to stay in Frankfurt this summer, it may be that we will see each other. I intend to make a little trip through Germany, and we may pass through the city of your future residence. I should be truly pleased to have a chance to talk with you.

Farewell, and *bon voyage*. I wish you all sorts of good and propitious things in your new place; much literary and little diplomatic activity! Please remember us particularly to Mme. de Gobineau and believe in my very sincere friendship.

XVII

Gobineau about his own progress

Frankfurt am Main, 7 March 1854

Monsieur,

Before writing you I wanted to reconnoiter my terrain a little. Your instructions are so wise and so fitting to my cir-

---

[2] Paul Louis Courier (1772–1825), enthusiastic pamphleteer in favor of the *Charte*, the constitution issued by Louis XVIII in 1814.

cumstances that I would be a lunatic not to observe them. I shall follow them in every detail. It is no longer possible to say now, as M. de Reinhard[1] used to say, that I am not even a good copyist or, as M. de Fénelon kept repeating, that, save for knowing Chinese, I am good for nothing; from now on, as you rightly observe, my reputation in these things is nearly assured and little remains but to stay put and do nothing. My inclinations fortunately correspond to your wise admonitions. Thus things will take care of themselves. Otherwise I found M. de Tallenay welcoming and rather friendly. M. Cintrat[2] had written him a very benevolent letter about me.

You cannot imagine the pleasure which the prospect of seeing you brings. I have a thousand things to tell you and a million points to discuss. You probably read the article about my book in the *Débats* of 24 February. The review was not very intelligent. I think I am impartial when I say this, for I am by nature insensitive to printed blame and printed praise alike. After all, the polite form, the awkward arguments, and the lengthy nature of the article may have helped me, as the bookstore sold a good number of books in the days after the review had come out.

I left M. de Rémusat well disposed towards me. This seems to agree with your plan and, with what you so kindly told me about M. de Beaumont, it is a very good plan indeed. In Paris I was flattered by a number of comments on my book. M. Mignet and M. Guizot were very kind to me, and M. Mérimée, who courteously offered to help me with the research for my third volume, graciously gave me a really very interesting picture signed by himself. It is a water-color portrait of a Vosges gypsy, a remarkable specimen of German *Zigeunerin*. He copied it from a pastel by

[1] French Minister to Switzerland 1849 to 1853, whom Gobineau had irritated no end.

[2] A high official, and Director of the Archives of the French Foreign Ministry.

Maréchal[3] which is in my possession. I have always been very sensitive to such marks of friendship. But, above all, I am attracted to yours. Of course, for who is more bound to you than I am? Adieu, monsieur, Mme. de Gobineau joins me in sending you as well as to Mme. de Tocqueville a thousand regards and best wishes.

XVIII

Gobineau about politics in Germany

Frankfurt am Main, 12 July 1854

I have been awaiting your answer, monsieur, to two or three letters of mine, but it seems you don't want to spoil me. And so I am expecting you in person. I imagine that the bad weather may have retarded your travel plans, yet not, I hope, to the extent of canceling them. We constantly talk about you and about the pleasure of conversing with you. Don't let fate rob us of all of this.

I am constantly governed by the maxim you gave me before I came here: "No dinners, no dispatches." Your prediction has been perfectly verified. Sometimes I meet M. de Tallenay in the house of others but very rarely in his own. He hardly ever puts his feet in the Chancery, and when we see each other we talk of the weather. But I don't complain, and having passed from under the regimen of the Know-It-All to that of the Do-Nothing, I much prefer the latter. But one should be fair. There is absolutely nothing

[3] Charles Maréchal, the painter (1801–1887). This portrait forms part of the Strasbourg Gobineau collection.

to do here save to record what is going on, and that is very little indeed. The Diet is a German bureaucratic chancery, and it is very far from being a real political body. It has little influence; the two dominant members do not want it to have any; Bavaria and Saxony, when they want, act independently; there remains little else than the minor German states playing for small stakes. Their relative impotence lends to this unlucky German assembly a somewhat ludicrous tinge which it would be glad to get rid of. A common sight is that of the two really serious persons in this assembly, the Ministers of Austria and of Prussia,[1] serious because of their characters and their positions, acidly complaining about the emptiness of their functions.

Should you arrive soon, you may see all this with your own eyes. I am beginning to believe that the zero is not necessarily the least interesting of all numbers. But one must get used to it. I should also wish to know where you are in your work. I frequently think about it, and I am awaiting the results with vivid impatience. About my own (*si parva licet componere magnis*),[2] I shall finish my last two volumes in about three months.

Farewell, monsieur; my wife sends you and Mme. de Tocqueville her very best wishes. To you I reaffirm my devoted, respectful, and enduring affection.

[1] The Austrian Minister was Baron von Brenner-Felsach; the Prussian was Bismarck.
[2] "Were the small permitted to compare to the great."

XIX

Tocqueville about his German impressions

Bonn, 22 July 1854

Your letter of the 12th, my dear friend, has finally reached me here, after it followed me across half of Europe. I do not understand your reference to several letters which I should have answered. After my last letter I received but one from you, the one in which you speak about Germany and about your wish that I come to Frankfurt. If you wrote after that, your letter must have been lost.

I left France around the middle of last month and practically without stopping came to Bonn, from where I am now writing and where I have been staying for about a month. I thought that before penetrating farther into Germany that I should try in this way to dissipate a little the obscurity in which this part of Europe has always been shrouded before my eyes. I think I was right in staying for some time in the same place and to observe the country through books and through the conversation of the people in this way. A rapid impression of many different people and of many different provinces might not have helped me so much. I knew some members of the university here and I also found a large library and men ready to inform me and to help in rounding out the always very imperfect impressions one gets from books. So I chose to reside in Bonn. We rented a small house on the banks of the Rhine and, except for the German habit of late supper,

I am living like a veritable native here. Unfortunately I lack the ability to speak the language; I am beginning to understand books but I am still quite far from being able to understand conversation. Yet I am slowly advancing each day toward what may have been the main aim of my journey here. I am not dissatisfied with this expedition. I should rather like to go to Frankfurt but I am not at all sure whether I shall be able to, despite the pleasant prospect of seeing and talking with Mme. de Gobineau and yourself. My interests tend to draw me to the north, and I think I shall move from here toward Dresden and Berlin. I think I shall stay in Bonn for another month, except perhaps for a little side trip into Westphalia, where I should like to observe a number of things that interest me. But Bonn will remain my headquarters and my wife will probably stay here. Up to now my health as well as my spirit has been quite good because of the sort of life I am leading, and I hope that when I return to France the two will agreeably continue to complement each other. For without good health I cannot work, and when I cannot work my still impatient mind ruins my health.

Your interesting sketch of the Diet did not surprise me. I imagined things there rather in the way you depicted them. They are so much the necessary consequences of German political conditions and of German federal laws that it is difficult to see the Diet otherwise. The German federal constitution is one of the worst imaginable; but things would not be much different even if it were one of the best as long as everything depends on Austria and Prussia, that heavy-set couple walking together with their minor charges. Legal fictions are not always as powerless as people think but they are certainly no substitutes for realities. Mere machinery cannot replace a living organism. A federal system will work only when its members are relatively equal and homogeneous (and even in such a case it is not always very strong) or if the pretended federal powers are, in reality, exercised by a powerful member whose power and prestige is sufficient to sustain the command it gives in the name of all. To the devil with this! Am I going to give you a lecture in politics? My loquacity at least proves how I like to talk with you even by mail. If I can, I shall do my best and come to talk with you in person. Please give my respects to Mme. de Gobineau and to you a thousand cordial greetings.

XX

Gobineau about the German North and South

Frankfurt am Main, 28 July 1854

I was not a little disappointed to learn that two of my letters were lost, monsieur; and, most of all, that the summer may pass without the delightful experience of seeing you again though we are hardly more than a half a day's distance from each other. If this is not an indiscreet suggestion, I should like to pay you at least a brief visit within the next fortnight. In any case, I very much regret not having you here at least for a two- or three-day visit. I think that many things would interest you here, above all, meeting the president of the Diet,[1] certainly one of the most important persons in Germany, not merely because of his position but because of his character, career and talents. You might like to hear what he has to say about his country. I feel that

[1] His friend Count Anton von Prokesch-Osten (1795–1876), onetime tutor of the Duc de Reichstadt, Napoleon's son. See also above, p. 182.

you are very seriously occupied with your work or at least with your preparatory studies. I rejoice with you and with all of your friends in seeing how this contributes to your health. You say that you intend to visit only Prussia. If I may be permitted to say so, I should think that this is not enough: because, though the visible movements in Germany are in the North, the powerful and determinant forces may be in the South. This always seems to be overlooked, and I should much like to have your eventual impressions about it. The past furnishes, of course, many proofs of this fact or, rather, of this condition, but even recent events, like those of 1848, curiously affirm it. It seems to me as if the present impulse were coming from the South and that with the growing reluctance of the North to yield this becomes more and more evident. I hope you will forgive this idle talk. My thoughts often run like the thoughts of those who when dreaming of a woman they have not yet met attribute to her such qualities of attraction which they might not quite wish her to have in reality.

Meanwhile we pass our days very much as Do-Nothings. But this is inevitable. For, to express it in terms of physics, we represent the central point in Germany where the negative and positive electrical forces neutralize each other. The only present activity concerns the Austrian loan, which is a great success. I have so many things to tell you that I have filled four senseless pages without having said anything. Forgive me once more in the way you always forgive me and tell me definitely if, for any reason, I should not be able to see you. Mme. de Gobineau sends her warmest regards to you and to Mme. de Tocqueville. I am very happy to see that she, like you, enjoys the Rhine, and I ask that she share with you the respectful affections of the man who is most attached to you and loves you most.

XXI

Gobineau about his attitude to the public

Frankfurt am Main, 15 October 1854

As the season advanced without news from you I surmised, monsieur, that you would not pass through Frankfurt. Both of us are much distressed by the sad cause of your sudden return to France. We much regret that a supplementary Italian trip will not come about to help re-establish the health of Mme. de Tocqueville, since we can hardly believe that the foggy dampness of the French winter would achieve what the waters of Germany failed to do. Physical afflictions are among the greatest burdens of life.

About your nephew,[1] I think he should be advised without hesitation to enter the bureaux and not to start out as a voluntary attaché. There are now between one hundred and one hundred and thirty of the latter and each year there is only one vacancy for such a salaried post. This illustrious category furthermore enjoys a detestable reputation, which it truly deserves. Thus it is preferred to recruit able members for the service from the bureaux where it is true that there are few lions but where one can learn or at least acquire the air of having learned something. This is much more valuable than what is now offered by the voluntary attachés. I believe that this would be the best way to start out.

[1] Hubert de Tocqueville, a modest and engaging young man of whom his childless uncle was extremely fond. He survived his uncle by only four years.

[247]

It is very true that we no longer live in very intellectual times, and I well understand the dislike and the annoyance which this condition inspires in you; but, as you yourself say, my work is little disturbed by it. There are many reasons for this. The first is that the methods I have chosen are exclusively scientific, and this has made me discount all considerations of popularity, since the field in which I am working is obviously independent of the consent of the majority. Then I am so much convinced that the present enfeeblement of minds is, on one hand, universal and, on the other, that its spread is inevitable, irreparable, and unlimited that only two roads remain open to me: either to throw myself in the lake or to go ahead on my own way without the least concern for what is called public opinion. I am resolved to stick to the latter, and I am interested only in those few hundred minds that are still alive amid the general atrophy. And, on this road, so far so good. My last two volumes are completed. I am trying to have them published and also trying to get the proofs, which is not easy. I should like to dispose of this book, as I have another subject in mind which is really quite close to the former but which should nevertheless be treated independently. It is, I think, a new discovery in natural history, resulting from purely linguistic researches. But I keep imposing on you about my work, and you, you never say anything about yours despite my vivid desire to know something about it. You are, I think, less just with your own work than I am with mine. Adieu, monsieur, my wife sends her warmest wishes to Mme. de Tocqueville and to yourself, to which I join my respectful and devoted affections to both of you.

XXII

Gobineau about his prospective Persian mission

Frankfurt am Main, 8 January 1855

Monsieur, I have not written you for ages as I am always hoping to come to see you in a few days, but the few days pass and a thousand obstacles impede my departure. The last obstacle has been a grave one. My daughter has been very ill for the past twelve days, but this very morning she began to feel better, and I hope to take to the road on Thursday. I cannot linger long, and I am writing in haste.

I shall be in Paris for a very short time. At the end of this month I shall be leaving for Persia with Bourée,[1] and the government has agreed to keep my position in Frankfurt vacant. There were various reasons to accept this Persian offer. My acceptance was made easier by my close friendship with Bourée. I do hope to be able to talk with you about this. In a few days everything will be definitely settled.

My last two volumes are being printed. They will appear while I am away; I shall offer them to you before I leave, as you say, not for their own sake but for that of their author. On the other hand, I have not given up all hope that some future day, when you despair of this century, you will be tempted to agree a little with me. In any case, you must forgive me for saying what I say, for I am

[1] Minister of France to China; appointed to Persia and later to Greece.

mathematically certain about the correctitude of my propositions. Not a gay conclusion, but what is gay in our days?

I learn from Serre[2] that your nephew has been appointed attaché to Vienna. It seems to me that you put him in possibly the most difficult post for a young man. These great embassies are hard on the character, on the manners, and on the habits of a beginner. I doubt that he will find many edifying examples. We too have a voluntary attaché, M. Gaston de la Rochefoucauld, who arrived full of good counsels and of good intentions; I wonder how long they will last. But your nephew, with more young colleagues around him, could eventually shine in comparison. Attachés belong to a race of their own, whose existence contradicts the doctrine that in this world everything that exists serves some purpose.

I like to hope that my letter finds you and Mme. de Tocqueville in good health. We are still under the rude impact of my daughter's grave illness, but we seem to be recovering. Mme. de Gobineau sends her duplicate best wishes. I myself hope to be calling on you before the end of next week, a great pleasure of which I was deprived so sadly in Germany.

Adieu, monsieur. You know that no one is more attached and more respectfully and tenderly devoted to you than am I.

P.S. I must not forget that M. de Tallenay always insists that I tell you of his enduring high esteem for you. M. de Valbezenne[3] writes the same from Calcutta. I hope there are more who remember you like this.

[2] First secretary at the French Embassy to Vienna; a close friend of Gobineau.
[3] French Consul at Calcutta.

XXIII

*Tocqueville about diplomatic careers; about
the future*

Compiègne, 19 January 1855

You must be in Paris by now, and I should like to be there
myself to grasp your hand, my dear friend, to wish you all
kinds of good fortune in the great voyage ahead. But I cannot yet come to Paris, and when I shall arrive there next
month I am very much afraid that you will have already
folded your tents. You must thus accept my written adieux
if I cannot do otherwise. My wishes are not the less vivid
and sincere for being put on paper. I knew for some time
that you were being considered for this mission, and though
I would have preferred to hear the news directly from you
I kept wishing for your success. In your profession, as in
the army, the number of campaigns counts; and the hardest
campaigns count most. Please keep me posted on your
progress; my old predilection for you persists.

You credit me unduly when you say that I *put* my
nephew in diplomacy. He put himself there; I have only
helped him indirectly upon his insistence. Besides, the
dangers which you so rightly describe are not to be feared
in his case unless diplomacy were able to transform the
metal of men in a sort of alchemy. My nephew is a hard-
working young man who has to be pushed into social life
rather than kept away from it; he is deficient exactly in those
lighter qualities which are often so necessary in your pro-

fession. Thus I hope that he will escape the frequently inevitable transformation of attachés into fools. I rather fear that he may fail to acquire that illuminatory varnish needed to make his solid and fundamental qualities emerge. I am very happy that Serre is in Vienna, and *I am very much touched* by the reception he gave to my young attaché. Please tell him when you write that nothing pleases me better than to have him give guidance to this young man. He will find a zealous collaborator and a loyal character, one capable of strong attachments when some interest is shown in him. Just yesterday he wrote me: "I am very happy with M. de Serre. Of all the people here he is certainly the man I like best."

I look forward to your last volumes with impatience but, at least for the present, without the temptation to be convinced by you. My personal impressions are on the opposite side. Yes, I sometimes despair of mankind. Who doesn't, even when he lives as isolated from it as I do? But I do not despair of this century, which, after all, may be marked as one of the great centuries of history, when men have conquered so much of nature and achieved the conquest of the globe. Should you need another *academic* push during your absence, let me know. You know that, as always, I shall be glad to be of help. Farewell. Good luck; do not altogether forget me, and write when you arrive at your destination.

P.S. I am sending this letter to M. Brénier[1] as I do not have your Paris address.

[1] A high Chancery official and former Secretary-General of the French Foreign Ministry.

XXIV

Gobineau to Tocqueville

Paris, 24 January 1855

Monsieur,

M. Brénier forwarded the letter that you were kind enough to have sent to me in his care. It has touched me for various reasons; I thank you deeply indeed. The reason I had not told you earlier about my Persian voyage was that it was still a castle in Spain. The Department was inclined to consent, but I asked for certain guarantees which were not answered until recently, and I wrote you only when the final decision eliminated all the elements of doubt.

I should be much disappointed to have to depart without having seen you and Mme. de Tocqueville. I must leave between the 5th and the 10th of February. Would you permit me to come for a few hours to Compiègne?

I am writing in great haste, surrounded by reports and by two sets of proofs to be corrected. Be good enough to forgive me in the name of that sincere and respectful affection which, I think, I need not prove anew.

Rue Miromesnil, 5.

XXV

Tocqueville to Gobineau

[Compiègne], 27 January

I have to tell you in a few words, my dear friend, that I am incapable of doing anything now. A few days ago I came down with a strong grippe, and though it is not grave I should not neglect a minor illness of this kind after my more severe respiratory maladies of the past years. I am thus wrapped up here speechless, and trying not to think too much either! Another reason why I cannot consent to your coming down here is that with the weather, and with such a long journey ahead of you, this short trip would be an added hardship which I should not let you take by any means. Nevertheless, I do hope to see you if God helps with a little thaw and if my grippe passes. Unless my health makes this absolutely impossible, I should be in Paris on the 7th. On the other hand, long journeys like yours are often begun with some delay. Thus I hope to find you still in Paris on the 7th, and immediately after arriving at my father's (19 place de la Madeleine), I shall send someone to find out whether you are there in effect.

So *au revoir*, and if, against my hope, I should not be able to arrive before you leave, *bon voyage*, and a thousand good wishes for your success. Write me about your health in any case. My best regards to Mme. de Gobineau, and to you many heartfelt greetings.

XXVI

Gobineau about his first Oriental impressions

Teheran, 7 July 1855

Monsieur,

I am writing you immediately as we arrived only four days ago. Yet (an unusual thing in the Orient), the court etiquette was accelerated for our sake; we have already seen the Shah[1] and his Grand Vizier; both could not have been more pleasant to us. We have traveled as well as if we had done nothing else all our lives. Mme. de Gobineau on horseback and my daughter on a donkey behind an Arab groom rode fifty days, climbing roadless mountains and crossing rivers with surprising ease. Diane was neither tired nor sick; instead she grew and gained much weight; and now when we no longer sleep under tents, she does not know what to do with herself. She became a veritable Turcoman, save for her color, which is Ethiopian.

I have seen many curious things, too many to relate all of them here. During our six weeks in Egypt I was able to make observations which do not reflect very well on the Europeans there. Nowhere have I yet seen such shameless dishonesty and rapacity. Thus we are much distrusted by the natives, who, to be honest, are also afraid of us, which, in some respects, provides a counterbalance. There was much talk about the cutting through of the Suez Isthmus; we saw the latter ourselves. As a citizen of the world, I

[1] Nasr-ed-Din, ruled 1848 to 1896.

have no opinions about it; as a Frenchman, I am against it, since the development of a Hellenic navy (I mean Greeks and Turkish Greeks) is more than evident, despite English opposition. Thus the advantages of a canal (advantages of which I am not in the least convinced) will in the future serve nations not necessarily friendly to us. In any case, the Oriental commerce of Marseille will be much compromised and the traffic of Bordeaux will be certainly ruined.

We spent very interesting days in Suez, in Jeddah, in Aden, in Mascat[2] and in Bushire. And now we are here, having traversed the whole width of Persia. We have certainly seen many ruins, by which I mean ruins of cities and of villages, places now without the least historic interest; we have passed through many deserts and we have traveled for long days without seeing anyone. Speaking about the spiritual state of the inhabitants, we are witnessing the spectacle of a great decomposition of ideas and of principles. Yet, all in all, in their practical inclinations these people seem much like the Turks and the Arabs, and while they share the greediness of the Indians they are far from sharing their rigid principles. In sum, they are rascals who could be considered our cousins, and I think we may say with some justice: this is what we ourselves shall become tomorrow.

One of these days I shall write you about the hard attitude of the British here. I do not yet see its purpose clearly, unless it is to prepare the way for the Russians.[3] For the moment I only want to tell you how much I remain attached to you, in deepest Asia just as anywhere else. Also, I ask you to give Mme. de Tocqueville my best wishes and

[2] He means Muscat.

[3] Reference to the Crimean War in course; also symptomatic of Gobineau's mistaken predictions and of his considerable Anglophobia.

regards, which go equally to you from your most attached and devoted servant.

I do not know whether you heard about the death of my uncle, who left me a sum which makes me independent. I know that this will please you.

⟶∿∿∿⟵

XXVII

Gobineau about India and Persia

Demavend, 5 November 1855

Monsieur,

I live in the hope of receiving some news from you soon and of learning that you and Mme. de Tocqueville are as well as possible. You must have received my first letter from Teheran some time ago and perhaps you have already answered it. I am very eager to know about the progress of your work. It seems to me that even with your great desire for high perfection you must have finished your preparatory studies and begun the final writing, unless you have come to modify your fundamental ideas. Pray tell me what happened and at what stage you are. My interest is undiminished by distance.

I am writing from hardly three days' distance from Teheran. We made a little trip to the mountains, partly to see the country and partly also to escape the great ravages of the cholera epidemic in the city, which, in our own legation, took the lives of one native and of two European servants. However, by now the epidemic has almost disappeared; the cold weather has set in, and we are here in snow-covered country, ready to return in a few days.

I do not know whether you were interested in the particular details about which I wrote; in absence of a negative answer I shall continue.

Politically the importance of Persia is that of a second-rate European state. Yet, if one is at all interested in what might be the politics not of tomorrow but of the day after tomorrow, Teheran is an observatory from which one can behold a very extensive vista of Russian and British positions and interests. To hear the British themselves, Persia is the key to India. Their consequent preoccupations, which to me are exaggerated, oblige the disinterested observer to follow British eyes to those points which seem to be of so much interest to them. The British anxieties concerning India are widely shared in the Orient, though, I repeat, to me they are extreme. For about twenty years now they have begun to admit that the absolute subjugation of the Indian native population—one of the main sources of the Europeans' prestige—harbors great future dangers since it may at any time lead to revolt. They have, therefore, changed their system. They have been trying to gain the sympathies of their Indian subjects by actively satisfying their needs, by respecting their ideas, and by taking interest in their welfare; I think that they have succeeded to a certain degree, at least in instilling some patience in their subjects. I think that the discontent of the Sepoy troops has been much exaggerated,[1] appearances having misled. It was pretended that they lacked good will and courage: true. Yet what is, and will remain, also true is the fundamental incompatibility of an Asiatic with a European people, especially with the British. This is at the bottom of British anxieties, and these emerge here at the slightest

[1] Reference to the brewing Sepoy discontent, which two years later erupted in the dreadful Rebellion.

movement which might have a repercussion on the imagination of the peoples of India.

What no one doubts, including the native populations themselves, is their absolute incapacity to liberate themselves. Divided as they are, supervised, weakened, impoverished, they will remain subjugated unless external events destroy British power on their great peninsula. Thus they follow external events with great interest, as does the Anglo-Indian community; as a matter of fact, having more information and foresight, and having everything to lose, the latter rather incline, as I said earlier, to exaggeration.

Of all external combinations a possible Russian move on India is first. Not that, in my opinion, the government of Calcutta should fear the descent of a European army on the Indus aiming to conquer the entire country. Though many people obstinately believe it possible militarily, I myself strongly doubt it, and I also regard it impossible politically. But the problem is not that the Russian Cabinet may ponder the conquest of all India but that an expedition of thirty to forty thousand men should appear with Persian troops, Afghans, Khivan and Bokharan Uzbeks in its train, bringing about an insurrection in the Sindh and in the Punjab and fomenting from there potential rebellions elsewhere. I believe that with such a purely destructive policy Russia would be able to push the British into a morass of difficulties from which nothing could result for Britain but, at best, a considerable loss of men, money, influence, and a sorry deterioration of her future prestige in the world.

The Asiatic peoples whom I mentioned, Persians, Afghans, and Uzbeks, have for centuries beheld India as the richest of all possible preys. During their brief periods of superiority each of them invaded India and returned with treasures which in retrospect their imagination exaggerates a hundredfold. They imagine that this Indian abundance has remained the same. They don't know and, if they are told, they don't believe that the English have extracted what they themselves had left behind earlier. To the contrary, inclined as they are to believe the British the richest nation on earth, they multiply the fabulous riches of India with the riches they attribute to her actual rulers. Thus they live with the constant desire to lay their hands on these imagined accumulations of gold, of silver, and of precious stones. And the more miserable their present existence, the more they feel pressed to act. Persia, ruined by the wars which at the end of the last century resulted in her present dynasty,[2] is ruined further by the present maladministration of her Shah and of his ministers, by a corruption hardly conceivable even in Asia. The warrior tribes are dying of hunger; and their chieftains, unable to provide for their people, are thirsty for a war to bring them riches. Furthermore, it is safe to say that the British are openly detested here. Their unpopularity is general. People think that their only intimidating weapon is their eventual descent on Bushire on the Persian Gulf. From the present war[3] they then draw the conclusion that the British have few troops at their disposal. And, finally, they flatter themselves by believing that even in the case of a not altogether successful invasion of India the British would not be able to retaliate too severely. So the general belief among the warrior tribes and among their chieftains is that sooner or later they ought to cross the Indus.

The Afghans believe this even more. First of all, they are even poorer than the Persians. Furthermore, they are better warriors and much less prone to ponder the possible outcomes of their actions, for each chieftain believes that if worst comes to worst they can still find refuge in their mountains.

Add to this that it is not typical of the Asiatic mind to think far ahead about the consequences of a desirable ac-

[2] The Qadjars.
[3] The Crimean War (see above, p. 256).

tion. This is even truer of the peoples of Khiva, Bokhara, and Turkestan.

At this moment there is an Afghan mission in Teheran. It has no contact with either the British or with ourselves. It is not so certain that it has no contact with the Russians. Everyone here knows what this Afghan mission wants. They are ready to place Herat and Kandahar under Persian rule in exchange for a joint expedition against Kabul, to chase from there the old Dost-Mohammed, former enemy and now devoted supporter of the British. In case of success, they speak about realizing the grand design of marching on the Indus.

Despite the present leanings to such a policy, two issues remain in the way of its immediate execution. First of all, the fall of Sevastopol resulted in uncertainty about the actual attitude of Russia to such an enterprise. The Anglo-French victory left a very deep impression here and, notwithstanding the excessive politeness of the Persian ministers, it is very obvious that deep down they feel rather uneasy. The European powers fighting each other is a sight which Oriental statesmen always enjoy; but, if any one of them must come out on top, they certainly prefer that Britain go down. Of this there can be no doubt. In the present situation the always very active imaginations of the Shah's counselors turn toward new possibilities. Because the ardently desired aim of their war must be rich booty above all, they ask themselves whether, if the sack of India should become impractical, there would be compensation in the prospective pillage of the Russian Caucasian provinces. They even go further: they have formulated quite a pretension, which I think you will find rather exorbitant. They have declared that if the armies of the Shah were to join the Franco-British forces they would be represented at the future peace conference and thus occupy a position alongside the great civilized states while having the integrity of

Persian territory guaranteed, first of all against Russia but also against all the other powers.

All of this is very unrealistic when seen from here. But the conclusion to be drawn from it is that, by necessity, Persia may from one moment to the next throw herself into the arms of Russia. This is but a question of time.

Here is another point. The Shah is very hesitant to enter into a campaign because, even if he is lucky in the field, he is not quite sure of being able to regain his own capital. Such is the unpopularity of his dynasty and of his own person. The South of this country has never been completely subdued. The Court is not only unable to reside in Ispahan without running great and constant risks; it is not even able to move there without the support of an artillery escort. The regiments recruited from these large provinces are posted as far away as possible and, unless absolutely necessary, they are not employed at all. This has been the normal state of things ever since the Qadjars occupied the throne. But what is new in the present reign is that the northern regiments are equally unreliable. The kingly tribe itself, as is common practice in this country where political opinions are very liberally expressed, loudly proclaims its disgust with the actual state of politics and its dislike of the ruling family, which has come from its own tents. Finally, the West and the North, the richest and most fertile Persian provinces, are worked by a sect more political than religious, by the Babis, who are veritable communists in their ideas and methods, and whom the Shah fears ever since four years ago when they laid an ambush for him from which he escaped only by a miracle. The mere appearance of one of these violent adventurers whom the Orient so abundantly produces would be enough to put the Persian dynasty in extreme peril. Here is one of the main causes of the present inactivity, which inactivity, however, is dangerous in itself, since it contributes considerably to general discontent.

Still, you will see that these things are transitory. What this effete dynasty may not dare to do might be a powerfully attractive weapon in the hands of a future pretender. On the other hand, it is not at all sure that the present rulers will not decide to act.

I repeat that the British understand the dangers which this situation means for them. During their ceaseless mental gymnastics they have almost revived the original ideas of their sorry policy, which, in 1838, had induced them to try to form under their protection a unitary Afghan state. Their plan was to create yet another buffer between Russia and India. You will remember the result, and the dreadful catastrophe of Kabul. I doubt that a return to such obviously impractical plans would be at all considered by serious minds in India or in London. But, faced with the necessity of doing something, one of the most distinguished officials of British India has announced now something new, and we have been assured here that Colonel Rawlinson's[4] proposals were received with interest and that they are the object of profound examination in London.

The idea, they say, is to erect the barrier between Russia and India in the Caucasian provinces, to establish there an independent Christian state, to obtain navigational rights in the Caspian, and to have there a British lake flotilla. The great enthusiasm which the British Legation in Teheran demonstrates for this project shows more than anything else the extent and the persistence of their anxieties.

If I may be permitted to express my opinion, not on Colonel Rawlinson's project but on what we are told it is, I must say that I hardly share the general optimism. A Christian state in Georgia would be flanked on both sides by Mohammedan populations; what is worse, by depredatory peoples whom even Russia could not yet fully conquer. This state would be exposed to everlasting conflicts with

[4] H. C. Rawlinson (1810–1895), the archaeologist. See also Note on Gobineau, pp. 182–84.

Persia, and the latter would be apt to bully it unscrupulously. It would be little inclined to have a Caspian fleet of its own, since there is not enough commerce to sustain it. The Russian tariff policy would exclude it from Astrakhan, and the steppes of the Turcoman tribes are not very attractive. It would thus be necessary for British forces to sustain this new Christian state permanently. But a permanent Russian army of 150,000 men has for twenty years been unable to reduce and pacify the Caucasian provinces. Would the British be disposed to maintain such a force? One must doubt it. And even if they were, it is obvious that their troubles would be twice those of the Russians, having Shamil,[5] the Circassians, and all the other mountain people on their hands while having the Russians always at their back. Thus if Colonel Rawlinson's project is what we are told here it is—and I think that it cannot be very different except for some details—I feel that you would be inclined to believe with me that it is quite a defective one.

I shall conclude with a very profound maxim which you told me one morning on the boulevard des Capucines: "The Russian Tsar may now call himself *The* Emperor." I am much afraid that he is indeed the most powerful of all the rulers, not because of the personal qualities of the present Tsar,[6] not because of this or that branch of his power but because of the very weight of circumstances. I shall not elaborate on them. If, when peace is made, by one pretext or another the Russian Cabinet should decide to compensate their losses in the Black Sea at the cost of Persia, they might lay their hands on the two magnificent provinces of Mazanderan and Ghilan. Their troops would enter and remain there. The people expect and even want them there; they have already threatened to invite Russia in spontane-

---

[5] Shamil, the nineteenth-century leader of the Caucasian nationalist guerrillas against the Russians: his memory was respected by Lenin and disavowed later by Stalin.

[6] Alexander II, ruled 1855 to 1881.

ously. We shall certainly not start a new war to impede this. And what is even stranger but no less certain is that Persia herself may take advantage of such a situation if she thinks she could thus secure solid Russian support for her own expansion eastward. This is the constant obsession; this is the *Rhine frontier* of everyone down here. They dream of Tamerlane, they dream of Nadir Shah,[7] they daydream of suddenly enriching themselves in a day, while realities count little to them.

I am working much; I am most active in trying to perfect myself in the language, which now I speak fluently enough. I find my daily discussions with the natives extremely interesting, and I am far from entertaining such a low opinion about them as is complacently done in Europe. They are not angels, nor are they perfectly honest, but neither are they the perverse ghouls which they are represented to be. If you are interested in this aspect, I shall write you about it someday.

I think that you received my last two volumes. This is why I am so much worried that you may not be satisfied with me. Please tell me what you are thinking. I prefer to be roughly treated by you than not to be treated at all.

Please do not forget my desire concerning the *Académie* whenever the chance arises. It seems to me that I have now, more than ever, sufficient title to the scientific grade I solicit. I wish you would agree. I hear from Paris many pleasant things which make me think that my nomination is not out of the question. I intend to remind M. Mignet of the benevolence he showed me in the past.

Farewell, monsieur; Mme. de Gobineau commends herself to Mme. de Tocqueville and to yourself. To her and to you I send my respects and my affections, which, as you know, will never diminish.

7 Powerful Afghan ruler, ruled 1736 to 1747.

P.S. I think I told you that my uncle died, having left me a sum which comes in handy. You probably received the American translation of my first volume. They wrote me that it should have come out in New York around the month of August.

<hr/>

XXVIII

Tocqueville about Europeans and Asians

Tocqueville, 13 November 1855

I received, my dear friend, your letter written from Teheran on 7 July about a month ago. Had I known how to send letters to you I would have written earlier. But I have withdrawn from the world so completely that I do not know who the director of the couriers' service in the Foreign Ministry is, and I waited for the visit of my nephew, who, as you know, is sufficiently pedantic to be safely charged with the present missive.

I have been worried about you. You have not treated me to your news since you left France, and I felt compelled to write our friend De Serre in Vienna to ask whether you were not drowned in the Red Sea or Persian Gulf. Your letter was very reassuring. What you say surpasses my hopes. Fifty days in the desert, under tents, and without much wear and tear, there is something really admirable. Please convey our congratulations to the two lady explorers and do not neglect their two mounts, who merit particular praise during such ventures. Now when I no longer fear the perils for your caravan, my imagination is a little alarmed by the news of the cholera. I read in the paper that it has raged in your present city and that a number of Embassy servants died from it. Please do not let six months go by again without having news from you.

I shall give you in a few words my own story since we last saw each other. Shortly thereafter I established myself in Paris until the summery weather brought me down here. I have been here for five months, and I hope to stay for a couple more. I spend the morning in my study, where I work much, and the afternoon in the fields, where I am surveying more work of another sort. I have been passably well. Time has flown prodigiously; I don't ever remember it passing so quickly and so agreeably. What a pity that one does not master the art of living until late in life.

I find it laughable to dispatch, my dear friend, such a dull piece of paper as this to thousands of miles away. It is hardly worth it. But what can a provincial rustic such as myself tell you that is interesting? You are the person who is surely full of interesting matters. Please let me know some of them. You are in the heart of the Asiatic and Musulman world; I am very curious to know to what you attribute the rapid and seemingly inevitable decadence of the races you have seen; a decadence which, as it already has delivered some, may deliver all of them to the domination of our little Europe, which so often trembled before them in the past. Where is the maggot that is eating this large Asiatic body? The Turks have become bad soldiers and now seem destined to be cheated and defeated by everybody. Yet you live now with a Mohammedan nation which, if the travelers' accounts are to be believed, is intelligent and even refined. What is this irredeemable decadence dragging it down through the centuries? Is it possible that we have risen while they remained static? I do not think so. I rather think that a dual movement has occurred in opposite directions. You say that one day we shall resemble your Eastern mobs: perhaps. But before that happens, we shall be their masters. A few million men who, a few centuries ago, lived nearly shelterless in the forests and in the marshes of Europe will, within a hundred years, have transformed the globe and dominated the other races. Seldom has Providence shown us an aspect of the future so clearly. The European races are often the greatest rogues, but at least they are rogues to whom God gave will and power and whom he seems to have destined for some time to be at the head of mankind. Nothing on the entire globe will resist their influence. I have no doubts about this. I am afraid that this may sound to you a little heretical. But you shall rely on your theories, and I trust I shall rely on my facts, which may be trifling but not unimportant.

Here I am farther away from Ispahan than ever. I turn to embrace you cordially and to ask you not to wait so long before writing. You know that I am never indifferent to anything that concerns you. Upon my return to Paris I shall see what is to be done for you at the *Institut,* and anything that is possible shall be done. Remember us especially to Mme. de G. Embrace Mlle. Diane in our name, and trust my sincere friendship.

XXIX

Tocqueville about Gobineau's book

Tocqueville, 8 January 1856

I have, my dear friend, your second letter (the one dated 5 November), and I hardly know how to thank you adequately enough. I was very much instructed and fascinated by it, and all I ask is that the idea of such letters should occur to you more often. Whatever a man as intelligent as yourself can tell me about a country of which I know little is infinitely valuable to me. If you received my last letter you have seen how very curious I was to learn what you thought of that part of central Asia. Your letter does not answer those questions, but it does answer many others I was going to ask. Please continue along these good lines, save for official matters, about which I shall not ask anything. You have a thousand things of great interest to me. Or, rather, everything you tell me about the peoples around you, about their habits, government, tendencies, needs, passions, all this is of precious value to me; it is very important in my present position as an observer of the things of this world, especially as it is about things unknown to me.

For my part what can I do to repay you in the same currency? Unfortunately, nothing. People in France now have little information, and I have less than the others. For more than six months I have been living in the midst of the countryside, busy with many things, but not politics, and finding myself very well, it seems, physically and mentally. So far as private information goes, I know not one item which merits to be recorded and dispatched through all those deserts. I see that the eventual loss of Kars and also the conquest of Herat by the Persians are considered unfavorable, especially for the British. But why should I write you about matters which will be ancient history by the time you read this letter?

I received your last two volumes, though I have not yet read them as they arrived at the moment when we were packing to come here, and my maid foolishly put them in a trunk which stayed back in Paris. Thus I cannot send you the expected censure which you seem so much to desire. Otherwise I continue having divided feelings about your work; I dislike the book, and I like the author; and I have trouble, at times, in balancing such opposite sentiments. What I disapprove of in the book I told you before: it is less the work itself than its tendency, which I consider dangerous. If we were to suffer from excessive enthusiasm and self-confidence, as did our ancestors of 1789, I would consider your book a salutary *cold shower*. But we have disgracefully come to the opposite extreme. We have no regard for anything, beginning with ourselves; we have no faith in anything, including ourselves. A book which tries to prove that men in this world are merely obeying their physical *constitutions* and that their will power can do almost nothing to influence their destinies is like opium given to a patient whose blood has already weakened. So much for the book. About the author I must say that he is a man of many talents and that he is a great friend of mine, whom I should like to have as my colleague, which, in turn, forces me to praise the product in order to help its producer. Here is what occurs to me about the *Académie*. Nothing pleases a body of scholars more than a work which is dedicated to them. Could you not—*to be sure, excluding politics*—find a suitable subject for an interesting paper about the laws or the social conditions or the history of one of the nations amidst which you now live? You may send it to me; I shall read it and present it in your name. It should certainly be helpful with the *Institut*, but it must not prejudice your progress elsewhere. Before you begin you should ask yourself very seriously what they would think of it in the Ministry, since you should not sacrifice your principal interests for the secondary ones. In any case, choose a subject about which you cannot be reproached.

I am very pleased with the news of your inheritance. We live in times when money is needed even to do those things that are worth more than money. Money is a thing which we must scorn and have at the same time.

Remember us especially to your amiable traveling companions and believe my sentiments of vivid friendship.

P.S. Write to Paris, where I shall be within three weeks. Send your letter to 19 place de la Madeleine.

—*∼∧∧∧∼*—

XXX

Gobineau about Persia and England; about Asia and Europe

Teheran, 15 January 1856

Monsieur,

Your reproaches have been so kind and affectionate that I despair for having earned them, and yet I am infinitely glad to have them. Meanwhile I think that I wrote as soon as I saw anything about which I could write with conviction. From my last letter you will see that I wrote without waiting for your answer. I shall keep doing this now that I know how interested you are in these parts of Asia.

They certainly merit interest for a number of reasons. And I must say that I fully agree with your principal opinions although I may disagree with you on matters of detail. That Europeans seem destined to dominate, and even possess, this country is beyond doubt. It would come about even if they did not want it. I believe that, rather than remain isolated in Asia, this region would prefer to become part of a Russian sphere of interest. To me the attraction of European power to this empire or, rather, to these tatters of an empire, is as inevitable as if it were a law of physics. On this point we see completely eye to eye. And when I see British India better governed and, I must admit, better off than at any time during the last eight hundred years, by a political and administrative personnel of hardly more than nine hundred Europeans; when in the Persian North I notice the eager and envious attention with which these provinces of the Shah behold their compatriots over the border governed by the Russians; when, finally, I see all of them, Moslems and Indians, from Calcutta to the Turkish frontier, so respectful and fearful of Europeans and so disrespectful of the Turks, who in the past so fully commanded their admiration, I am led to two conclusions. The first, as you very rightly say, is that the Asiatic nations, and especially Persia and India, are not blind but able to understand and to learn. The second conclusion flows from the first: it is that their religious, racial, and educational preconceptions are by no means intractable.

Here are a few humble facts to support the first. I am speaking only of the place where I am and also because Persia is so much more malleable than India. Since the time of the Safawids, which Chardin[1] described, the Persians have learned how to use windows from the Russians and how to wear shoes from us; but for the last fifteen years they have taken to Russian tea and to Russian clothing. Inside and outside the harems they have renounced those dirty habits which the Gardanne mission[2] found so very repulsive. To wear undergarments and to change them frequently has become a general habit, not only in the rich families of Teheran. Even muleteers in the deep country have told me that all except the poorest Persians are ashamed not to change their underwear and their stockings

---

[1] Jean Chardin (1643–1713), judicious French traveler in Persia.

[2] General Gardanne (1766–1817) led a Napoleonic mission to Persia in 1807 in search of an eventual Franco-Persian alliance against Britain and Russia.

(another European importation) at least once, and generally twice, a week. They greatly admire European industry and imitate its products most intelligently. I have seen cloth manufactured in Shiraz which is a perfect imitation of English cotton to the point of weaving the names of the original English manufacturers into the fabric. They are greedy for printed cottons, of which even the smallest village bazaars are full. Here in the streets one hears the lilting cries of merchants, *Kugherta ferenghi!* ("European matches!"), selling only matches made in Vienna. Finally, to speak or to learn French has come to be regarded among the people as the highest personal quality. This we owe to the Russians—and to the Persian mothers. The latter are very ignorant, and yet they seem to push their husbands to give a kind of elegant education to the young, which to them principally consists of speaking French.

I do not see how religion could obstruct these developments. There are some brigands and rogues who will proclaim their hatred for the infidel as a pretext to rob or torture some Armenian; there are mullahs who, to create their own reputation of holiness, will curse intolerantly at any contact with anyone not a Shiite Muslim; there remain a few idiots who consider themselves impure and unable to pray unless they three times rinse a cup used by a European; yet brigands, priests, fanatics, and idiots are found in every country and in every age. During a horrible outbreak in 1828 the mob of the bazaar garroted the entire Russian mission to death as the violent and indecent behavior of the latter had for a long time exasperated the population. Under the pretext of searching for hidden Christians, these Russian gentlemen vexed the Teheranians in a thousand ways and forced the harems, where they behaved in a most brutal manner. A terrible riot ensued and their house was razed. Only one attaché escaped with the help of a mullah, who hid him for eight days in his own house with truly paternal solicitude. The chief of the local priesthood, a highly respected man, a sole imprudent phrase of whom had led to the outbreak of the mob, punished himself by renouncing his position and exiling himself at the holy place of Kerbela, where he remained until his death. To give you a further idea of the popular spirit during this catastrophe, two unfortunate Cossacks of the Russian Legation took refuge in the palace of the British, temporarily unoccupied as the British mission was away. Some of the fanatics pursuing the Cossacks stumbled into a rose bed in the mission's garden. Their companions immediately turned to curse them, protesting loudly that they were not after any Englishman or European but only after the two Russians. The latter were then dragged out of the building and murdered in the street.

So much about the fanatics and the mob. I do not know whether I gave you any religious statistics about the nation. At least one fifth belong to the sect of Ali Illahi, who pretend that Ali is an incarnation of the Divine. Because of some dogmatic resemblance, these people are very cordial to Christians. The number of the Ghebre sect has not diminished, and there is now even quite a rich Ghebre colony in Teheran itself. At the base of all Persian beliefs is magic. The very vividness of their doctrine had much to do with the religious schism separating them from the Turks. Beside the Ghebre are the Sufis, to whom the cultured people belong. Their philosophical inclinations vacillate between ecstasy and atheism. Yet the majority of Persians are indifferent, and at the most one fourth of them may be considered as practicing Mohammedans. As you will understand, in such a divided nation fanaticism is not very frequent. For myself, I have not even seen traces of it.

When I come to their racial prejudices, you must forgive me when I hold forth a bit in a field which I consider my own. There is no such thing as a Persian race in the scientific sense of the word, just as there is no French race any longer; of all the European nations surely we are the ones whose original character has been effaced the most. And it is within this very effacement that we, physically as well as morally, are now claiming to find our own character. The same holds true with the Persians. On a very old Semitic stratum were superimposed Aryan populations, mixing with the earlier inhabitants. Then the Medes and the Persians came to inject new blood; then the Indo-Germanic invasions from Scythia in the north while the Arabs surged into the south. The Parthians again began the struggle for a white ascendancy; they were ultimately submerged by the crescent waves of masses from the south and the west. The Turks, who were white, were followed by swarms of Mongols, who were not; the Mohammedan Arabs then inundated the country once more as far as Bokhara. Finally the Tartars, who are half Finno-Ugrians, returned. Here a perpetual invasion and evolution of racial mixtures has been taking place. I saw in the south people similar to the ancient types of Persepolis; in the north I saw entirely German physiognomies; and even in the smaller cities fully European types in their coloring, stature, carriage, facial and bodily structure (when I say Europe I mean, above all, our great mixed cities). This people has no racial prejudices and cannot have any. Democracy here has been fulfilled. The Ilats, or nomads, consider themselves the noblest of all people, claiming their privileges from the fact that in very ancient times the masters of Persia came from their tribe. This is correct. But, save for a very few exceptions, their blood is not in the least purer than that of the others; and when they are servants they drop some of their ridiculous pretensions. They are more violent than some of their other compatriots; they say that they are less greedy and more honest; and they try very hard to defend themselves from the worst possible reproach here—from the charge of lacking education, of which they themselves are a bit ashamed. They have no other social privileges over the city dwellers; even the members of the royal Qadjar tribe are considered lower than any newcomer who, having some claim to education, having some manners and having a little writing pad hanging on his belt, has the title of a *mirza,* or Writing Man. Well, by now everyone calls himself a mirza; I had to dismiss a stableboy who vaunted himself with his haughty title. Still there exist considerations of nobility, of which there are various kinds. The Sayids, or the descendants of the Prophet, are scattered everywhere in the Musulman world. The title may be acquired through marriage with a Sayid daughter; we have a colleague, Haydar Effendi, the Turkish chargé d'affaires here, who, though a third-generation descendant of a Christian Macedonian, is nevertheless a Sayid because his mother somehow belonged to the tribe of the Koreish. The Persians are quite equalitarian. If a Sayid becomes a common porter, his title helps him not one bit, but if he happens to have wealth, knowledge, and personal respect his title amounts to an ornament. There is also the element of old Arab origin. To belong to an important Turkish tribe as, for example, to the Karagözlü, near Hamadan, is another claim to pride. Yet, I repeat, this by itself does not make men respectable and it does not even facilitate their careers. The last Governor of Ispahan, one of the great Persian administrators, was a domestic servant four years ago. He speaks about his past with great dignity, and he offers his hand to his old servant friends, which astonishes no one here. Meanwhile he would have precedence over any Shah or Prince, were the latter to become indigent. Thus in no way, either tribal or aristocratic, does the Persian nation have any racial prejudices. She is too mixed for that, and she carries her own indifference so far that the numerous Negroes here are considered on a basis of perfect equality.

What goes here under education cannot be called great either in a moral or in a scientific sense. Very few, even among the lower classes, fail to know the elements of reading and writing. Generally people know a little Arabic, enough to understand the common prayers. They know a bit of geography and of Islamic history, about which the lowest porter of a bazaar would put many educated Europeans to shame. He knows the names and the main deeds, real or supposed, of the most famous princes, and at least some traditions about the Prophet; he will recite by heart a number of poems. Add to this a very nice writing hand, the ability to turn a few pretty phrases in letters interlarded with pretentious Arab expressions, and a general sense of business possessed here by everyone else, and you have a mirza. He will probably start by offering the opium pipe to the first person who comes along, yet all the honorable lucrative professions are open to him, and even if he becomes Prime Minister no one will ever question his origins.

The generally weakest part is their moral education. To lie nearly always, to cheat as much as possible, to find sexual inversion natural despite religious laws, to develop a moral carapace of the greediest individualism which ultimately destroys the last traces of patriotism and of every consideration of human affection—except for family ties, which, it must be said, can hardly be closer than they are here—these are the sorry qualities to which Persians, like most Asiatics, have reverted. Let us now look at the attenuating circumstances. In Persia everyone thieves. The city governor robs his administrators and subordinates, who, in turn, rob those around and beneath them. The funds which he collected for the government he largely keeps for himself; but, in order to prepare a good hearing for his eventual pretexts, he pays a sort of pension to the Prime Minister, who, afraid of eventual royal impatience, in turn does his own best to keep those royal lips silent. I tell my servants to do their buying right here, since custom does not permit me to appear in town except on horseback and surrounded by seven or eight houseboys. My man returns, announcing that he paid twenty francs for something worth fifteen. I say: "No, I know that this is only worth fifteen.

I shan't give you a penny more." He disappears, saying that he is going to reason with the merchant. But as I know that the merchant before even trying to sell me anything must pay the guards at the door and the head of the livery servants as well as the head of my domestic servants, I give eighteen francs and everyone is satisfied.

At the same time, no governor or official would ever permit himself to extort money by violence, and highway robbery is almost unknown. (I am not speaking here of some of the mountain tribes of the South, with whom robbery is a warlike action.) Embezzlement is very rare. It is customary to leave rare and precious objects on tables, in open chests and closets in houses with their thirty servants, all of whom cheat in their purchases and in their bills, but who would never touch a diamond left on a table. A dozen times we have left all sorts of valuables in our tents. The tents were guarded at night by poor soldiers, who were often not paid for a year and who were often reduced to eating nothing but melon rinds or cucumber skins. Never did we miss a penny. Dishonesty is, thus, restricted to certain specialties. This distinction is important. The great thing with the Persians is courtesy. Everyone, from peasant to prince, knows the most complicated formulas of address. The great concern of every person and of public opinion is regard for conventions. To be a thief, a drunkard, an infamous liar, is not serious; it is pardonable. But what is inexcusable is not to know the polite forms, and in fact, it is extremely rare to find anyone who does not know them.

I wonder whether I am wrong when I say that this tendency, existing equally in China, India, and here, a tendency which seems to be ascendant even with us (though to a much lesser degree, being still in its infancy), seems characteristic of enervated peoples, where virile sentiment has vanished. To substitute beautiful manners for private and public morality, to permit cruelty as long as it is not accompanied by marks of passion, to tolerate everything as long as all that is ignoble and even odious is cloaked by smiling and pleasant appearances—I confess that I see in this, on one hand, the last word in what is called civilization, but on the other the broad abandonment of those customs which make people repulsive in the true sense of that adjective—that is, physically repulsive as well as making them safe from conquests and subjugations.

I thus believe that the Persians, like the Indians, are ready to pass under European domination and that, even more, they are disposed to adapt themselves to such a future. Consequently it would be the greatest error to consider them similar to the Mohammedan populations on the shores of the Mediterranean. They have nothing in common with them. As you say, the Turks have become bumpkins and blockheads, good for being defeated and cheated, while the others are undisciplined and undisciplinable savages.

The day when the Persian North becomes Russian and the South perhaps British will not be an ordinary day in the history of the world. Its effects, its terrible effects, will not be late in coming. Here the conquerors will find hardy soldiers, easy to lead into battle; they will find dormant and really virgin earth; I saw people hardly scratching it with a bad rake and things soon shooting up. The mountains offer coal of fine quality, superb iron ore, native-made leather with beautiful patterns, sulphur and other minerals. Once these people receive permission together with enforceable protective laws they will develop their material interests as well as do Europeans. I do believe that they will never possess safe judgment, a healthy judiciary, and a reasonable consistency of ideas. I never met an Oriental, however distinguished, who does not have the most curiously incoherent mental processes. It is mainly to this that I attribute their incapacity to govern themselves. In one sentence, they are an intelligent people, they are able to comprehend their own interests in the restricted sense of the word, but they are a people incurably decadent.

Undoubtedly we Europeans shall dominate them, and they will let themselves be ruled. We shall rule them because we have more constancy in our imagination, more energy in our thoughts and, even though we ourselves have fallen far from the level of the white races from whom we descended, we have nevertheless conserved our will power better than have the Orientals. But to rule them will be all that we can do; we shall not be able to assimilate them. They will take from us what they find convenient and let the rest go, and if one of the two conforms to the other I do not doubt that it will be ourselves. We shall descend to their level on every point of contact. Did the Russians perhaps rise to the level of the Germans? Never, but wherever they could they slid down to the level of the Greeks. Once they become the masters of Persia they will do the same, and the result will be a compromise which, for Europeans, will be mere decadence. But will we profit materially at least? Will we be able to live, commercially and financially speaking, at the expense of Asia? Will we nourish ourselves from her substance? No; she will exploit us in the long run as all our ruling qualities fade away and, letting us indulge at our pleasure, she will naturally and thoughtlessly draw profit from those incontestable and *unmatchable* advantages which her own corruption will gradually acquire for her. The Asiatics' rapacious desire for gain, the economic practices of their families, their low level of salaries, their extraordinary sobriety are advantages which we will never be able to equal. Once we have built their roads and taught them how to invest their capital in those manufactures in which they excel, they will give us cotton and silk, agricultural products and everything that we want at such low prices that we will have to abandon the competition. Look at what is already happening to India.

For some time the mother country wished to establish there the supremacy of English capital. Considerable capital was brought together, and the whole enterprise was undertaken with that realistic common sense and energy for which the English are known. In a few years everything was devoured and lost. The whole enterprise floundered. Europeans who do business in India cannot but be agents for the natives; their position is so unfavorable and precarious that their number diminishes each day. Opium is a purely European manufacture in India today, an ephemeral advantage seen by the British themselves, for once the Chinese renounce their impossible customs' laws and decide to cultivate the Indian opium trade they can do that very well and very cheaply indeed. Another European product is indigo, and the indigo plantations are now doing very badly. The rest—factories, agriculture, banks, and commercial firms—are in the hands of the natives to the extent that they profit increasingly more from the traffic between India and Britain. At Jeddah I saw two lovely European-built ships of theirs flying the British flag. An average of forty ships a year call at that port, bringing Indian products to all of Western Arabia. Shipowners, speculators, peddlers, captains, sailors are, all, natives. By protecting them Britain gains nothing. At Aden I visited many shops; perhaps a third contained British wares; the rest were native, German or Swiss. Who owned the shops? Parsees; there is not one British shop in Aden; the same in Muscat, the same in Bushire, the same in Shiraz.

Here people use British cottons but they buy them from natives. As they are not too durable, they are not much wanted by the richer classes. My servants wear nothing but Persian products, which, because of the lack of roads and transport difficulties, are a little more expensive but incomparably more beautiful. The Russians sell German cloth and sugar here. But the day the Russians will be masters of this country rich with sheep and with wonderful wool, under the Russian flag the natives will export woolens so beautiful and cheap that we shall not be able to compete with them. Every Persian wants to see Europe, for they know about the wealth and security which they have been unable to create in their own house (I am repeating myself here for the last time). Let us be on our guard. Their great admiration for our material welfare is bound to their immense capacity of production and with the quantity of silk, of cotton, of sugar cane, of coffee in their South; once they begin to produce they will sell all these things to us. Now that we are adapting ourselves more and more to the maxim that "To eat well, to drink well, to dress well, and to live well is the supreme aim of humanity"—watch out! The ancient nations of Asia believe this, too, but they have been impressed with it deeper and longer than we have been. We shall teach them new procedures in that great art, but not much time will pass and it will be they who will give or sell us their lessons, meanwhile leaving to us all the burdens and the vainglories of government. After Greece conquered Asia Minor she sank in the quicksands of Asia Minor. After Rome conquered Asia Minor and Greece, her victories gradually suffocated her. After we Europeans become the masters of Asia we shall, like young men from good families, find there a caretaker who will introduce us to vices yet unknown to us which will make us sink down. When I see all that great interest in the opening of China, in getting involved with that ancient and voracious people, I confess that I should wonder why the possible consequences of this new camaraderie are not better examined, were it not that I may have lost the capacity to wonder at all.

Adieu, monsieur. My wife and Diane are grateful for the affectionate interest you have for them and from the height of their Asiatic glories they send their warmest regards to you and to Mme. de Tocqueville. Pray add my homages to theirs. You mention the *Institut*, about which I did not want to burden you in my first letter though I did so in the second. I am touched and indebted by your solicitude and I am awaiting the omnipotent effects of so generous an intervention. Yet you know that my devotion to you is independent of further indebtedness. Nevertheless, I hope for success, partly for the honors it may bring me and partly for other serious reasons. Think of me once in a while; I shall write again soon. No one is more deeply devoted and more respectfully attached to you than am I.

XXXI

Gobineau about the decline of the West

Teheran, 20 March 1856

Monsieur,

Your letters are sources of great pleasure and, at the same time, they put me in a constant state of perplexity. Before I turn to the latter I wish to thank you most gratefully for my nomination; I am doing what you had advised. With Adolphe d'Avril I am sending you today a paper about Persia for the *Académie*.[1] But, as you suggested, I shall also ask M. de Walewski's[2] permission. Although there is no actual politics in it, you are right in that such a permission may be necessary. I cannot ask my highest superior directly, for I would have to wait too long for an answer. The answer will therefore reach you, or so I hope, through a chain of intermediaries, among whom Mme. de

[1] This paper may be permanently lost.
[2] Count Alexandre Colonna Walewski (1810–1868), Napoleon's illegitimate son, twice Foreign Minister of France.

Kergorlay[3] will be the last. Again I thank you from the bottom of my heart.

I understand your reproach for not having answered all of your questions directly. I shall do so in the future. Yet I am much dependent on the thread of observations which I am following at the very moment when I write you; and when I think they might interest you I write without exercising much selectivity. Let me tell you that I am overwhelmed with the exorbitance of my impressions here. The result is disorder. I feel that I keep repeating myself and that I do not classify my impressions. I may be writing you about the same things twice as I forget that I have related them earlier. These are the hazards of this kind of research, so full of incoherent matters. But another issue torments me more. It is your constant reproach that I am weakening the power of already considerably drowsy nations. If I am doing that at all, I am certainly not doing it by humming nursery songs. Mérimée writes that there are people who want to devour me or at least to burn me alive. Maury, your librarian of the *Institut*, assures me that he has treated me badly in an article of the *Athenaeum*, and he tells me the most injurious things with that friendly good humor which is at the bottom of his character. If I am corrupting at all, I corrupt with acids and not with perfumes. Believe me that this is not at all the purpose of my book. I am not telling people: "*You are acquitted*" or "*You are condemned*"; I tell them: "*You are dying.* Far from me to pretend that you are incapable of conquering or unable to be moved and transported by sporadic spurts of energy. I neither impede nor do I push you. This does not concern me in the least. What I say is that you have spent your youth and that you have now reached the age of decline. Your autumn is more vigorous, undoubtedly, than has been the decrepitude of the rest of the world, but

[3] The wife of Tocqueville's earliest, and perhaps dearest, friend.

it is autumn nonetheless; the winter will come and you will
have no children. Establish kingdoms, dynasties, republics,
whatever you want; these things may be possible. I am not
opposing you. Go disturb the Chinese in their home, polish
off the Turks, drag the Persians into your schemes; these
things may be possible and even inevitable. I shall not contradict you, but in the final account, the causes of your
enervation are gathering and they will continue to gather
by these very actions. And no one in the world will replace
you when your degeneration is completed. That thirst for
material pleasures now tormenting you is a positive symptom. It is a sure symptom, like the roseate cheeks of those
who suffer from the maladies of the chest. All civilizations
in decline before you had it and, like you, they seem to
have enjoyed it. I am not inclined to read the journalistic
phrases on these subjects. After all, can I still do something
here? By telling you what is happening and what is going
to happen, am I taking something away from you? I am
not a murderer; neither is the doctor who announces the
coming of the end. If I am wrong, nothing will remain of
my four volumes. If I am right, the facts will not be subdued by the desire of those who do not want to face them."

I follow with great interest the impression which my book
produced in different places. In Germany, where, generally speaking, people are more concerned with intrinsic
truths than we are, it seems that they are a little shocked
but that they are very interested. I gained valuable friendships there. In France people are asking whether I am a
royalist, a republican, an imperialist, for or against the
Univers,[4] but all of them are perplexed because I have not
proved that the French are the leading people in the world.
Had I proved this to the British, I think they could have
made something of it, but what purpose would it serve in
France? It seems to me that people in Paris have convinced

[4] The famous right-wing Catholic paper edited by Louis
Veuillot.

themselves to the point where they cannot be contradicted.

In America the results are more curious than anywhere else. Three distinguished persons whom I did not previously know honored me by writing. One of them translated the entire systematic argument of the volume and requests my opinion about a second edition, ready to be published as soon as the first is exhausted. I have not seen the first, but from what he says, he kept the essential parts of my thesis about the perennial existence of races and about the effects of miscegenation. He did not dare to present to the public the part about the inevitable consequences. He did not want to tell them how, from the moment that two races are inequal, marriage with an inferior race means immediate degeneration. At the same time, I detect that he did not suppress the superiority of the American Anglo-Saxons over the Mexican race and that this proposition has been accepted without trouble. What he surely did not translate was my chapter on the United States. Nevertheless, he writes me that even the abolitionist newspapers recognized the exactitude of my principles. Despite all of these alterations and incoherencies, that very practical nation succeeded in fashioning from a purely scientific theory a political weapon which the contending parties now hurl at each other. This does not disturb me, but what disturbs me is that you, monsieur, who do like me, maintain a reserve about the very morality of my concepts. What can I say to you? If truth and morality are not connected, I shall be the first to agree that my book is devoid of the latter, but then it is also devoid of anti-morality, as are geology, medicine, archaeology. My book is research, exposition, presentation of facts. These facts exist or they don't. There is nothing else to say.

I shall not write about Persia today, as there is much about it in the paper which I enclose. In a few weeks I hope to finish a philological book which should form an appendix illustrating my main work. For, having raised the flag of revolt against antiquated historical theses, I shall go to the end and I shall not abandon those men who have come with me. As I have told you, there are great treasures here: manuscripts, inscribed stones, archaeological finds, medals, all of which serve my purposes, all to the good. But, damn it! if I am correct in believing that you do not share my viewpoint I still do not want you to condemn me for sins I have not committed, and at the same time I shall not rest satisfied with generous silence. Please look at my facts directly. And please look at the people to whom my doctrines apply. Is it possible to draw a spark from old pieces of hide? Adieu, monsieur; our fondest possible affections go to you and to Mme. de Tocqueville. Remember us together with my respectful devotion, which you know so well.

XXXII

Gobineau about the impact of his book

Teheran, 1 May 1856

Monsieur,

By now you probably have my paper that you so generously suggested for the *Académie des sciences morales et politiques*. From a letter by Adolphe d'Avril[1] it seems that the authorization of the Ministry will be granted. I shall certainly be pleased.

I am somewhat annoyed, though not really hurt, by the

[1] Gobineau's friend, later known for his early diplomatic history of the Congress of Berlin (1878).

slowness with which knowledge about the existence of my book and its principal tenets spreads in France. From America I received my first translation, commented and annotated by a Mr. Hotz of Montgomery and by a Dr. Nott of Mobile,[2] together with some letters which indicate that they are taking it really seriously. In Germany a writer I do not know complains in an article in an Augsburg paper about the frequent employment of my ideas without reference being made to their source, which means that they must be interested in them; I am also told that a book is about to appear which will elaborate my thesis; I receive similar notices from England and from Switzerland, while at home they remain rather indifferent. I know that you will not regard me thirsty for praise. You are perhaps more inclined to think that I am thirsty for combat. Neither one nor the other is really true. But I wish that they would discuss my book seriously in my own country. I know only too well where the silence comes from. It is not much to our credit. The French, who are always ready to set anything afire—materially speaking—who respect nothing either in religion or in politics, have always been the world's poorest when it comes to scientific matters. Everything that is new fills them with a strange fear, to the point where they do not even want to attack a new theory, since they are afraid even of touching it. Thus did it happen that though they had no natural inclinations to Protestantism they let it establish itself everywhere during the sixteenth

[2] Josiah Clark Nott (1804–1873) was a pro-slavery doctor and "ethnographer." This early American Gobineau edition is now almost extinct. It was published in 1856 in Philadelphia with the title *The moral and intellectual diversity of races, with particular reference to their respective influence on the civil and political history of mankind. With an analytical introduction and copious historical notes by H. Hotz, to which is added an appendix containing a summary of the latest scientific facts bearing upon the question of the unity or plurality of species, by J. C. Nott.*

century. They toyed with it; they ridiculed it; in the beginning they even approved of it a little; they became disgusted with it and, not knowing how to combat it, they felt they could resort to nothing but civil war—when, had they acted in time, a few able men would have been enough to convince everybody how incompatible were the aims of that new movement with the national spirit. The same thing happened to science. From the great to the little, the same things are happening now. For wanting to be such revolutionaries we are not even capable of being innovators.

Thus I am asking for your protection. Knowing that you do not approve of it, it would be very bad form if I were to ask that you defend my book, but this is not at all what I want; what I want is that my thesis be discussed and that I be given an opportunity to demonstrate that I am right. But if they are not discussing my work, to me this is like receiving unearned praise. Do I have to wait until my opinions come back to France retranslated from English or from German? I know that there have been some examples of this, but I would do anything to avoid such an unnecessary handicap.

I should like it very much if you could talk about this with M. Mérimée. I am writing him today, after having sent him some, I am afraid, excessive details about Afghanistan. And here is another idea. General von Prokesch-Osten announced at the Vienna Academy of Sciences, of which he is a member, that he proposes to submit a critique of my historical philosophy. To this they consented because of his prestige, remarking though that this is a departure from their usual procedures. Last year M. de Rémusat promised to do almost the same at the *Académie des sciences morales et politiques*. I doubt whether he has done it. M. Mignet was kind enough to press him. Rémusat promised it to me, yet I do not doubt that his spiritual inclinations must have filled him with a certain reserve, "for,"

he said to me, "if what you say is true, I prefer that someone else should affirm it." I know that if you were to assume
this task instead, you would not fear the new character of
my doctrine. Nothing, then, remains to make me perfectly
happy but to see you convinced by my recent argument
to the effect that morality is not engaged in our debate and
that my own method of history is exactly as much opposed
to evil as are the methods of Tacitus and of Thucydides,
while it sheds a little more light on the causes. I confess
that I am powerfully attracted by this idea of seeing my
work illuminated by your lucid mind. To whom else could
I turn?

Farewell, monsieur. We are attached to you in Teheran,
as in Frankfurt, as in Paris. All is well with us; I hope to
camp at Hamadan within a fortnight. When I shall be able
to talk to you about ancient Ecbatana, about Kurds, and
about all these things I do not yet know. Pray present my
devoted homage to Mme. de Tocqueville and accept my
most respectful and devoted affections.

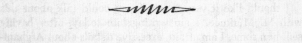

XXXIII

*Tocqueville about the fatalistic and anti-Chris-
tian fallacy of racial theories*

Tocqueville, par Saint-Pierre Église (Manche)
30 July 1856

This is a much delayed letter, my dear friend; I am certain
that you will forgive my long silence once you know about
the sad event which caused it. You may have heard about

my great misfortune of losing my father about the same time that your paper arrived and that I received your last letter, the one of May 1st. You may have seen enough of our family life and of the place which our good and dear father occupied in it to understand what a terrible tragedy his loss has brought to us. Almost immediately after his death we left Paris and came down to enclose ourselves in this retreat from where I am now writing.

Let me turn to you. Your paper interested me very much, and I do not doubt that it will produce the same effects on the *Académie*. It has already produced it on Mignet, who volunteered to read it in my absence. He could not do this yet because of the accumulation of overdue lectures, but I think that it will not be long delayed. All these details must be known to you from the letters of d'Avril, who continues to prove a truly devoted friend of yours. What he will not tell you is my own disappointment of being unable to read the paper myself and to have it preceded, as I had planned, by a short introduction about the author. The reasons for this inability are, alas, too evident.

Yet I confess that even without these reasons I should have been somewhat embarrassed to introduce within the body of the *Académie* the discussion which you desire. I could not do it without strongly attacking your ideas, something which I find quite repugnant. You know that I cannot reconcile myself to your theses in any way and my thoughts are so much *obsessed* on this point that the very reasons with which you are trying to make them more acceptable tend to confirm my opposition even more, an opposition which remains *latent* only because of my personal affection for you. In your penultimate letter you compare yourself to a physician who announces to his patient that he is mortally ill. You ask: What is immoral in that? My answer is that even though this act in itself may not be immoral, its consequences assuredly are most immoral and pernicious. If one of these mornings my doctor were to say to me: "My dear sir, I have the honor to announce that you are mortally ill and, inasmuch as all of your vital organs are affected, I must add that there is absolutely no chance for you to recover," my first temptation would be to knock that doctor down. Thereafter I should think I would have no choice but either to pull the covers over myself and wait for the announced end or, if I possessed the temper which animated the circle of Boccaccio during the Florentine plague, to think of nothing else but to sample all the possible pleasures before this inevitable end, to burn, as they say, the candle at both ends. Or again, I could profit from this doctor's sentence by preparing myself for eternal life. But societies do not have eternal lives. Thus your doctor will certainly not number me among his clients. I must add that physicians, like philosophers, are often greatly mistaken in their prognostications; I have seen more than one person condemned by physicians who nevertheless became quite well subsequently and who angrily criticized the doctor for having uselessly frightened and discouraged him. Thus you will see, my dear friend, that though I am much disposed to admit the talents of the author I cannot uphold the validity of his ideas. Since I sincerely wish to attract attention to you I shall nonetheless do my best to bring about either a eulogy or at least a good critique by one of our colleagues. In the subsequent discussion I shall gladly insert a word which, though it may register my reserve about the book's thesis, will much emphasize the author's merits. But these things one cannot do from afar, and we will have to wait for their realization until winter.

You justly rankle at the silence with which your book is being treated in France. But it would be wrong for you to be much affected by this, since the main source of this silence lies in those general causes which I have already indicated to you and which do not at all diminish your stature. There is no place in France today for alive and enduring interest in any sort of intellectual achievement. Our temper, so intellectual, especially during the past two centuries, is now going through a transformation which is manifest in lassitude, in disenchantment, in a dislike of ideas, in a love of statistics. This is caused by our political conditions. The present ruling class does not read and does not even know the names of writers. Now that it no longer plays a part in politics, literature has fallen in the eyes of the masses. How can you, then, expect a book like yours, full of transcendent philosophy, in four erudite volumes, to disturb the deep, lethargic somnolence which is now weighing down the French spirit? Twenty years ago people might have regarded your theses as a means of attacking the Church, and this (beyond the scientific merits of your book) would have furnished you with propagandists as well as with readers. But you must, of course, know how we have now become extremely devout. Every day the pastor of our village upholds from the pulpit the Christian virtues of the Emperor, his faith, his charity and the rest . . . as an example . . .[1] Granier de Cassagnac has become a communicant.[2] What else can I say? At this time when we are more exclusively than ever preoccupied with the material goods of this earth we advance every day along this road of sanctimoniousness. I assure you that even Mérimée himself, who boasts among intimates of not having been baptized, would not dare to publicly propose doctrines like yours. For it should be recognized that, despite the pat on the back you give to the Church and though you, perhaps in good faith, make great efforts not to put yourself outside her pale, the very essence of your theses is hostile to the Church. And nearly every one of the consequences that may be drawn from your theses are more or less opposed to her doctrines. Therefore you will find in France many people who will tell you, like Rémusat: "I

---

[1] The interruption occurs in the original manuscript.
[2] Bernard Adolphe Granier de Cassagnac (1806–1880), an intelligent but unscrupulous political and journalistic adventurer.

believe in what you say, but I prefer not to be the one to proclaim it," and you will hardly find anyone willing to champion you. Therefore I think that your book is fated to return to France from abroad, especially from Germany. Alone in Europe, the Germans possess the particular talent of becoming impassioned with what they take as abstract truths, without considering their practical consequences; they may furnish you with a truly favorable audience whose opinions will sooner or later re-echo in France, for nowadays the whole civilized world has become one. If in Britain and in America your book will meet with interest, the interest will only echo the ephemeral views of partisans. For those Americans whom you mention and who translated your book are known to me as perfervid leaders of the anti-abolitionist party. They translated the part of your book which suits their prejudices, the part which tends to prove that the Negroes belong to another, to a different and inferior race; but they suppressed the part which tends to argue that, like every other, the Anglo-Saxon race is also decaying. A book of real merit such as yours is destined to evoke considerable interest in the thoughts of thinkers of every nation but, except perhaps for Germany, it is not destined to interest the mass of readers in whose minds not more than the name may register.

You will know that I myself have returned to my writing profession in spite of the sad events I mentioned before. I have asked d'Avril to send you a copy of my book.[3] Until now I have certainly no reason to complain either of the public or of the press. Yet you will credit me with enough sense to know that I have illusions about this sort of success. I have written a short book; I took the only subject which even now is capable of electrifying public opinion to a certain degree, and which subject one is still permitted to discuss: the French Revolution. Until now its more visible

[3] *The Old Regime and the Revolution,* published a few weeks before.

history has been shown; I have turned it around to show what was beneath it. Certain passions, still alive, have grasped the occasion to attack or to praise me, from which a certain amount of noise has resulted. But I know very well that the readers interested in my book are those who are even more interested in the latest information on stock dividends. I am anxious to have your opinion about this book, which, even if it does not give me a durable reputation, has at least helped me to pass difficult times and to transform into good years the always so hard passage from an active career to retirement. I have come to enjoy very much the life which I am now leading; it is so salutary for my mind and health that I would find it difficult to abandon it if this were necessary. Having departed from politics both agitated and ill, particularly in the beginning I would have had a rather rough time had I not prepared this long writing task which has not only occupied but in a way electrified me. Here I am at the end of the ninth page. I shall not conclude without a cordial embrace for you and without asking that you remember us to Mme. de Gobineau. Rest assured that when I return to Paris I shall not forget your desire for an Academic discussion. I hope to bring it about. In your turn, write me please once in a while. Your letters give me great pleasure. Will your duties bring you closer soon?

A thousand good wishes.

XXXIV

Gobineau insists on his Catholicism

Teheran, 29 November 1856

Monsieur,

Despite the immense pleasure which your letters always bring me, I waited a long time before answering your last though I wanted to answer it perhaps more than I did any other. Do not, please, reproach me. The roughest and most perilous phase of my Asian adventures has just been concluded. Mme. de Gobineau had become expectant and abandoned at the same time by her French maid; it was impossible for us to stay here. So we took off for the Russian frontier. After sixteen days of fortunate traveling we passed through a region full of streams and Diane was struck with malaria. With great difficulty we brought her to Tabriz, where for twenty-five days she remained closer to death than to life; I leave you to imagine how we felt and how we lived. In the end God restored her to us. I took my family beyond the Araxes, into Russian territory; I have a letter from Tiflis which tells me that Diane is very well; and, thanks to an incomparable friend, General Prokesch-Osten, I hope that by now my wife and my daughter are safely in Constantinople, from where they shall continue to Paris. Meanwhile I returned here in fourteen days, dragging with me, my civil and military household who were hardly in a state to follow: while Diane absorbed all my thoughts, eighteen of the twenty-two men in my caravan were ill; one died, the wife of the British Consul of Teheran died; the maid whose desertion was the primary cause of all these troubles also died, and my Persian caretaker has not yet recovered. However, I am finally back and here I am now in charge of everything, all alone except for a dragoman; the rest of the legation, including all European servants, are either dead or have returned to France. I confess that, except for missing my family, I do not suffer much from solitude. Essentially I get along very well with the Persians, Afghans, and Parsees with whom I am living; the only result is that I neither speak nor hear French except when the Russians come to see me, which is not a great tragedy. The Persians greatly appreciate the way in which I live and treat them, and as I am the first diplomatist since Darius who has spoken and dealt with them directly without an interpreter they tell me how much they like me and they shower me with cordialities.

I read your book with an eagerness you can well imagine, and I left it in Tabriz with a man of rare intellectual distinction, M. de Khanikoff,[1] the Russian Consul-General, who was insistent in asking me for it. Since you allowed me to discuss it I shall do so, but first of all let me answer a phrase in your letter which concerns my own opinions. It is necessary that I clarify this point, for it is closely related to what I want to speak about.

It seems to me that you are inclined, if not to doubt, then at least to suspend judgment on the real portent of the statements about Catholicism in my book. It seems that in this respect I may not have been clear enough, which I regret; if, on one hand, Professor von Ewald, the illustrious Hebraist,[2] accuses me of being an initiate of the Jesuits— which he does, I must say, in very courteous terms—another gentleman, whose name now escapes me, says in the

[1] Nikolai Vladimirovich Khanikov (1822–1879), Russian diplomatist and Orientalist, friend of Gobineau.
[2] Georg Heinrich August von Ewald (1803–1875), a German Orientalist and philologist, later a bitter anti-Catholic.

Journal des débats that I am a materialist; again, others, like yourself, incline to believe that I am yielding to the present mode of ideas and that my religion has no consequences.

How can you, who know me so well, entertain such doubts? Does this seem in line with my character? Am I really a man who would pay lip service to opinions which he knows to be false or am I not, rather, too much inclined to attack everything that to me does not seem quite true? What is my *Essai sur les races* if not proof that I am not afraid and that I do not accept the commonplaces and the ideas so dearly held by our century? Do you think that I would stoop so low as to construct cowardly excuses— which, incidentally, were not in the least required of me— for monstrous statements which I did not at all make? No: when I say that I am a Catholic, it is because that is what I am. Not, certainly, a perfect Catholic, which I regret and which I desire to become one day; when I say Catholic I mean entirely Catholic, with my heart and with my mind. And if I ever thought, like you, that this is incompatible with my historical philosophy I would immediately abandon the latter. True, I used to be a rationalist, a Hegelian, an atheist. I have never been afraid to go to the very end of the road. It is through its terminal gates that I left these doctrines that open into emptiness, to re-enter into the realm of doctrines having value and substance. Beyond these metaphysical reasons I have had two more, and I should even say three, were it not that the third is hardly of interest to you since it is merely personal. Here are the two others. M. de Rémusat, who has at times influenced me in a certain way which he probably did not at all expect, told me one day: "You are a typical product of your age: you are an anti-Christian with feudalist ideas." This observation, the irony of which is quite just, struck me deeply, and I have often thought it over. Not because I should have pretensions of systematic coherence, which does not quite seem to me a quality attainable by men (at least not perfectly), but because I naturally do not like to witness obvious contradictions within me. The question is whether in the end I should cease to regard feudal liberty as the most maligned and worst understood matter by generations no longer worthy of it or whether I should not rather discard Feuerbach and the others whose political doctrines fill me with horror. This was my first reason.

The second one is this. Since I have not merely visualized but actually seen the revolution,[3] those dirty shirts disgusted me so much and led me to so exaggerate, if you wish, my notions of what is just and what is true that, had I not been married, I should have been capable of becoming a monk in order to take the diametrically opposed road. And this was only the preparatory stage. My very active life brought the rest gradually, and now Asia has been the capstone. Here one is reminded of prayer every day. Life is full of dangers. Philosophical opinions which may be good enough at the fireplace are very sterile when one is on horseback in the desert. This is why I am very sincerely, very completely, very profoundly Catholic; and while, to my deep regret, I confess that though there are no empty areas in my faith, there are lacunae in my behavior; I feel that, were I pushed only a little more by people and by circumstances, I could come to the point where I would be regarded a veritable fanatic by the anti-Catholic party.

Because of these things your book gave me the greatest pleasure. Though you did not say so, I saw that you are disposed to consider the fourteenth, fifteenth, and sixteenth centuries an era of transition, that is, of decomposition: that in those centuries, of which the last is so stupidly praised for its political achievements, every one of the previously so free institutions (yes, I say free and stable and well-entrenched ones) was destroyed by legalists, by royal

[3] Reference to the Revolution of 1848.

power, and by nascent democracy. You have shown admirably that the French Revolution invented nothing and that its friends and its enemies are equally wrong in attributing to it such things as return to Roman law, centralization, government by committees, the absorption of private rights within the singular powers of the State, and I do not know what else. You have shown the omnipotence of the State or, what is worse, the general belief that this is to the good. You say very well that the notion of *public utility*, which can in a day force anyone out of his house if the engineers so decide;[4] that the situation in which everyone finds this quite natural, with monarchists as well as republicans considering such a monstrosity a right of society—you say very well that this antedates 1789, and you have given such solid proofs that after you it is no longer possible to write the history of the Revolution in the way it has been done up to now. In brief, they will come to agree that the father of the revolutionaries was Philippe le Bel.[5]

But because all of this is so clear to me and because you have made it even more evident, allow me to ask you what it is that you find so admirable in the Constituent Assembly of 1789? They did not invent any of the ideas that are commonly attributed to them. You make this brilliantly clear. They only precipitated the ruin of those who had resisted the final affirmation of those ideas of which you yourself certainly do not approve. These ideas would have come about in any case, in a gradual manner, and their complete application was inevitable. What these gentlemen did was to open the door to violence and to every democratic atrocity. Could they even erect a temporary dam before the torrential elements which they let loose?

[4] Reference to the then novel concept of public utility, to the prospective expropriation and purchase of private properties for railroads and highways.

[5] Philippe IV, le Bel, ruled 1285–1314, considered by some the first modern national monarch and centralizer of power.

Not at all. After remaining in session for two years, they arrived at the sorriest lucubrations which the world has ever seen, at an inapplicable constitution; they then dissolved while committing the grossest blunders which a political body has ever committed in history. So why do you have any sympathy for these people? They invented nothing; they resisted nothing; they foresaw nothing; they made phrases, and their actions consisted in opening the gates for things they did not want—or what I credit at least some of them for not having wanted. But since they shouted about tyranny when there was no tyranny—as you so profoundly show—since they gesticulated with clubs to kill a few flies; since they wound up by disastrously repeating every one of the wrongs which had been committed in what at least was a more tranquil manner before they came in— I do not see the sense of showing any interest in them. Moreover, I confess that I see something very vile in this assembly which applauded the first violences, the mad comedy of the capture of the Bastille, the first massacres, those burnings of the castles. Simply because they did not see that it was all of their own making and that their own heads would soon be cut off, do you think that these wrongs done may be qualified by saying that these were generous mistakes? Why *generous?* I certainly hate the Montagnards more than I do the Constituent Assembly, but I am not sure whether the former are most despicable than are the latter, and of the Girondins I am sure that they are the most despicable of all.

These are the primary reflections which I wish to submit to you. There remains another point which struck me. You, very justly, observe in your preface that with your love for free institutions you separate yourself from those who do not consider them practical because of the low opinion in which they hold their fellow citizens. It seems to me difficult to qualify by free institutions the mere mechanism superimposed on a society such as ours. A people like ours that, whether under the Republic, representative government or the Empire, will always maintain an immoderate desire for the intervention of the State in all of its affairs, that will be passively obedient to the gendarmerie, to the tax collector, to the surveyor, to the engineer, a people that does not understand true municipal administration, and to which absolute and irrevocable centralization is the last word, such a people will not only never have free institutions but will not even understand what they are. In essence, it will always have the same government under different names and, because of this, it would be better if this government, always the same in principle, should in practice be as direct as possible. Do you remember the times I had the honor to work under you in the Foreign Ministry? What lovely problems we had to face! When all Europe was aflame, when your work was so urgent night and day, everything had to be dropped to prepare an answer to the interpellation of a M. Savoye, of a miserable party hack! What did public liberty gain by that? When the Austrians threatened to break their armistice with Piedmont and march on Turin and you wrote that beautiful and courageous dispatch[6] which I shall never forget, didn't you perhaps expect to be absolutely disavowed by the majority of the Assembly and to be obliged to resign? What does liberty or what does national honor gain from such a form of government, if not the deadliest exigencies of parliamentary politicking, which means the most narrow-minded questions, worse than the worst kind of royal suspicions? People cloaking themselves in what they call collective responsibility, which means no responsibility at all? Had there been two chambers instead of one, it would have been

[6] This was the Boislecomte dispatch by Tocqueville, dated 25 July 1849, to the then French Minister to Piedmont. One of the great state papers of diplomatic history, it is reprinted in Tocqueville's *Souvenirs*.

the same thing, and contrary to M. d'Haussonville,[7] there are more things to be criticized in the foreign policy during the reign of Louis Philippe than he says. To sum up, I do not see any reason to give the title "free institutions" to any of the forms which the French nation, composed as she is, has granted during the past five hundred years or will continue granting her governments. Whether outbursts of anarchy or of perennial despotism, the question is merely the clothes they wear; I prefer black clothes to shirt sleeves and lace to black. It is this black worsted which gave us the present spirit of France.

You see that I have a very angry temper. This is why I submit my protestations to you. You must forgive me by recalling the respect and the devotion which you know I have for you.

XXXV

Tocqueville about the incompatibility of Christianity with doctrines of race

Tocqueville, 14 January 1857

Your letter of 29 November, which I received about a month ago, has certainly touched me deeply, my dear friend. What a terrible journey! My worst voyages are child's play compared to it. Were it not that I received a letter from d'Avril at the same time, informing me of the fortunate arrival of Mme. de Gobineau and of your daugh-

---

[7] The Count Joseph d'Haussonville (1809–1884) wrote a conservative *History of French Foreign Policy from 1830 to 1848.*

ter, I confess that your letter would not have assured me
yet. I must say that I cannot understand how the cause
which you describe could make you decide to precipitate
your wife and your daughter into the perils of such a journey, in the middle of which you knew you had to leave
them. I admire the temerity of Mme. de Gobineau, and I
am happy and almost surprised at the success of her
bravery. I now consider Mlle. Diane immortal. Your friends
can tell you how much concerned I had been to see her
leave. I admit that, knowing the frequent effects of the
Orient on travelers of her age, I wondered whether I would
see this charming child again, and that the image of M.
de Lamartine's daughter[1] had occupied my imagination as
I waved you farewell. But now she is safe from these dreadful dangers—many thanks to God.

You have taken indeed seriously I do not know what
facetious remark I may have made about your religion.
This proves that one should not joke with friends who are
three deserts and three oceans away, since in such a case
a misunderstanding of a single word might not be corrected
in less than a year's time. No, my dear friend, calm yourself; I have never taken you for a black hypocrite; as you
say, I know you too well to have ever had such an opinion
of you. God save me from that! I have taken you for one
of those people, numerous in past and present and numerous even during the centuries of faith, who venerate the
Christian religion and who are loyally devoted to it without unfortunately being absolutely convinced Christians. In
such a spiritual state one does not consider oneself a hypocrite by paying many respects to such a generous and
saintly religion (I am at least using religion in the sense
in which it is one of the greatest instruments of morality
and civilization which God ever decided to employ). Many

---

[1] Reference to Julie de Lamartine, the poet's only daughter,
who died of a sudden illness during an Oriental journey at the
age of ten.

of the finest minds of modern times have certainly been
hypocrites in this way: I am speaking of those, above all,
who have professed doctrines which to them seemed true
but which to them, too, seemed contrary to Christian
dogma and consequently dangerous to the souls of the remaining faithful if no efforts are made to mitigate such
detrimental results. I put you among these rascals. Forgive
me. I admit that I could not believe how you could fail
to see the difficulty of reconciling your scientific theories
with the letter and with the spirit of Christianity. About
the letter: what is clearer in Genesis than the unity of the
human race and the descent of all men from the same an-
cestor? About the spirit: is it not its unique trait to have
abolished those racial distinctions which the Jewish religion still retained and to have made therefrom but one human race, all of whose members are equally capable of
improving and uniting themselves? How can this spirit—
and I am trying to use plain common sense—be reconciled
with a doctrine that makes races distinct and unequal, with
differing capacities of understanding, of judgment, of action, due to some original and immutable disposition which
invisibly denies the possibility of improvement for certain
peoples? Evidently Christianity wishes to make all men
brothers and equals. Your doctrine makes them cousins at
best whose common father is very far away in the heavens;
to you down here there are only victors and vanquished,
masters and slaves, due to their different birthrights. This
is obvious, since your doctrines are being approved, cited,
commented upon by whom? by slaveowners and by those
who favor the perpetuation of slavery on the basis of radical
differences of race. I well know that right now there are in
the south of the United States Christian pastors and perhaps
even good priests (though they are slaveowners) who
preach from their pulpit doctrines which are undoubtedly
analogous with yours. But be assured that the majority of
Christians, consisting of those whose interests do not sub-

consciously incline them toward your ideas—be assured, I say, that the majority of Christians of this world cannot have the least sympathy for your doctrines. I am not even speaking of those materialistic opinions which, according to you, do not exist in your book. This may be so, but it is certain that the materialism of many people will nonetheless gain strength from it. Thus I confess that the reading of your book left doubts in me about the solidity of your faith, and that I have irreverently placed you among those men whose doubts do not keep them from treating Christianity with a true and profound respect and who do not believe that they are hypocritical when they endeavor to make their ideas as compatible as possible with the latter. You tell me that I am in error and that you have become an absolutely convinced Christian. May Heaven hear you! You will be the happiest man in this world, not to speak of the one hereafter; of this I am profoundly convinced, and you may be certain that no one will rejoice more in seeing you persevere along this road than I. Alas! it is not a road open to every mind; many who are sincerely searching for it did not yet have the good fortune of finding it. If I spoke badly (I do not recall it now) about the devout, it is only because I am revolted every day when I see petty people in their gossipy circles with their foolish affairs who are capable of every sort of despicable and violent action talking devoutly of their *holy religion*. I am always tempted to shout at them: "Rather than be Christians of this kind, be pagans with pure conduct, proud of your soul and with clean hands!"

I am descending from these levels to a very minor subject, to the *Institut*. I find that your chances are very good. Until recently our plans seemed to have had nearly insurmountable difficulties. Entry into the *Académie des sciences morales et politiques* must come through a section. The two logical sections for you, philosophy and history, seemed to me hardly accessible for many reasons which are too long

to be explained here. But a new state of things has arisen
to give you very good chances. A year ago an almost invisible little *coup d'état* was directed against the *Institut*,
and particularly against the *Académie des sciences morales
et politiques*. We were saddled with ten additional colleagues under the name of a section of politics. Villemain[2]
calls them the *garrison*, since they have entered the citadel
by force in order to keep us under their eyes. As very few
of these unacademic academicians have been *elected* according to the usual rules, we do not consider them colleagues and we show them little regard. But the same
sentiments do not prevail for those members of the section
who will be elected at each occasion of vacancy. A number
of corresponding members, ten I think, have been created
who will be elected and not nominated. Our plan would
be to make you one of them. If the section presents you,
you will be probably elected as we would have a majority
for you within the *Académie*. The requirements are so
broad that I cannot see how your study would not qualify
in one way or another. The problem now is to be presented
by the section. To Rémusat and to myself M. Lefèvre[3]
seems to be the natural intermediary. D'Avril must have
told you that, on our advice, he saw Lefèvre and was much
pleased with him. Rémusat is very well disposed. I shall
return to Paris in two weeks, and you can rest assured that
I shall promote your affair vigorously and that I shall do
my best to see it through.

2 The *Académies* were, at that time, frequently called by con-
temporaries the last bulwarks of "intellectual Catholicism." Abel
François Villemain (1790–1870), Permanent Secretary of the
French Academy, had introduced Tocqueville in 1841.

3 Jules Lefèvre, or Lefèvre-Deumier (1797–1857), a moderate Bonapartist scholar.

XXXVI

Tocqueville about his refusal to despair

24 January 1857

I ask you to permit me, my dear friend, to discuss your
political theories no longer. Not being able to maintain the
liberties which existed five hundred years ago, you prefer
that we maintain none: good. Afraid of submitting to the
despotism of parties under which it was possible at least to
defend, in speech and in the press, one's own dignity and
one's own freedom, you prefer to be oppressed directly by
one single individual at a time, but so absolutely that no
one, yourself no more than anyone else, could say a single
word. Good again. Different tastes ought not to be disputed.
Rather than to witness the intrigues of parliaments, you
prefer a regime in which the greatest events may be over-
shadowed by a stock exchange speculation or by the outcome of an industrial enterprise. Even better. I must admit
that I am not very successful with you. Since I have known
you, your temperament has always seemed independent
(you see that I regard you incapable of hypocrisy). It
must be in our present state of affairs that I finally find
you satisfied with things and with people as they now
are! But, seriously, where can our political discussions
lead us? We belong to two diametrically opposed orbits.
Thus we cannot hope to convince each other. Now when
one deals with grave questions and with new ideas one
should not discuss them with one's friends when one has

no hope of persuading them. Each of us is perfectly logical in his mode of thinking. You consider people today as if they were overgrown children, very degenerate and very ill-educated. And, consequently, it seems proper to you that they should be led with blinds, through noise, with a great clangor of bells, in nicely embroidered uniforms, which are often but liveries of servants. I, too, believe that our contemporaries have been badly brought up and that this is a prime cause of their miseries and of their weakness, but I believe that a better upbringing could repair the wrongs done by their miseducation; I believe that it is not permissible to renounce such an effort. I believe that one could still achieve something with our contemporaries, as with all men, through an able appeal to their natural decency and common sense. In brief, I wish to treat them like human beings. Maybe I am wrong. But I am merely following the consequences of my principles and, moreover, I find a deep and inspiring pleasure in following them. You profoundly distrust mankind, at least *our* kind; you believe that it is not only decadent but incapable of ever lifting itself up again. Our very physical constitution, according to you, condemns us to servitude. It is, then, very logical that, to maintain at least some order in such a mob, government of the sword and even of the whip seem to have some merit in your eyes. Still I do not think that you would offer your own bare back in order to render personal confirmation of your principles. For myself, I do not think that I have either the right or the inclination to entertain such opinions about my race and my country. I believe that one should not despair of them. To me, human societies, like persons, become something worth while only through their use of liberty. I have always said that it is more difficult to stabilize and to maintain liberty in our new democratic societies than in certain aristocratic societies of the past. But I shall never dare to think it impossible. And I pray to God lest He inspire me with the idea that one might as well despair of trying. No, I shall not believe that this human race, which is at the head of all visible creation, has become that bastardized flock of sheep which you say it is, and that nothing remains but to deliver it without future and without hope to a small number of shepherds who, after all, are not better animals than are we, the human sheep, and who indeed are often worse. You will forgive me when I have less confidence in you than in the goodness and in the justice of God.

Although it seems that you are enjoying your solitude in Teheran, I must say that I am not happy and that I am somewhat disturbed to see you there, alone in such a far-away country. My only consolation is my hope that you are rapidly earning your rights of transfer. It seems that Persia has lately assumed an importance which must naturally add to the professional reputation of the person who directs the affairs of France there. Continue distinguishing yourself, but do not stay there too long. And, in the meantime, write about yourself. I should never dare send you such long and indecipherable hieroglyphics were it not that I know your expertise in the art of reading my writing. Take good care of yourself. Many, many thousands of best wishes. Be assured that I have not forgotten your academic ambitions.

⟶ᴠᴠᴠᴠᴠ⟶

XXXVII

Gobineau about his prospective books

Teheran, 20 May 1857

Monsieur,

You answered my arguments with six pages of irony. From them I conclude that you do not wish to debate any longer. Let us not debate then, and let us talk about other matters.

I should have written you much earlier, particularly because I do not want our correspondence to languish, but I was truly overwhelmed by my official duties and weighed down by work. Here the excitements of the international crisis were embellished by diplomatic conversation in the European manner on one hand, by intrigues and by violent undertakings in the Oriental manner on the other, and by occasional murders which, since I was not personally involved, left me inactive but not inattentive. We bravely concluded with a voluntary pact which provoked only some minor turmoil outside the city, but now everything is for the best. While I was in the middle of this confusion—and affairs in Persia cannot be treated either hurriedly or facilely—I remained concerned with my own studies, which were in that exciting period during which, after having discovered many new materials, they have to be confirmed, organized, and plausibly presented. I was lucky enough to find many Persian manuscripts hitherto hardly known or studied. They had already transported me to that very different sphere from which I usually regard the history of old Persia when two other books, unknown even to the scholars of this country, came to further expand my horizon and to bring me profound pleasure. To this are added my discoveries of a series of medals, yet undeciphered, the reading of which will fundamentally change the whole classification of the Arsacid kings; finally a very beautiful collection of engraved antique stones, all of them from the period between Cyrus and the first Caliphs. These allow me to reform radically all the existing notions about the importance of Media and of Persia in the empire of the Achaemenides. Roughly speaking, my work is finished, and what is left is the endless corrections, modifications, and *additions* which the eventual discoveries of my continuing researches could produce. Yet, in the end, on my table here rests the manuscript of three large volumes, *Histoire généalogique des nations iraniennes,*[1] which, with God's help, I shall bring back to Europe and which is the proof to myself that I have not wasted time here. It goes without saying that they essentially affirm what I said in my book on the races about the Aryans of Central Asia. One day I hope to do the same thing about the primitive populations of the Western world. I have a secondary concern right now, which is to find out whether or not there is someone who during these last two years has deciphered the medals which I have found. I sent the information to General Baron von Prokesch, who is very erudite in these as in so many other matters, and I am awaiting his reply. If, as I hope, I am first, I shall send you a copy of my letter which will appear in the German journal of Asiatic studies. It goes without saying that the French spirit is too elevated and too delicate to be bothered with such petty things as these. Therefore I did not even think of burdening the presses of Paris with my studies. The only thing I might have at-

[1] They ultimately grew into six manuscript volumes which were, however, published in an abbreviated form.

tempted would have been to find some intelligent person who, in the interval between my letter and its publication, would have taken it on under his own responsibility.

I know that I am speaking only about myself, but I am doing this perforce. I know nothing else of interest about which to write you. I was without European papers from January until the last few days, and the first ones I read have given me the sensation that if I were to stay here for another year I would need a dictionary to understand them. It seems that an endless number of lovely new things are taking place. I read, for instance, in a description of a ball that the *Lancers* were very diverting. The chief of my chancery, who is my sole companion here, asserts that Lancers is a game like Chinese puzzle.[2] I am more inclined to think that it is rather like Blind Man's Bluff. Such are the depths of barbarism to which we gradually fall.

Adieu, monsieur, all this letter is dreadfully silly from the first word to the last. But forgive me in the name of my present incapacity to do better. Please ask Mme. de Tocqueville not to forget me and to share with you my most affectionate and tenderest regards.

[2] "Lancers" was, instead, an English dance, similar to both the quadrille and to the *écossaise* (schottische).

XXXVIII

Gobineau about the Persian Court

Camp de Dzyjer (Teheran)
20 September 1857

Monsieur,

This may be my last letter; since Baron Pichon has been named the new Minister, my duties are terminated and I am coming home. Still, the new Minister, who does not know this country, may be a few months late; if I should have to leave within two months, I would face a somewhat hazardous voyage through Turkish Armenia, rough as Siberia. But I have seen worse.

I hope I collected a big enough pile of materials to illuminate the ancient history of Central Asia from a new angle. Since my last letter I was fortunate in being able to discover the key to the most difficult cuneiform scriptures. The results will be, I hope, quite valuable, especially those which tend to affirm my basic theses. Yet while paying much attention to the manuscripts and remains of antiquity, I am still very much interested in the present world, life here being an indispensable and complementary commentary on the former.

The present government of Persia is a combination of different levels of institutions of different origins. This results in the strangest constitutional theory I have ever seen. The laws and administrative regulations, especially in the rural provinces, go back to the Parthians, in a way to Cyrus.

Executive power originates from the Sassanides; the State is a Sassanide state; the Parthian administration has been adopted by the Sassanides; this combined version was, in turn, adopted by the first Mohammedan conquerors, who were content with changing the religion of the State and with substituting the religious legitimacy of the Caliphs for the legitimacy of the Sassanides, whose descendants they declared themselves to be. Thus the Caliphs merely continued the line of the ancient kings of Persia.

But the Caliphs rule Persia no longer—you know why. Different Turkish, Persian, and later, Mongol and Tartar dynasties declared themselves governors or regents in the name of the traditional kings of Persia; each of them had a turn at rule by the right of race. Meanwhile the Persian jurists have not recognized the legitimacy of any of these dynasties, since two essential conditions have been lacking. The first is their legal investiture by the Sassanide line through the Caliphs; the second is the sacred Mohammedan prerogatives which alone enabled the Caliphs to lawfully inherit the rights of the last of the Sassanides. Thus, since the demise of the Baghdad Caliphate, there have really been no legal rulers of Persia. There is more to that. Inasmuch as the Persians are Shiite Mohammedans, it results that since the fall of the last Sassanide ruler, Yezdedjerd, Ali has been the only legitimate sovereign; all the other Abbasside Caliphs are considered usurpers, including the kings of the present dynasty. The practical consequences of this doctrine are peculiar indeed.

Since he is not really lawfully regnant, the Shah rules merely by the right of force. Thus his prayers would not be valid, as he pronounces them in a place which he does not rightfully hold, were it not that he carefully pays nominal rent for a part of his palace in Teheran and for the ground where he sets up his tents when traveling. This money goes to the mosques. There he can make his lawful prayers, for there he is finally considered a lawful tenant.

A religious person aspiring for saintliness cannot sit down with the king nor accept anything offered by him, not even a drop of water, since whatever the king possesses is not lawfully his. It happened during the reign of the father of the present Shah that one of the chief priests of Ispahan, when invited, would not be seated until he pushed back the royal carpet with his stick and sat down on the bare earth. The courtiers admired this gesture very much, and the Shah himself was not altogether angry. Now comes the worst. Through certain notions of reincarnation, which are more Indian than Moslem, the race of the Imams is still thought to exist. An unknown person may reveal himself as an Imam. There are certain advance signs determining this revelation. Four years ago an Imam appeared; the Shah barely escaped assassination; and about three hundred of the Imam's captured followers were atrociously murdered. Two rebel villages had to be stormed, at the cost of much blood; and even within the highest circles of the government a follower of the Imam remained who was finally shot at Tabriz. The government is also dreadfully afraid of the sectarians called Babis; it is even afraid of searching them out. Thus the Persians maintain their antiquated constitution since they feel they cannot do otherwise. On the day of Neurouz, or of the Persian New Year, the grand royal benediction ceremony truly reflects this state of affairs. The soldiers, the grandees, and the people assemble at the square in front of the palace. The Prime Minister is at the head of the crowd, thirty or forty steps from the throne. The Shah arrives. He sits down. A number of princes surround him, carrying his sword, his buckler, his arms, and his shield. There begins a familiar conversation between the king and this minister representing the nation. The Shah asks how things are in general. The minister naturally answers that nothing could be better. Still, says the Shah, we heard that the cholera killed a lot of people during the past year, is this not true? People have exaggerated, answers the minister; thanks to the reigning fortunes of Your Majesty, the ravages were few. Still, the Shah pursues, if they want to remain fortunate, public officials should have enough integrity in order to merit Divine protection, for if they lose their integrity, etc.—and there follows a moral discourse which is interrupted only from time to time by "Assuredly!" "Without a doubt!" "Your Majesty is certainly right!" from the minister. After this scene the Shah smokes a pipe. In golden and enameled vases sherbets and fruits are passed around. Finally the Shah rises and leaves. You will see that though during this scene the Shah does not play the role of the leader of the nation he also rejects that of the usurper since he adopts the air of being a stranger to all of these things; he pretends to ignore them and feigns to be uninformed about what everybody knows. He assumes the personality of a foreign and essentially benevolent chieftain. I forgot to say that on these occasions he also distributes some money to the needy. This state of affairs is also reflected in the national finances, where the Shah receives not a penny from the State but, on the contrary, he himself frequently lends money to the Treasury. But I see that I am running out of paper and you, probably, of patience. Yet if, by chance, these things should interest you, we shall have time to talk them over during the coming winter. Farewell, monsieur, you know my respectful attachment and my traditional and unreserved devotion to you.

XXXIX

Gobineau about his home-coming

Château de Trye (Oise),[1] 8 May 1858

Monsieur,

After having arrived, I came down here at once to embrace my wife, my daughter Diane, and my newlyborn.[2] I stayed here for a few days, and then I went to Paris, where I hurried to the Hôtel Bedford. You had left two days before, which was a dreadful disillusionment as I had a great desire to embrace you. Will you now stay at Tocqueville for the entire winter? Will you not come to Paris at all? I should be terribly disappointed, for I do not know what my future destination will be and, from what the Minister[3] tells me, my stay in Paris may end on a day's notice. I am in what they call a reserve status, that is, I draw my full pay but I may within twenty-four hours receive an order to leave. Thus I ardently hope to see you before this winter, since who knows where I shall be then?

I had a hard enough journey, and I certainly do not wish to do it all over again. Yet my fatigue did not catch up

---

[1] In 1857, after having alone inherited his uncle's fortune, Gobineau had bought this castle. He was obsessed with the somewhat insubstantial idea that this castle and its lands had once belonged to his Norman ancestors. See also p. 181. p. 000.

[2] Christine de Gobineau, later married to M. Serpeille, mother of Clément Serpeille; about him see p. 184.

[3] Walewski. See above, p. 283.

with me until now. Otherwise I am perfectly well and nothing is wrong. In waiting for my next destination, I am preparing to have some of my works published. I have almost finished six volumes on ancient Iran, and I have an article on a new method of reading cuneiform scriptures to which problem I think that I have found the solution. I say I think, and I may be wrong. If I were not so sure, I would not do anything about it since I am not a professional scholar. Thus I am very busy, and my family occupies the rest of my time. I am enchanted with my new daughter, Christine, and I found my wife reasonably well after the fatigues of maternity.

I have a million things to tell you and I cannot but repeat again how much I should like to see you. But I am told that you are very busy with your continuing studies of administrative history, and also with your agriculture. Both are fine occupations. Yet right now I look at them with a jaundiced eye, for they indicate that you will not move from home. I have not as yet seen anyone aside from my superiors, for I did not stay in Paris except for official business. Everything draws me to and everything keeps me at Trye.

My wife tells me that she found you very well, much better than when we had left, and, above all, in very good humor. She sends you her best regards as well as to Mme. de Tocqueville to whom I offer my services and homage.

Adieu, monsieur, write me, please, a word on your plans in order that I may know what I should look forward to. Trust always the sincere and respectful attachment of this most devoted friend of yours.

*Tocqueville about his life; about academic
affairs*

Tocqueville, par Saint-Pierre-Église
12 May 1858

I was certain that you had returned, my dear friend, as I
read in the British and German papers that a French diplomatist, M. Nobineau, attaché of the Embassy to Persia,
had landed at Marseille. I recognized you in that not very
exotic disguise. I inquired about you when I came to Paris.
I was told you that you had naturally gone to see your
wife and your children. It seems that I left Paris two days
before you returned. I am much disappointed; you can believe with what great pleasure I should have embraced you
upon your return from these distant adventures. I am
doubly disappointed as I cannot yet exactly say when we
shall be able to meet. I expect to return to Paris next month
but I am so content with this rural life that I am constantly postponing my return. By the end of July the Caen
railroad will arrive here. Possibly this will make me post-
pone my Paris trip until the autumn. But it is certain that,
due to necessity, I shall spend quite a long time in Paris
this year. I must make the necessary researches for my
work, which you, I don't know why, call an *administrative*
history, though it has less administration in it than anything else. I may also remark that it is not correct to say
that I am delving deeply into agriculture. My agriculture

consists of a field and of a few sheep. The truth is that I have taken a deep liking to the life I lead in the country, where I mix mental activity with moving around in the free air. My mind and body profit therefrom. I think you will see me in better health and, above all, in better spirits than when we used to burden ourselves together with all that bad scribbling.

I see that you do not devote yourself entirely to your profession and that you have not lost the beneficial habit of working for yourself. You are still the greatest drudge whom I have ever known. It is amazing to see someone who after such a long, hard voyage immediately spends his free time turning out an article on cuneiform scriptures. The subject is very interesting. But you are intelligent enough to know that someone who is not a professional must make his case doubly strong before the scholars. I do not doubt that the works which you have brought back from your diplomatic pilgrimages must be, as yours always are, very illuminating. I am looking forward to chatting with you about what you have seen, about what you now see, and about a thousand other things.

Mme. de Gobineau must have told you where the affair of the *Institut* now stands. She knows that my zeal for your academic interests may have even been dangerous for you, though this has not cooled my zeal. Rather the opposite is true; it tends to keep me in a state of latent fervor. The truth is that we have been deprived of our majority by that microscopic *coup d'état* which imposed on us ten new-comers, among whom some have had sufficient merit not to have had to come in this way. It must be granted that this *garrison*, as they are called, has been very modest. They do not interfere at all. But when it comes to the choice of new candidates, every one of the suppressed passions appears very strongly indeed. To impose our candidates on them is impossible. We cannot ignore them. Yet they rarely find enough supporters to elect their own. It flows therefrom that it is important that you have this *garrison* present you or at least agree to you. After that I should be very willing to be charged with bringing my friends to your side. This is the natural procedure now, and it would be neither practical nor salutary for you to try reversing it.

Let me have your news soon and trust my sincere friendship. Our affectionate regards to Mme. de Gobineau.

<del>————</del>

XLI

Tocqueville about his own work

Tocqueville, 5 August 1858

I read your letter,[1] my dear friend, with the greatest interest. But, at any rate, this is the effect of every one of your letters. I am anxious to know what will happen with your linguistic endeavors. It seems that you could hardly be wrong if, after having severely curbed your imagination, you really find that certain characters always correspond to certain meanings. A hypothesis which permits the prediction of certain effects that always reoccur under the same conditions does, in a way, amount to a demonstrable truth. Even the Newtonian system has no more than such a foundation. If you have really discovered such an important secret which has been vainly searched for during centuries, and if this is admitted by the world of scholarship, this will certainly give you the highest reputation. I wish therefore very much for the success of your discovery for the

[1] Probably permanently lost.

sake of science on one hand, and for the sake of my good friend on the other. Keep me posted of developments.

I am, like you, afraid that you may be sent to a far corner of the globe before we shall be able to see and chat with each other. Still, the time of my little trip to Paris may be coming. I am thinking of going toward the end of next month. If you are still in France we shall, I hope, finally meet. I have a great desire to see you again. As you say, perhaps rightly, at times it seems that I may not have grasped what was going on in your mind; and our letters help little, especially in a merry country like ours, where now people write with the knowledge that the secrecy of correspondence is not being respected. At the present there remains in France only one way to exchange thoughts freely and completely; it is to be closeted in the privacy of a room.

I confess that in my last letter I may have grumbled perhaps a little about what you had said about my work. You must forgive me. But is it not permissible to grumble a little when an intelligent man such as yourself, who has read everything that I wrote and who is so capable of judging what I am doing, calls a general study concerning the causes, the movements, and the effects of that immense human eruption which is called the French Revolution a work about "administrative institutions"? One need not belong to that *genus irritabile*, well known to you, to be at least a little irritated by such a definition of a work envisaged so differently by its author.

I shall not continue today; there is little more of interest that I could tell you. Do not be tardy in reporting about yourself. Please give our best regards to Mme. de Gobineau and, above, all, trust my indeed sincere friendship.

XLII

*Tocqueville about his enduring trust in the gen-
ius of France*

Tocqueville, 16 September 1858

It is not due to any chagrin that I have not answered your
letter before last, my dear friend. I expected to leave for
Paris any day and it is my principle not to write when one
can talk. And I did go to Paris two weeks ago, but I stayed
only for forty-eight hours. I went, above all, to consult my
physician as I have not been quite satisfied with my health
during the past three months. He found me ill enough to
order an immediate treatment, achievable at home but impossible in a hotel. I plan to return to Paris now around
the 8th of next month for a longer stay. I hope to find you
still there and, if this be so, I should be more than delighted; I have conserved my deep friendship for you despite that quarrelsomeness of which you accuse me with
some justification. This bad habit of mine is not of recent
origin, and I shall watch lest it become chronic. I am devoted to you; I have much esteem and affection for you.
But there exist differences between our tempers, and there
exist even contrary tendencies which produce what you are
complaining of, often not without reason. I love people; I
rejoice in finding them praiseworthy, and nothing is so delightful to me as are sentiments of admiration when they
seem warranted. When I can neither esteem nor admire my
fellow men, which happens rather frequently, I confess

[324]

that I prefer to look for the few good traits among their vices, trying to train my eyes on these white speckles visible against darker backgrounds. Perhaps because of the painful struggles which you so courageously faced in your youth you are naturally accustomed to distrust humanity in general, and your own country in particular. Would you not expect, for instance, that I should be somewhat impatient when I hear you say that our nation has always been petty and mean, that it never produced a genius, if not perhaps that ignoble Rabelais, in whose works I have never found a single piece of gold after having waded through his heaps of muck? As if some of the greatest works of the human mind did not come from our nation? As if, above all, we had not produced a constant stream of great writers during the past three centuries, stirring and moving the spirit of mankind most powerfully—whether in the right or the wrong direction may be arguable, but their power one cannot doubt. I do not know any foreigner, except perhaps some prig of a German professor, who would pronounce such judgments on France which you, a Frenchman, are making. I am not saying this to challenge you but for an example of what I mean when I say that, while I like you so much, I cannot avoid being quarrelsome. In your letter I find that you are similarly unjust to your contemporaries. When have Thiers, Villemain, and even Cousin done better than in their last works,[1] despite the somewhat debatable value of their subjects? And, so far as their intrinsic value is concerned, what European historian is more famous than Thiers, more brilliant than Villemain, a better writer than Cousin? Is Lamartine perhaps not the greatest poet of our days, though he may no longer write anything but detestable poetry and a prose which is no

---

[1] Thiers had just finished his *Histoire du Consulat et de l'Empire;* Villemain had just published his excellent studies of contemporary history and literature; Cousin was completing his studies on eighteenth-century society.

better? It is unfortunately only too true and sad that these very talented persons, who, to be sure, are not extraordinary geniuses, are getting old and that they are not being replaced by anyone. In the generations that come after those now in their fifties or sixties, after men of high intellect who are now becoming old dogs, who is there of any fame at all? Those old novelists and old comedy writers like Scribe, who are surely no Molières or Le Sages but who have been at least eagerly read everywhere in the civilized world, are not being replaced by anyone even capable of making the same noise they did. This saddens and worries me, for this is a new condition and, consequently, its duration is not predictable. It is, I think, partly due to the widespread apathy of souls and to those clouds which hover above us, languishing every spirit. Strong hatreds, ardent passions, high hopes, and powerful convictions are, all, necessary to make human minds move. Right now nothing is strongly believed, nothing is loved, nothing is hated, and people wish for nothing but a quick profit on the stock exchange. Yet France has never had a temper so permanently depressed as to be interested in nothing but material welfare, and I keep hoping that a new movement which will raise her will power will also reanimate her literature.

It is difficult for me to explain why I wrote all of this down. This is nothing but an inordinate monologue. Do not answer as we shall soon see each other after such a long time, and we shall talk about this and about hundreds of other matters. A thousand cordial wishes. Do not forget to remember us to Mme. de Gobineau.

XLIII

Tocqueville from his sickbed

Cannes, Var, 28 February 1859

My dear friend, if I really said that you should wait before receiving my new address I must have been absolutely wrong. But this is what happened. Having arrived here, I found that Cannes is a small village where everyone knows where everyone else lives. From this I imagined that my friends would simply have to address their letters to Cannes, Var. Otherwise I am well satisfied with the explanation you gave for your silence, for my breast heaved[1] when I told myself that you were the only one among my friends who had not been very solicitous about me. My condition may have frequently warranted solicitude. First I was very well for two months. Then came a New Year's present of two or three attacks which were more painful than any I had ever had before. This lasted for a month. Luckily February seems to have repaired the damages of January. I have regained my powers. My lungs, which brought me here, seem to be recovering, and I am almost beginning to feel as if I were reborn.

I want everything that you wrote, the travel book[2] and the book on the cuneiform writing (though I am not very capable of judging the latter). So, my dear friend, please

[1] A pun (*je m'en plaignais amèrement*, in petto), referring to Tocqueville's serious tubercular condition.

[2] Refers to Gobineau's *Trois ans en Asie*, which had just been published.

send me with the least delay everything which is printed and which is being printed; you can surely count on me as a reader avidly desirous to learn about these Oriental countries which you covered.

I was worried about you because of the affair in which you found yourself. Thank God that this storm has passed.[3] But what is *essentially* your situation? You know that there never has been a former Minister without a weakness for his *chef de cabinet*. I certainly share this kind of sentiment. And, meanwhile, is it really true that I used to be Minister? There are times when I doubt it. Farewell, my dear friend, give our respects to Mme. de Gobineau and believe in my sincerest friendship.

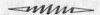

XLIV

Gobineau about his own intellectual endeavors and troubles

Château de Trye, 4 March 1859

Monsieur,

I evidently have the honor to be the one among your friends who inspires you with the least confidence, and yet I am not reproachful when I say that the exact opposite should be true, as there is no one whom you have tested so constantly and for so long. But I am not really lamenting this as I feel that for a year I have, in a way, been hexed with you. For one reason or another I find it difficult to

[3] Refers to a minor personal intrigue against Gobineau in the Foreign Ministry.

depart from my apologetic mood. Thus I shall only say this: no one loves you more, more loyally, or more constantly than do I; all the rest counts little.

I do not know what is going on with regard to my career. The Minister seemed to be very satisfied with me, for on my return he sent me to the Tuileries, where the Emperor expressed much pleasure with my performance. I must admit that I took this quite seriously since I thought I had done my duty under difficult circumstances. Despite all this, they now want to send me to China as first secretary. This is not a disgrace; but it is a punishment. The Minister returned to this decision, but he let me know that because of some of my observations I had acquired a bad mark and if I were to be recalcitrant about my next destination he would have to put me in reserve status. Well, here I am, quite perplexed. They imply that they are not quite sure of me politically. This is unjust for two reasons: first, because I am incapable of not serving loyally whomever I do serve; second, because I sincerely believe in absolute government for the French people. So this whole affair is quite obscure to me. Still, I hope that they won't treat me any worse without reason.

I am sending you my book on cuneiform. My *Voyage* is being printed and you should have it soon. When I began my work on cuneiform I had no idea where all of this would lead me, and had I divined it, it is quite probable that I should have kept my discoveries to myself and said nothing, peace being worth more than anything else. Once my book was published, the scholars met in conclave and decided that they would not speak a word about it, letting it die in silence. But I had an article in the *Moniteur* where I proposed the idea that the monuments attributed to Nineveh were not Assyrian but mostly Persian from the times of Xerxes, and I translated a number of short inscriptions from the Louvre Museum to corroborate my opinions.

This must have irritated a M. Oppert[1] of the French archaeological expedition to Mesopotamia, one of the pundits who immediately sat down to write an article full of the grossest insults though without discussing my thesis or my arguments at all. I sent to the *Journal asiatique* an article which contains the principal theses of my system about the particular conditions of the Persian languages. After having kept it for three months without sending an answer, they now tell me that they cannot publish it since I contested certain points which to them are incontestable. I answered that, whatever my opinions about these points may be, the article did not deal with them; I should be disposed to withdraw these points but, on the other hand, I do present important translations and discoveries, and I ought not to be accused of not revealing my methods of transcription when I am refused the chance to publish and to present these to the public. On this matter my interlocutor (it is M. Mohl of the *Institut*)[2] asked me to let him keep my article so that he could give me his personal opinion. This I have done. And this is where I stand. You can see that things do not move smoothly. While I am waiting for this I am publishing another work about the monuments erected by Xerxes at Nineveh (Khorsabad). In my *Moniteur* article I did not mention his name except with many reservations. Yet I have read new inscriptions since which show that I have not been mistaken. I am now translating a very long inscription (of 150 lines) from ancient Arabic which seems to date from the youth of Xerxes, preceding his war with Greece. Due to an extremely fortunate circumstance, this piece is rhymed prose like the oldest parts of Genesis, of the Koran, etc. When they are ready to give me a hearing, I shall produce a transcription into modern Arabic script and, in case my method of transcription should be wrong,

[1] Jules Oppert (1825–1905), French Orientalist of German origin, a Sanskrit scholar.
[2] Jules de Mohl (1800–1876), Oppert's colleague.

I shall ask them how in the world this method could produce from a cuneiform text such a piece of eloquent rhythmic prose in ancient Arabic, relating historical facts found in Herodotus? Such a demonstration should make sense unless they think that I myself composed the piece. But I do not know enough Arabic to do that. I am looking, both in Germany and in Paris, for the help of some benevolent Arabic scholar who would, instead of hiding behind sterile rejections, consent to try finding out whether with my method he could read and understand it. If I succeed with this, all will be well. But it seems just too easy at first sight.

In sum, I confess that I do not find the way competent people behave towards me very edifying. While M. Rémusat, in a recent article, does me the compliment of declaring that I have proposed a new historical system which, whether good or bad, is my own discovery, the Orientalists, like M. Renan in his book on the *Origins du langage*[3] and M. Maury in the *Revue des deux mondes,* are copying chapters from my book on the *Races* and are most careful to omit my name. They go to the point that, when they are obliged to cite the book which Professor Pott of Halle wrote about mine and where my name figures in the title, they abbreviate the title[4] to preserve my namelessness. These are small matters and, of course, I shall say nothing

[3] This book, first published in 1848, was reissued in 1858 in an enlarged form, manifesting the growing affinity between the ideas of Renan and of Gobineau. Gobineau first wrote Renan in January 1854 (see above, p. 234). His letter is printed in a little book by Jacques de Lacretelle, *Quatre études sur Gobineau,* Liége, 1927.

[4] No wonder. The title reads: *Die Ungleichheit menschlicher Rassen, hauptsaechlich von sprachwissentschaftlichem Standpunkte, unter besonderer Beruecksichtigung von des Grafen von Gobineau gleichnamigem Werk. Mit einem Ueberblicke ueber die Sprachverhaeltnisse der Voelker. Ein ethnologischer Versuch von Aug. Friedr. Pott . . .* (1856).

about them. But this is the spirit of science in the nineteenth century, a spirit which is not at all scientific but mercantile and commercial. What annoys me is that I devoted a lot of trouble and time to all of this work. You wanted news about what I have been doing; here is my news, perhaps there is too much of it.

I should still like very much to see you. It occurred to me to suggest that you go to Egypt. I am certain that your health would profit marvelously from such a trip, which is quite easy now. Nine days! Yet I know how Mme. de Tocqueville dislikes the sea and, then, thank God, you are almost recovered, and there may be little left to do. Yet it may still be necessary that you courageously keep yourself away from your work for some time, at least from fatiguing work. There is, true, the burden of boredom, but one's health is worth the price. I also desire very much to see the next part of *The Old Regime and the Revolution*. I well understand that you have not said anything about it to me yet but I know that you are thinking much about it even under your present burdens. Still, allow me to repeat once more what I said earlier: do not consider yourself so well as to renounce rest altogether. Farewell, monsieur, a thousand regards go to Mme. de Tocqueville and to you with my desire that you believe a little more in the entire and devoted attachment of your *chef de cabinet*.

XLV

Gobineau about his prospects

Château de Trye, Oise, 21 March 1859

Monsieur,

I trust that you received my book on the *Textes cunéiformes* and I hope above all that your health continues to improve. I have been in Paris recently and I saw M. Mérimée and also M. de Rémusat, who gave me news about you. I expect you to say that the improvement, about which you rejoice in your last letter and about which everyone is talking, continues. I know that Cannes is a fine place and that your rest and idleness without boredom will suffice to restore you completely. Yet I also should have liked (I think I had mentioned this earlier) to see you go to Egypt for a winter's stay. But I know that Mme. de Tocqueville does not like the sea and, in sum, if everything seems well, why not leave good enough alone? Perhaps I am merely partial to the Pyramids.

Let me announce that I have a new destination. I am supposed to go to Newfoundland for six months as an official to study the limits of the zones of fisheries. I have for my naval colleague M. de Montaignac, whom you know well and who is the commander of the French naval station there. I am sure that we shall get along very well with each other. For myself, I shall do my best. This is considered quite an advantageous assignment for a variety of reasons; I shall say nothing about its inconveniences, the main one being that I have to leave my family, which is never pleasant.

M. de Rémusat tells me that you are working. I am very happy about this; but on the other hand, I should not like to see you tire yourself out. I know that you never take literary work lightly and that you devote to it all of your soul and all of your efforts. This is why I ask you to restrain yourself, lest you pay the boring price of another winter in quarantine. To avoid this is important for your very work.

My *Voyage* will come out in June or July. I hope it will be as successful with you as it is with my publisher. First he wanted to have an edition in duodecimo. Now he is making two editions, one in duodecimo, one in octavo, and he is even toying with the idea of putting in engravings. You will see that I am well appreciated. But I am still concerned with the affair of the *Cunéiformes.* I am in regular contact with M. Renan in order to explain my system to him. He read a paper at the *Institut* in which he tore into the *errors* of Messrs. Rawlinson and Oppert.[1] I hope that these are the preliminaries for a closer alliance between us. But to criticize is not only easier but also more pleasant than to agree. At any rate, I shall do my best to acquire this important new ally, and if you could directly or indirectly stoke the fervor of M. Renan by letting him know that you are interested *not in me, and not in my eventual triumph but that this matter deserves serious consideration,* I am certain that this would be most helpful. Adieu, monsieur, our thousand regards and our warmest affections to Mme. de Tocqueville.

[1] The latter (see above, p. 330, note 1) had just published a book on similar subjects.

XLVI

Gobineau to Mme. de Tocqueville

Sydney (Nova Scotia), 27 May 1859

Dear Madame,

I learned here of the tragedy which struck you, and together with you all those persons who are attached to you. You know that I am among them and that for how many years my heart has been devoted to him who is no more. Few among his friends were so close to his life as I have been and few have had so many occasions to know the greatness of his soul, the nobility of his heart, and his merits of so many kinds which put him so far above the majority of men; few are those who loved him more than I did and who have had more reason than I to offer him their affection and limitless gratitude. I think that he knew that these were my sentiments and that I belonged to him with all of my heart.

You have known all of this, madame, and I am asking you in these sad days to remember the share I take in your sorrows. Always consider me your devoted servant and believe that I would never be happier than when you would wish to recall this. You will also know that I am very anxious to learn about your own health, which has not been strong and which, at this time, has to undergo such a cruel trial. If you were to find a minute to write me a few words about yourself, I should be very grateful indeed.

Adieu, dear madame, believe that I remain deeply and respectfully attached and devoted to you.

P.S. My traveling companion, M. de Montaignac, joins me in offering his profound respects. Here is my address:

> Aboard the *Gassendi*
> French Naval Station, Sydney, Cap Breton
> Halifax (Nova Scotia)
> via Liverpool.

ANCHOR BOOKS